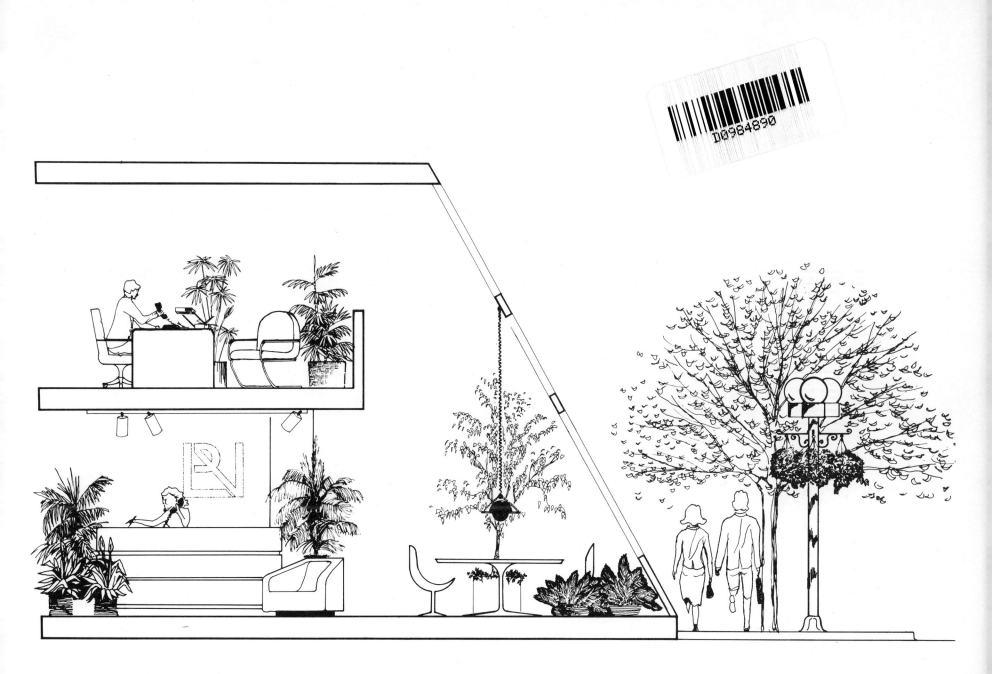

# INTERIORSCAPES:

# Planning, Graphics, and Design

# INTERIORSCAPES:

# Planning, Graphics, and Design

**Gregory M. Pierceall, ASLA**

*Purdue University*

A RESTON BOOK
PRENTICE-HALL, INC.
Englewood Cliffs, NJ 07632

*Library of Congress Cataloging-in-Publication Data*

Pierceall, Gregory M.
    Interiorscapes: planning, graphics, and design.

    ''A Reston book.''
    Includes index.
    1. Interior landscaping.    I. Title.
SB419.25.P54 1987      747'.98      86-25533
ISBN   0-8359-3232-X

Editorial/production supervision and interior design: **Kathryn Pavelec**
Page layout: **Peggy Finnerty**
Cover design: **George Cornell**
Front cover photographs: **Gregory M. Pierceall**
Back cover master plan: **The Collaborative, Inc.**
Endpaper drawings: **Mario F. Nievera and Timothy D. Lee**
Manufacturing Buyer: **Barbara Kelly Kittle**

© 1987 by **Prentice-Hall, Inc.**
A Division of Simon & Schuster
Englewood Cliffs, New Jersey 07632
Printed in the United States of America

10  9  8  7  6  5  4  3  2  1


ISBN   0-8359-3232-X


Prentice-Hall International (UK) Limited, *London*
Prentice-Hall of Australia Pty. Limited, *Sydney*
Prentice-Hall Canada Inc., *Toronto*
Prentice-Hall Hispanoamericana, S.A., *Mexico*
Prentice-Hall of India Private Limited, *New Delhi*
Prentice-Hall of Japan, Inc., *Tokyo*
Prentice-Hall of Southeast Asia Pte. Ltd., *Singapore*
Editora Prentice-Hall do Brasil, Ltda., *Rio de Janeiro*

This text is dedicated to my rascal daughter Robyn,
"CHA" daughter Hillary,
and ever-loving and devoted wife Harriet.

# Contents

# Preface

Interior landscape design as it relates to indoor spaces is a space and activity definer within which people work, live, relax, and recreate. Interiorscapes are only as alive and dynamic as the imaginations of the client and the designer. Design proposals should not be an end unto themselves, but a means of creating a setting that is useful and pleasing. Designs that are developed should reflect the space, the client, and surrounding influences. Design ideas are refined through a systematic thought process and expressed in plans. These plans are the means used to implement the actual developments.

*Interiorscapes: Planning, Graphics, and Design* is a reference for individuals involved in the design and development of interior plantings. Landscape architects, architects, interior designers, landscape nurserymen, landscape contractors, and landscape maintenance firms collectively are involved in interior landscape design. The interiorscape industry is part of the larger "green industry" composed of all nursery and landscape professionals.

To a landscape architect, interior landscape design is a specialty area. Interiorscaping may be an extension of other more primary planning services provided to clients. As part of the landscape professionals, landscape nurserymen, contractors, and maintenance firms are also involved with the products, the development, and the establishment of interior landscape designs. As a professional group they not only produce and sell plants and construction materials, they also provide the technical expertise of installation and care beyond the initial design stages. As specialists within their respective fields, these landscape industry individuals make recommendations that influence interiorscapes now and in the future.

The planning, graphic, and design concepts used to present planting and construction ideas for interiorscapes are the focus of this text. Illustrations and actual case study examples are used to communicate the planning, graphic, and design information. Section One of the text is an introduction to interiorscaping and the landscape industry, design principles and elements, and the planning and design process. Section Two of the text covers graphics, materials, procedures, and the communication skills and graphic language used to communicate a design. Section Three discusses design through actual project examples. Collectively, these three sections represent eleven chapters of information regarding the planning, graphics, and design of interiorscapes.

This text represents my interest and expertise in interior landscape design. My experiences as a landscape horticulture professor, and landscape architect, are expressed in the planning, graphics, and design information and their interrelationship in developing a design proposal. The pictorial case studies illustrate the planning, graphic, and design concepts used to develop an interiorscape. An understanding of these basic concepts provides the necessary basis to communicate a design proposal. In the thought sequence from ideas to drawings to development, planning, graphics, and design are only a means to make an idea reality.

Gregory M. Pierceall
*West Lafayette, Indiana*

# Acknowledgments

With the completion of this text, I would like to recognize and thank everyone who has contributed to the text's content and development. My appreciation and thanks are extended to those who encouraged me in the profession of landscape architecture, especially my wife Harriet. I also extend my thanks to the numerous design clients that have trusted my judgment and expertise in the practice of landscape architecture. Lastly, my sincere thanks goes out to the many students and colleagues with whom I have shared ideas and they their thoughts regarding design.

For their review and direction during the manuscript's early planning, I thank Susan Jo Cita of Laubman, Reed & Associates, and Douglas G. Smith. To Ed Engledow, President of Engledow Inc., and Richard Wade, Melvin Simon Associates, I thank you for all the contributed photographs and plans that make this text complete. To all the clients who freely gave their projects as examples in the text, I extend my appreciation. Thanks also goes to Kevin Fry, Tim Lee, Mario Nievera, Raymond Paul Strychalski, and Thomas G. Kramer for their delineation skills in the development of some of the text's graphics. To the production staff of Printing Services at Purdue, thank you for your cooperation and efficiency in the handling of the many blackline prints and PMTs used in this endeavor. A special thanks is extended to Jane Carter, who typed all the drafts of this manuscript and to whom special recognition is due for her reading of my "hieroglyphics," otherwise known as handwriting. Lastly, I would like to thank the technical and production staff of Prentice Hall Publishing Company, especially Kathy Pavelec, Peggy Finnerty, Ed Moura, and Debbie Monte for their ever-present advice and encouragement during the manuscript's development.

# Chapter 1

# Interiorscape Professionals and Industry

*Interiorscaping, interior landscape design,* and *plantscaping* are terms used to describe the professional activities associated with the design, installation, and establishment of tropical plantings indoors. No one term completely describes the specialization and diversification of practitioners within the interiorscape profession. One characteristic of the profession that is consistent is the fact that the interior plant industry is interdisciplinary (Figure 1.1). Interiorscape design often involves the coordination of architects, landscape architects, environmental engineers, interior designers, and interiorscapers (Figures 1.2 and 1.3). Interior plant specialists, service practitioners, and associated professionals are involved in specific areas such as plant propagation, nursery management, production, sales, and plant and supply wholesaling. Interior plant installers and maintenance personnel, in combination with these other related profession-

**Figure 1.1**

Architects, landscape architects, interior designers, and other professionals are involved with clients in developing interiorscapes. This shopping mall food court uses plantings as a focal point as well as a separation between seating areas. (Courtesy of Engledow Inc.)

1.2

1.3

als, are partially included in the larger "green industry" (Figures 1.4 and 1.5). *Green industry* is a general term used to define the group of professionals and practitioners involved with plants in our interior and exterior environments. Interiorscapers, architects, landscape architects, landscape contractors, interior designers, and landscape maintenance personnel, in conjunction with other professionals when developing interiorscapes, are part of a team composed of the design, green, and interiorscape industry specialists (Figures 1.6 and 1.7).

It is necessary for interiorscapers to appreciate the planning and design of an interior landscape in order to understand how and why plants are placed in particular interior spaces in relation to the architecture and interior design of

**Figures 1.2 and 1.3**

The design of an interiorscape proposal often is part of the architectural and interior design process. These photos illustrate the integration of plants and built-in planters in a hotel lobby. (Courtesy of Engledow Inc.)

**Figures 1.4 and 1.5**

This renovated industrial park building includes an interior planting. It serves as an entry to the building and is a focus to offices on two surrounding levels. (Photos of The Bradford Exchange, Niles, Illinois, courtesy of Tropical Plant Rentals, Inc., Chicago, Illinois.)

1.4

1.5

1.6

1.7

**Figures 1.6 and 1.7**

In this building addition to corporate offices, a plant installation company, in conjunction with project architects, created a dramatic interior courtyard. It was designed so that plants are within sight of all employee work areas. The court also provides a focus for visitors. (Photos of John Deere, Moline, Illinois, courtesy of Tropical Plant Rentals, Inc., Chicago, Illinois.)

1.8

1.9

**Figures 1.8 and 1.9**

In this shopping mall the interior planting is located as a focal point associated with the stairs and escalators. Planter integration with the architecture is critical to traffic patterns. The designed skylights provide the plants with light levels necessary for growth and development. (Photos of Town Square Mall, St. Paul, Minnesota, courtesy of Tropical Plant Rentals, Inc., Chicago, Illinois.

the space (Figures 1.8 and 1.9). Conversely, design professionals need to understand the cultural concerns and growth habits of tropical plants in order to appreciate the task of trying to maintain them in indoor environments (Figures 1.10 and 1.11). The increased use of plants in today's buildings is a result of more stark construction materials, the inclusion of designed open spaces, and natural or added light previously not available in buildings (Figures 1.12–1.14). Interiorscaping and its design should function to define space and activity within the parameters established by the architecture, interior, furnishings, client needs, and inhabitants of the space.

To accomplish an interiorscape design that is both functional and attractive, designers use a logical thought process that combines the architecture of the building, the interior design with the space, and plants with constructed features. This ideal sequence, often called the *design process*, strives to create useful and attractive settings that reflect the projected image, design scheme, and client-user needs, while

**Figure 1.10**

The wide selection of plants available for an interior requires an understanding of plant cultural requirements as well as the project lighting, ventilation, and use.

**Figure 1.11**

The most critical interior cultural consideration necessary for plant growth and survival is light. Plant species should be selected to match the interior and light intensity with the plant. If the existing light is minimal, plant cycling, where plants are rotated, may be a design option.

**Figure 1.12**

In this public building, skylights and permanent planters provide an environment for plants to grow, and highlight seating areas in the corridor. (Courtesy of Engledow Inc.)

1.13

1.14

**Figures 1.13 and 1.14**

The inclusion of natural lighted spaces in architecture allows plants to become a permanent part of the building design. These photos illustrate the exterior and interior appearance of this greenhouse-like space. Glass has become a part of our contemporary architecture.

making a positive contribution. Thus design drawings are not an end unto themselves, but ideas for the development of a space. In planning, it should be the designer's responsibility to understand and to include as design criteria how people work, move, relax, and interact within the space. The benefits to people to be gained from indoor plantings are identified in an article by Brent Merchant in *American Nurseryman* (November 15, 1982). "The use of plants indoors goes beyond man's inherent need for green. Aesthetics qualities plants provide create a feeling of hospitality and helps reduce the cold feeling building material can have [Figures 1.15 and 1.16]. Secondly plants provide an effective and economic decoration for interiors as compared to the expense and availability of original art and sculpture [Figures 1.17 and 1.18]. Lastly plants are practical, they booster employee production by creating a positive work environment.

**Figure 1.15**
In this art museum foyer on the campus of Indiana University, the designed balcony planters and planted grape ivy contrast and accent the contemporary interior of cast concrete and glass.

**Figure 1.16**
In this roof-top atrium the interior is defined by glass and brick, and is furnished with wicker. This space is complemented by plants, which add a splash of color and provide scale to the area. (Courtesy of Engledow Inc.)

**Figure 1.17**
The atrium provides adjoining offices with an extended view that is both functional and aesthetic. (Courtesy of Engledow Inc.)

**Figure 1.18**
In this office park lobby in the specimen fig (*Ficus spp.*) provides a sculptural accent from all vantages. (Courtesy of Engledow Inc.)

**Figure 1.19**

In this bank office area, plants create human work spaces. (Courtesy of Engledow Inc.)

**Figure 1.20**

In this office, planters and wall-divider plantings provide visual separation, contrasts, and color for employees and patrons alike. (Courtesy of Engledow Inc.)

Plants also project a human image for corporation to employees and consumers [Figures 1.19–1.21]." Plants are also part of the urban renaissance of developing "people" places, especially shopping malls and redevelopment or renovation projects (Figures 1.22–1.25). Interior plantings, besides serving the project focus, may be part of the tourist attraction in large atriums and conservatories (Figures 1.26–1.28).

In order to achieve the results outlined above, designers need to understand that designing with and growing plants requires knowledge of both design and plant specialties. Interior landscape design is the use of planned plantings in an interior to help create an attractive and functional area for the people who use the space. While the design elements and principles used in interiorscaping are the same as

**Figure 1.21**

This sitting room includes plants as a personal accent to this "people"-gathering space. (Courtesy of Engledow Inc.)

**Figures 1.22 and 1.23**
These photos show the seating court and vaulted skylight at the Alemida Mall in Houston, Texas. The detailed designs of the skylight, tile, fountain, and planters provide an "island" for customers to rest and relax while shopping.

1.22

1.23

**Figure 1.24**
In this two-level mall, a simple "street tree"-like planting is used to create "people scale" in the corridor. Plants, banners, and lighting help accent and scale the space. (St. Clair Square, Fairview Heights, Illinois.)

**Figure 1.25**
In this urban redevelopment project, an atrium helps preserve the facade of a historic building while including new shopping spaces. The plantings at the doors help provide scale and serve as a continuation of the street-tree planting on the exterior. (The Galleria, Louisville, Kentucky.)

9

**1.26**

**1.28**

**1.27**

**Figures 1.26–1.28**
These photos illustrate the development of a hotel atrium/conservatory at the Opryland Hotel, Nashville, Tennessee. The 2-acre ground area and 1-acre glass roof provide a flexible year-round attraction for tourists and guests of the hotel and restaurant.

those used in other design professions, the crucial consideration here is that plantings are living components within a man-made environment. The emphasis of this text is to synthesize planning, graphic, and design concepts regarding interiorscaping, thus "bringing the outdoors in," as is illustrated in the text cover photos of Portside in Toledo, Ohio.

Chapter 1 covers interiorscaping as a concept and encourages the "art of seeing"; that is, being aware of our surroundings in relation to interior planting design. As an introduction to the concepts, procedures, and techniques used in the planning and designing of an interiorscape, Chapter 2 discusses basic design elements and principles relevant to all design areas. Chapter 3 then discusses the logical sequence used by designers in designing an interiorscape, commonly identified as the *design process* in design professions. While plans and drawings are important parts of the design process and are used in client–designer interaction, the actual installation, establishment, and maintenance of the project is equally as important in the long-term use and enjoyment of the space. Interior landscape designs are only as alive and dynamic as the limits of our imaginations. Chapters 4 through 7 cover graphics used in communicating interiorscape ideas, and Chapters 8 through 10 cover design illustrations and case studies.

## HISTORICAL BACKGROUND

Decorating with plants may date back to ancient times with the use of cultivated plants in containers by the Chinese. Today bonsai plants are as popular as potted plants were in ancient Greece and Rome (Figures 1.29 and 1.30). During the Victorian era plants—especially palms—were integral elements in a parlor: thus the term "parlor palm." Miniature indoor greenhouses, "Wardian Cases," were used to grow and display plants. Today, the excitement of the Victorian conservatory can be seen in the contemporary Disney World reconstruction, which houses a cafeteria.

The most recent growth in the production and use of plants indoors has been during the ecology boom of the 1960s and 1970s. Parallel to the increased awareness and use of plants indoors were advances in plant production and

**Figures 1.29 and 1.30**
Decorating personal living spaces with plants is a tradition that dates back to ancient Chinese potted plants. Potted plants illustrate our societies' continued interest in containerized plants for interiors as accents to our personal surroundings. (Longwood Gardens, Kennett Square, Pennsylvania.)

1.29

1.30

availability, and architectural changes conducive to plant growth indoors. Figures 1.31–1.36 illustrate the use of plant spaces and glass in architecture. During the 1970s large-scale interior plantings were begun. One such example is at the Crown Center Hotel in Kansas City, Missouri (Figures 1.37 and 1.38). Today plants indoors have become a part of our lifestyle as seen in stores, advertisements, and on television. Indoor plants help create a feeling of nature inside.

**Figure 1.31**
The Du Pont House, a historic atrium structure at Winterthur, Delaware.

**Figure 1.32**
Newly-constructed contemporary attached housing. The south-facing glass provides passive solar heating and light for plants in the interior. (Rockford, Illinois.)

1.33

1.34

**Figures 1.33 and 1.34**
The Penzoil Building in downtown Houston, Texas. The atrium bridges the twin towers and meets the street with attractive plantings.

**Figures 1.35 and 1.36**
The main pedestrian portion of the Penzoil atrium. The large planters were selected to reduce seating opportunities, as the space was meant to be a focal point for pedestrians, not a seating area.

1.35

1.37

1.38

1.36

**Figures 1.37 and 1.38**
The design and development of the Crown Center Hotel in Kansas City, Missouri in the 1970s included one of the first large-scale interiorscapes. The 90-ft high waterfall and lobby area illustrate a good example of the integration of architecture and interior plantings.

Indoor gardens project a human image; their beauty provides personal satisfaction, and space is better utilized when their functional benefits are considered (Figures 1.39–1.41).

Ed Engledow, president of Engledow Interior Landscaping, defines their interiorscape activities in his public relations material as "... the art of using plants to make inside space more useful and beautiful. Especially within an office building or other business location. Interior landscaping may be effectively used for easing blank walls, filling open spaces, creating more privacy, and/or adding 'character' to

**1.40**

**1.39**

**1.41**

**Figures 1.39–1.41**
In new hotels and restaurants interior plantings have become an integral part of a company's image and public visibility. (Photos of the Registry Hotel, Dallas, Texas, courtesy of Donald J. Molnar.)

an overall business environment. Interiorscaping is not haphazard or by chance but follows a definite arrangement, plan, or design considering the desired effect, available space, and lighting conditions and plant containers. An interior landscape is most effectively achieved by skilled professionals." The practicing professional in the interiorscape industry requires an understanding of the diversity of the industry and how they, as a practitioner, fit into this interdisciplinary profession.

*Interiorscapes: Planning, Graphics, and Design* is an introduction to the process of interior planting design for inte-

rior landscape professionals and students. As many or all of our decisions are made with our eyes, and in combination with preconceived ideas, the images and examples included should help you in identifying planning, design, and graphics information for interior plantings. Through sketches and photographs of architecture, interiors, plantings, and designed situations, the "art of seeing," will hopefully be identified. Figures 1.42–1.49 show how in our contemporary society commercial spaces and business organizations include interior plantings as a part of their total image. Indoor plantings have now become an expected component in our cul-

**Figures 1.42 and 1.43**
Plants are used in display to provide a background and to complement the merchandise as a sales tool.

1.42

1.43

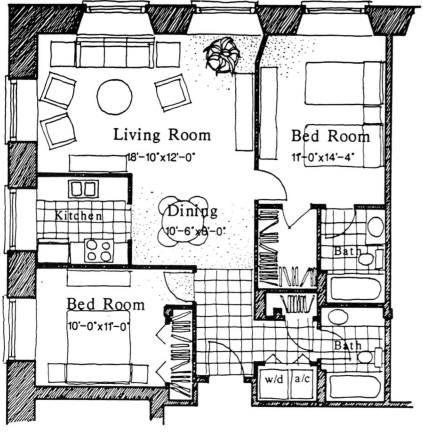

## TWO BEDROOM UNIT A2

1042 to 1071 sq. ft.

## THE MILL BUILDING

1.44

These figures show an interior plan that includes plantings as a focus for potential uses of the space. (Courtesy of Kennedy, Brown, McQuiston Architects. Sketch by E. Schleef.)

1.45

1.46

1.47

**Figures 1.46 and 1.47**
Collected advertisement graphics include plants as a design element.
These ads use plants in the interior to give a personal image to the
offices and furnishings being sold.

**1.48**

**Figures 1.48 and 1.49**
An interior planting can be as complex as a hotel lobby or as simple as an office park atrium. The key to the design and selection of plantings for an interior is the evaluation of the space and its use.

**1.49**

ture. The examples will focus on planning, graphics, and design and their interrelatedness in proposing planting design ideas for interior spaces. The four major text sections include: I. An Introduction to Interiorscaping and Design Concepts and Processes; II. Graphics Skills; III. Project Case Studies; and IV. an Appendix, industry associations, and support information.

To achieve this overview of the interdependence of planning, graphics, and design in proposing an interior planting, this text emphasizes the concept of "bringing the outdoors in" as a design consideration. This concept will be introduced in the text through Portside, a private-public development project in downtown Toledo, Ohio. This private development, in concert with the city, comprises the Promenade Festival Park, a commercial area, and hotels. The plan on the back cover begins to convey the project's context from the existing downtown buildings, streets, and walks to the open plaza and building spaces with river frontage. The site plan, in combination with the site photos, illustrates that built projects do require plans and designs executed with the site, surroundings, clients, and users in mind. While the graphics illustrate the overall space, the photographs show how the designers have used a theme to tie the indoors and outdoors together. Interiorscaping is not an end unto itself but is part of the total design picture, involving architects, landscape architects, interior designers, planners, and the users of the space.

In this text, the term *interiorscape* or the term *interior landscape design* will be used to describe the activities associated with the selection and placement of plantings as features within an interior (Figures 1.50–1.54). The word *interiorscaper* or *plantscaper* will be used to identify the practitioner or professional involved in the planning, design, and development of an interiorscape. Other terms included in the associated design professions are *architect, landscape architect,* and *interior designer.*

In practice, the interiorscape design process is usually initiated by the project owner, project manager, project architect, or other associated individual. Requests for infor-

**Figure 1.51**
In this delicatessen the hanging plants help create a setting and scale for the open atrium space. Here, plant species and placement is critical so as not to conflict with food service or patrons.

**Figure 1.50**
In this office reception area the interior plantings are rented and maintained by an interiorscape specialist. (Courtesy of Engledow Inc.)

**Figures 1.52–1.54**
Large-scale office complexes as seen in these photos use atriums and plantings as foyers and reception areas.

1.52

1.53

1.54

mation usually relate to what professional services are available regarding the development of the project. As a design professional, the information and services provided should focus on the client's request, the project site and its surroundings, as well as other conditions important to the development of an attractive and useful space.

## THE INTERIOR LANDSCAPE INDUSTRY

The interior plant industry includes specialists in plant production, design, installation, and maintenance converging in the development of indoor plantings as an integral part of designed interiors. While many of the professionals often are involved in the planning and development of interiors, they may not always be familiar with specific details of growing tropical plants. Many plantscapers, although they are plant specialty personnel, aren't familiar with design considerations or the process of proposing plants for interior spaces. The roles of each professional in an interior design should be understood: Production and nursery professionals are the suppliers of the basic planting elements; planning and design professionals pull together ideas, ending with the installation; and establishment and maintenance personnel care for the project once it is completed. Interior plantscape plant selection should be based on both plant function and interior design considerations. Many interiorscape problems can be caused by placing a plant in a location where it cannot survive or does not relate to the room's design scheme. Plant and design knowledge are equally important in the selection, production, merchandising, and installation of plant materials. With all these considerations, the designer-plantscaper designs and selects interior plants as the clients' representative (Figures 1.55 and 1.56).

For the interiorscape contractor, knowledge of design provides an understanding of the use of plants as a design element in a space, but not exclusively as a major design focus of the space, as is the case with outdoor plants and constructed features. As for interior landscape maintenance firms, design awareness gives them direction and focus in the management of plants as they relate to the space and the design concept (Figures 1.57 and 1.58).

**Figures 1.55 and 1.56**
The lobby area of this hotel is staged with balconies that include movable floor planters. Ledge plantings also add scale and soften the edges within the atrium space. (The Peachtree Plaza Hotel, Atlanta, Georgia.)

1.55

1.57

1.56

1.58

**Figures 1.57 and 1.58**
While design and development of interior plantings should relate to the architecture and interior design, maintenance is also an important consideration. These photos illustrate the use of plantscape specialists who water, groom, and manage the planting in the Galleria in Louisville, Kentucky.

21

Interiorscaping and interior landscape design concepts have evolved since the time when plants in containers were the norm; today designers and their interiorscapes must provide a more functional and attractive indoor human environment. Rather than show the diversity and complexity of available plants, containers, and construction materials, interior plant designs should reflect the building—its use, the construction materials, and its furnishings—and the client's needs (Figures 1.59 and 1.60). Just as the plantscapers and designers of the past proposed designs that were suited for the situation and times, today's interior landscapes must utilize new technologies, practices, and considerations that are necessary with a more design-educated public. Today the public sees interior planting daily in magazines, catalogs, stores, and so on. Today's designer must assess a client's preconceived ideas about interiorscapes and then evaluate them through an understanding of design elements, principles, and process. Designers should convey the basic functional and aesthetic benefits of a planned interior development to clients as well as informing them about recent developments in the industry. As shown in Figures 1.61 and 1.62, the designers of this project see the interior and plantings as part of the building's and the site's landscape development and use.

Interior landscapes are planned, designed, supplied, installed, maintained, and serviced by a wide range of industry practitioners and professionals. Architects, landscape architects, interior designers, contractors, project managers, salespersons, and nurserymen are a few of the people involved. As a person interested in interiorscaping or other professional areas including architecture, horticulture, landscape design, landscape architecture, and interior design, it is important to understand how these specialties relate to the larger "green" and interior landscape industries. And to best align your personal interests and abilities with the appropriate career areas, it is necessary to understand the expertise and knowledge required for each of the "green" and associated industry professions.

*Architect:* A practitioner of the design profession of architecture, which is considered to be the art and science of designing enclosed structures to control the environ-

**Figure 1.59**
In this mall seating area, movable planters allow the mall management flexibility in organizing seating and staging of activities. (The Galleria, Louisville, Kentucky.)

**Figure 1.60**
In this hotel lobby atrium, permanent planters are used as part of the architecture to create an interior image and focal point in the space. (Embassy Suites, Indianapolis, Indiana.)

1.61

1.62

**Figures 1.61 and 1.62**
The design integration of the exterior and interior of a project is seen in these photos of the Galleria, downtown Louisville, Kentucky. The allée scheme of street trees outside the atrium are continued into the interior planting at the atrium entries.

ment for human activities. These design professionals are registered in all states.*

*Landscape Architect:* A practitioner of the art and science of designing and developing landscapes and gardens.* The primary design focus here is site planning.

*Landscape Architecture:* (1) The art of arranging land and the objects upon it for human use and beauty, and (2) the art of space utilization in the landscape. Landscape architecture is concerned with the use to which landscape space is developed and the creation of environments within landscape spaces.*

*Landscape Design:* Creative environmental problem-solving process to organize external space and attain an optimum balance of natural factors and human needs.*

*Interior Designer:* Creatively solves problems relative to the function and quality of man's proximate environment. Included are recommendations of interior spaces with an understanding of other related aspects of environmental design.* Interiorscaping may be a specialty area within any of these design professions or a practice of its own.

*Interiorscapers–Plantscapers:* These may be designers, installers, salespersons, nurserymen, and/or maintenance people offering a variety of services as part of an umbrella organization of their company. Because of the wide variety of services often requested, few interiorscape designers specialize in design only.

One potential conflict inherent in the design process is that the design proposal can become secondary to installing, selling, and maintaining an interior. Rather than providing the client with a design that fits this situation, the "services" become the focus. The expertise provided by designers and other professionals to clients should be consistent and creditable so that the professional proposal is provided without personal conflicts of interest.

Within the professions of architecture and landscape architecture, design based upon site and client considerations has long been accepted as a means to propose functional,

* Warner L. Marsh, *Landscape Vocabulary* (Los Angeles: Miramar Pub. Co. 1964).

aesthetic, and buildable landscape developments. Novice or experienced plantsmen can often overlook project and client considerations when developing proposals because their plant experience and knowledge often overshadows their planning and design backgrounds. In comparison, designers may understand design and construction materials but lack the understanding of plants and their cultural requirements that is necessary for sound plant growth and establishment. The practice of interiorscaping as an industry requires an understanding of both design and plants. The project location, building orientation, interior spaces, and client information—in conjunction with planning concepts and design considerations—are used to develop useful and aesthetic interior plantscapes. Used as a communications tool in concert with planning and design considerations, graphics help the designer to visualize and communicate ideas to other designers, clients, and contractors.

The planning, design, and development of interiorscapes involves many different people: client-owner, building architect, interior designer, landscape architect, and interiorscaper. While the interior landscape industry has a diversity of evolving professionals, the green industry that has developed around the focus of exterior landscape design and development also has a great variety of information concerning what landscape design both exterior and interior can use. Within each industry, specialty, and profession each defines their process and product with respect to their expertise. Collectively there is no real consensus regarding specific goals and objectives to be satisfied by an interiorscape design. As a person interested in interiorscaping, be aware of the diversified nature of the industry and the wealth of resources available: it is in the best interests of your clients, the industry as a whole, and yourself.

## Associated Professional Organizations

Many "green" industry organizations are available to provide information directly related to your professional or personal interests. Included is a partial listing of professional design and green industry organizations; their addresses can be found in the Appendix.

| | |
|---|---|
| AAN | American Association of Nurserymen |
| AIA | American Institute of Architects |
| ALCA | Associated Landscape Contractors of America |
| ASID | American Society of Interior Designers |
| ASLA | American Society of Landscape Architects |
| CELA | Council of Educators in Landscape Architecture |
| FFF | Florida Foliage Foundation |
| IBD | Interior Business Designers |
| IFLA | International Federation of Landscape Architects |
| ILD-ALCA | Interior Landscape Division-ALCA |
| IPA | Interior Plantscape Association |
| LAF | Landscape Architecture Foundation |
| LIAC | Landscape Industry Advisory Council |
| NCIHC | National Council for Interior Horticultural Certification |
| NLA | National Landscape Association |

## Industry Publications

The "green" and design industries are serviced by publications that provide information on trends, products, and other subject matter relative to interior landscape development and other areas of design. A listing of some of these industry publications follows:

*American Nurseryman:* A bimonthly publication concerning plant production, maintenance, and development areas within the landscape and nursery industries.

*Architectural Record:* A monthly publication that records and presents trends and concepts on current architectural practices.

*Florida Foliage:* A monthly publication with an annual special foliage locator, published by the Florida Foliage Association. The annual issue includes feature articles, planting availability listings, directory of foliage and applied industries, and regional Florida maps; the monthly publication covers current topics in the interior foliage industry.

*Garden Design:* A quarterly magazine that reflects the diversity of residential landscape architecture and design. This is a specialized area released by *Landscape Architecture* magazine.

*Interior Design:* A monthly publication serving the interior design profession which presents design projects, industry news, and professional announcements; it also provides a good overview of available merchandise.

*Interior Landscape Industry:* A monthly published by the American Nurseryman Publishing Company featuring industry news updates, coming events, and articles on the interiorscape and applied industry areas.

*Interiorscaping:* A bimonthly magazine published by Brantwood Publications. Included are feature articles as well as special concerns and viewpoints from educators, landscape architects, the industry, and the readers.

*Landscape and Turf:* An industry publication that focuses on the planning, design, maintenance, and establishment aspects of site and landscape development. Published seven times per year.

*Landscape Architecture:* A bimonthly international magazine of regional and land planning, landscape design, construction, and management.

*Nursery Manager:* Published monthly by Branch-Smith Publishers. Topics include production, business, landscape, law, and ornamentals; interiorscaping is also covered by contributing editors.

*Progressive Architecture:* This monthly magazine features articles on current trends in architecture.

*Weeds, Trees, and Turf:* A monthly publication that emphasizes the production, installation, and maintenance of landscapes.

## SUMMARY

Interiorscaping, which involves professionals in a wide range of professional areas, must combine the concepts of planning and design with plant knowledge in order to develop interior planting designs that are both functional and attractive. As you read about *Interiorscaping: planning, graphics, and design,* put the information in perspective to your selected area of interest. The end result of any interiorscape should be a quality space for client use and plant survival. Interiorscaping as a process should take client-owner, project site and locale, principles of interior design, and cultural details, into consideration to provide a useful and attractive area for enjoyment. The illustrations and examples included in this chapter identify the interrelationships between industry professionals and the use of planning, graphic, and design information in an interior landscape design. As you reflect on this information, try to identify what design considerations you use when proposing plantings and selecting materials for an interior landscape design situation.

# Chapter 2

# Design Elements and Principles

## INTRODUCTION

Attractive and functionally-organized interior planting designs are usually not accidental occurrences. Much forethought and planning goes into design proposals for architecture, interior design, landscape architecture, and interiorscaping. While there are no magic formulas for good design, certain principles have evolved over time through all of the arts—music, painting, architecture, sculpture, and so on. When used these principles facilitate orderly and aesthetically pleasing results. Planting design for indoor spaces may include the development of a range of interior areas and spaces. Designs for individual buildings may include foyer areas, reception spaces, open-floors, office systems, and even large building atriums (Figures 2.1–2.6). Interiorscaping in concept can define the spaces in which people

# HOLIDAY PLAZA COMPLEX

**Figures 2.1–2.6**

Interiorscape design should strive to unify and complement the architecture and interior design. These photos illustrate a hotel/commercial complex. The Holiday Plaza is a combination of a hotel and commercial offices. The images shown are part of a promotional brochure. *Figures 2.1 and 2.2:* The interior atrium space bridges the office tower and hotel use areas within the building. *Figures 2.3 and 2.4:* These photos illustrate the use of plants in a corridor with vaulted skylight and soffit planters and the use of floor planters to define seating areas in the foyer of the hotel. *Figures 2.5 and 2.6:* The functional use of plantings as screening help create subspaces in the restaurant / lounge area of the atrium.

2.3

2.1

2.2

2.4

27

**2.5**

work, relax, or recreate. The design drawings that convey these ideas should not be an end unto themselves but a means of planning, designing, and developing a setting that is useful and pleasing (Figures 2.7 and 2.8).

A successful design for an interior landscape—one that is useful yet visually attractive—requires the application of the elements and principles of design. Line, form, texture and color are the design elements used with the design principles: scale, proportion, dominance, rhythm, repetition and balance. The compositions developed in architecture, interior design, landscape architecture, landscape design, and interiorscapes are three-dimensional; the spaces will be experienced visually and physically as we live and work in these "compositions." Interiorscapes are spaces composed of materials which express inherent line, form, texture, and color (Figures 2.9–2.12). In designs that are functional and attractive the designer has manipulated the

**Figure 2.7**

In these collected graphics, the examples illustrate that attractive and functional interiors are first designed, then developed. (Courtesy of: Signode Corporation, Glenview, IL. Designer: Jeanne Hartnett and Assoc., Inc. Photograph: David Clifton. Drawing: John Murford.)

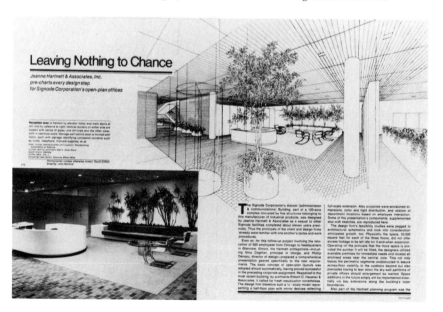

**2.6**

**Figure 2.8**
Interiorscaping in a sophisticated way is bringing the outdoors in, just as landscape architecture tries to extend indoor spaces and activities outdoors.

**Figure 2.9**
In this office interior the triangular-shaped atrium is contrasted with banners to unify balcony levels. Repeated plants are also used to unify the balcony and corridor spaces. (Courtesy of Engledow Inc.)

**Figure 2.10**
In this office lobby, balcony areas are edged with plantings to soften the architecture. These plants provide a living element to this area. (Courtesy of Engledow Inc.)

**Figure 2.11**

Office interiors can include plantings to accent file areas and screens, as well as to separate areas within open offices.

**Figure 2.12**

Retail stores now use plants as accents within sales areas as part of the store display. (Courtesy of D. G. Smith.)

design elements using the principles of design in order to satisfy the characteristics of that specific site, its surroundings, and client conditions.

When a design proposal or actual design project looks attractive it is usually an anticipated and planned effect created through good design. Two-dimensional disciplines such as photography and graphic design use these same principles and elements. As you experience designed spaces, evaluate the actual space or photos and plans of the area, reviewing them in terms of the design elements and the application of the principles of design. These same skills are, in turn, used to convey design ideas that eventually will be actual interiorscaped spaces. After your reading of the chapter, try to remember these ideas for a better understanding of the applications of basic design (Figures 2.13–2.16).

Design ideas are organized and refined through a systematic thought process called *design process,* or *site planning* within the profession of landscape architecture. These thoughts are expressed in plans which are used to implement the actual site installation. An understanding and ordering of the locale, the project, and client information, in conjunction with knowledge of design elements and principles is important when making a design proposal. This information is used in the design process to result in a planned environment that fits its context. Each project and its solution should be unique: it should be evaluated on an individual basis.

Some common traits of good design can be discussed in general terms. First, good designers take the needs of the client and user into consideration. Second, the proposal should be functional and constructable. Third, it should be sensitive to the project situation. Fourth, it should aesthetically please and enhance the quality of life. These considerations are similar to the objectives used by Thomas Church, a California Landscape architect, in site planning and design. Design proposals are only as alive and dynamic as the imagination of the client and designer.

Interior landscape design as a "design discipline" includes design composition in the project's development, its presentation, and actual installation as a "total" proposal.

**Figures 2.13 and 2.14**

From a vantage from above and at floor level these plantings help screen use areas and create pleasant pedestrian zones. (Holiday Inn Plaza, Matteson, Illinois.)

2.13

2.14

2.15

2.16

**Figures 2.15 and 2.16**

The development of an interiorscape is creating a garden space indoors. The concept of creating indoor gardens had its early roots in the traditional flower shows which brought exterior plants and construction materials indoor for temporary displays. (Courtesy of Frits Loonsten Inc. Landscape Contractors, Indianapolis Flower and Patio Show.)

Interior space design and information composition involves a layering of ideas. An evaluation of what the existing physical conditions and design implications are comes from the floor plans and related drawings of interior conditions. In addition, the client's needs or anticipated uses help direct the design composition towards appropriate revisions to satisfy functional and aesthetic requirements. While working on paper, it is important to remember that the plan represents actual building areas and spaces that have height as well as depth and width. As seen in Figures 2.17–2.20, plans represent project areas that the design proposal must accomodate.

Although a design's worth is frequently judged by the project's appearance alone, the design criteria used are of equal importance and should be taken into consideration. Interior planting design proposals should be functional, visually pleasing, and economically feasible. Remember, good looking plans do not necessarily make successful designs.

**2.18**

**Figures 2.17–2.20**

These four photos represent a planned and designed office atrium. The interiorscape is the focal point of the lobby and surrounding offices. The design is asymmetrical and attractive at floor and corridor levels alike. Construction material selection and plant details add to the unified feeling of the space. (Courtesy of Envirodesign, Dallas, Texas. Designers: A. L. David and Dick Author.)

**2.17**

**2.19**

2.20

Similarly, a design which works functionally but is unattractive visually is not desirable. Successful designs combine functional and aesthetic qualities in the total composition. Overall, a pleasing interior landscape should improve our day to day surroundings: The plantings should enhance life by providing a setting that may reduce tensions, anxieties, and conflicts in our daily environment.

## THE ELEMENTS OF DESIGN

Interior landscape designers, as other professional designers, should consider the attractive and functional considerations in developing three-dimensional spaces. Through design elements and principles designers process ideas into plans, and plans into implemented proposals. To help introduce this design language, brief definitions and simple illustrations of design elements and principles are included. The first consideration in proposing an aesthetic and useful proposal is the use and the users of the space, as established through an evaluation of the space and client needs. The topic of design process will be included in Chapter 3. Both in the presentation and active installation of a design, de-

signers should strive to achieve a completely functional and aesthetic solution using the principles and elements of design and design process.

## Line, Form, Texture, and Color

Plans of project proposals are composed of line, form, and texture, with color or descriptions of colors as representating the actual project space. Line is used to define forms and to add texture to drawings.

**Line.** In interior landscape design, as well as other design fields, line is found in the edges of elements and materials. Plants with their individual habits of growth give a certain feeling of line: Overall feelings of upright, horizontal, or irregular line are conveyed by plants and their containers. Floor surfacings and their patterns, ceilings, wall panels, and related openings all have line, and result in inherent edges established by projected lines from within the space or building. Vertical line can be found in the shape or construction materials of the room and in other enclosure elements (Figures 2.21–2.26).

Line in a design can create visual movement as well as defining forms and areas through the delineation of shapes and edges. It can be straight, diagonal, parallel, perpendicular, curvilinear, or a combination of these. Line may create a feeling of formality when straight or of naturalness when curved, while intersecting lines can create points of hesitation.

All materials used in design have lines, thus an understanding of the inherent line quality of shapes and materials is important. If, early in your planning, you are informed that the construction materials will have straight edges, your understanding of line should tell you that tight curves would not be a realistic design solution due to the inherent character of the materials.

Selection of line within a composition should take the shape of the room, its circulation, and the areas to be developed for activities into consideration. Often, the configuration of a room and its furnishings, or its uses, dictates the lines to be used in an interscape project design. Line is one way to manipulate the visual and physical composition and to organize design proposals.

2.21

These photos collectively show that plants and architecture have inherent line that should be considered in the evaluation of spaces and in the selection of plants. *Figure 2.21:* This succulent species has a vertical and somewhat inherent recurving form. *Figure 2.22:* This specimen *Dracaena* has an overall upright form. *Figure 2.23:* This *Dracaena* has a vertical line with recurving lines seen in the *Pothos* ground cover. *Figure 2.24:* This atrium corridor is taller than it is wide, giving an upward feeling and directing attention toward the anchor store. Due to the narrow floor area, hanging baskets rather than floor plants are used. (Alemida Mall, Houston, Texas.) *Figure 2.25:* The horizontal lines in the balcony edges provide an ideal location for bands of Grape ivy. *Figure 2.26:* The vertical lines in the Peachtree Plaza Atrium are contrasted by the horizontal lines of balcony seating areas with lines of hanging plants and movable planters of figs that define seating areas.

2.22

2.23

2.24

2.25

2.26

**Form.** Form is the actual three-dimensional aspect of an object or space. The height, depth, and width of an object or area can be perceived as a solid, hollow, or transparent element within a design or component.* Buildings "read" as solids from the outside, and as covered structures with openings on their faces from the inside. An interior space is often perceived as a hollow within this solid. Figures 2.27 and 2.28 show the exterior form of a building, the related interior area, and the interior space.

**Figures 2.27 and 2.28**

The architectural form or shape of these pavilions sited on the inner harbor area in Baltimore, Maryland, creates distinctive exterior and interior shapes. The interior is scaled and accented with the addition of tree forms. In this photo the trees are illuminated with small holiday lights. (Photos courtesy of Tom Kramer.)

2.28

2.27

---

* G. Earle, "A Manual of Design Theory for Landscape Architecture" (unpublished handout, SUNY College of Environmental Science and Forestry).

Plants themselves have rounded, straight, or irregular forms (Figure 2.29). A plant's overall form can also be influenced by the inherent line found in its trunk configuration or branches, as seen in Figures 2.30 and 2.31. When plants are used in containers the plant–container combination may also need to be evaluated (Figures 2.32 and 2.33). When developing an interior planting, the form of a space determines the use and the number of users and/or furnishings and associated plantings. It is your evaluation of an area—its dimensions, size or scale—upon which design proposals that are comfortable for human use or activities are based. These conditions should be reviewed before the addition of plants is considered.

**Figure 2.29**
In this collected magazine ad, an interior scene was selected to complement the chair design which is the point of the advertisement. The cactus adds a sculptural element and adds scale to the image. (Photo courtesy of Vecta Contract.)

**2.30**

**Figures 2.30 and 2.31**
While "a plant is a plant" in a general design sense, individual plants need to be chosen with discrimination for a specific project. While each of these photos show a fig tree the plant form and trunk characters are quite different.

**2.31**

2.32

2.33

**Figures 2.32 and 2.33**

Plant / container relationships are also important design considerations. In these collected graphics, the interiors shown illustrate both plant composition and container selection. The plant and container selection needs to relate to the space, furnishing, and materials. Many container source catalogs are available through their manufacturers. The brochures distributed can be a valuable resource in communicating to clients the choices available. (Photos courtesy of: Louver Drape Corporation and Architectural Supplements, Inc.)

**Texture.** Texture is the visual and/or tactile surface characteristic of an object or element within a design. Visual texture is a surface configuration that evokes a tactile sensation. Clouds are often perceived as being fluffy and soft although they cannot be touched; similarly, one perceives a placid pool of water as smooth. Some plant materials viewed from a distance seem to have a flat texture, yet may be quite different when seen closer or actually touched. Texture can relate to the overall character of the object, or it can be specific to individual components of the whole: its branches, leaves, and so on (Figures 2.34 and 2.35). Without textures and surface variations, design illustrations and actual project areas would seem flat and uninteresting. In combination with light and shadows textures add depth and interest to compositions. Texture in plants and surfacings can provide interest and variety within a design scheme (Figures 2.36–2.39).

The textures of plantings in an interior space may be perceived in varying ways. Fine-textured plants may visually recede from the viewer, while coarse-textured plants may advance due to the size of the component plant parts. In planting design proposals, if fine-textured or detailed plantings are to be included these plants should be located close

2.34

2.35

**Figures 2.34 and 2.35**

These photos exemplify the diversity of plant-leaf shapes and sizes available. Plant-leaf shape and size translates in overall plant texture, which is a design consideration within an interiorscape.

**Figures 2.36–2.39**

Finely-textured plants: the rabbit-foot fern, maidenhair fern, spotted croton, and peperonia.

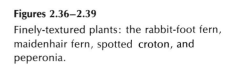

2.36

2.37

2.38

2.39

to a viewer's vantage point. If coarse-textured plantings are used they are best located further from the viewer's vantage point so that their mass is perceived as background (Figures 2.40–2.45). Similarly, sculptural features or accessories should be located where they can be seen rather than in illogical areas, and staged with an appropriate background (Figure 2.46).

Plant selection by texture falls into three basic categories, according to Professors Tom Weiler and Judy Watson of Purdue University: "Plant textures can be categorized as

**Figures 2.40 and 2.41**
The cactus, while having a sharp texture to the touch, has a medium texture visually, as does the Austrian umbrella plant. Both have average-sized leaves and result in a medium texture.

2.40

2.41

2.42

2.43

**Figures 2.42–2.45**
Large-textured plants have expansive individual leaves as seen in the fiddleleaf fig, cycad, monsteria, and palm species shown.

2.44

2.45

**Figure 2.46**

This sculptural element in a mall is seated in a base of plants in a planter. It is important from a design sense to recognize that the sculpture is the primary focus and the plantings are secondary. The plants selected provide a textural contrast to the space and sculpture. (Photo of Northbrook Court, Glencoe, Illinois.)

fine, medium and coarse as conveyed by leaf arrangement, grouping, branching patterns as well as flower and fruits of certain seasons." Fine textured plants usually have tiny leaves or leaflets and a delicate appearance. Medium textured plants have intermediate leaves, and coarse plants have large, massive leaves. Plant texture may be used to enhance a room's appearance or to blend with the surroundings.*

**Color.** Color, the last of the design elements, is a completely visual element. Technically it is the observed reflection of light waves from a surface. When light strikes a surface, some light waves are absorbed and others reflected. The reflected light is what gives an object its color. In Figure 2.47 natural light composed of a spectrum of colors is strik-

---

* Tom Weiler/Judy Watson, "Interior Plants, Texture" (Purdue University).

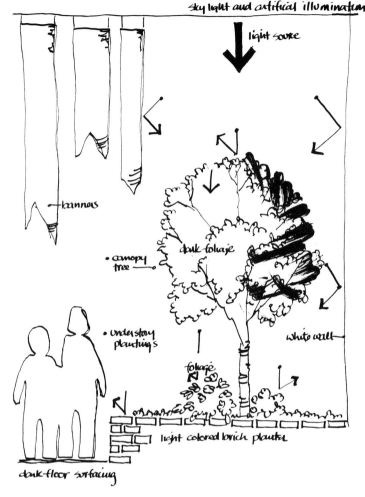

sky light and artificial illumination

light source

banners

dark foliage

• canopy
tree

• understory
plantings

white wall

foliage

light colored brick planter

dark floor surfacing

**Figure 2.47**
As both natural and artificial light strike interior surfacings, light waves
are both reflected and absorbed. The actual color seen is the light waves
being reflected from surfaces.

ing the opaque surfaces of the plants, the floor, wall surfacing, and furniture from behind the person in the scene. As
the light hits the various surfaces, light waves are absorbed
and reflected. The actual color seen—in this case the greens

of the plants and the browns and oranges of the walls and
furnishings—is reflected light waves.

Color in design creates excitement and contrast. Warm
colors (reds and oranges) are visually advancing colors,
while blues and greens are cool colors that visually recede.
The selection of plants and materials in interiorscaping
should establish a theme to complement or contrast with
the interior, its fixtures, and its surroundings. Seasonal additions may also be a design consideration.

Color in the interior landscape is often thought to mean
a selection of varying shades of green. With the great diversity of available plant species and the potential additions of
seasonal accent plants, an interior scheme can come alive
with a wide range of colors throughout the year. Leaves,
flowers, fruits, and stems all contribute to a plant's color and
effect. Composition considerations should include a review
of the background and foreground elements with color perceived as part of the composition.

Permanent plantings and interior elements are usually
coordinated with the use of seasonal spots of color and
accessories. Potted spring and summer bulbs and flowering
plants are seasonal options that set off the permanent plantings. No matter what the color theme is, select a palate that
adds interest while maintaining unity in your design. When
considering an acceptable palate of color look at the regional characteristics of the locale for hints. Different regions may have specific color preferences relative to their
landscape setting and/or climate that you need to be
aware of.

The characteristics of color are hue, value, and intensity.
Hue is the name of the color: red, yellow, purple, etc. Value
describes the lightness or darkness of the color, indicating
the quality of light reflected. Intensity is the degree of pu-
rity, strength, or saturation of the hue. A monochromatic
composition is one that uses different values and intensities
of one hue, or color. Complementary colors are hues that
are on opposite sides of the color wheel and are used side
by side for emphasis. Red next to green or blue next to
yellow are complementary colors that have an increased intensity because of the strong contrasts created by their prox-
imity to each other (Figure 2.48).

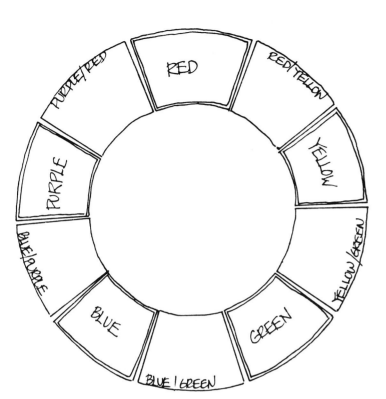

**Figure 2.48**
Color wheels are often used to illustrate the basic relationship between primary and secondary colors. Color schemes that use colors on one side of the color wheel are called monochromatic, while schemes using colors selected across from each other are complementary color schemes.

## THE PRINCIPLES OF DESIGN

Planning and design of an interiorscape should begin with an understanding of the overall design context and the interiorscape's relationship to the architecture, interior design, and use of the space. The design principles which are then used to manipulate line, form, texture, and color within a space are scale, proportion, order, unity, dominance, repetition, rhythm, and balance. The designer should appreciate

the existing character, condition, and inherent characteristics of the project and apply design principles, using the elements of design for defining and detailing a design. Any recommendations made should attempt to enhance and complement the interior scheme established. Interiorscapes, like designed spaces, should express a sense of place and create a feeling of unity between the building, its site, the interior, and the interiorscaping.

The basic principles of design are the foundation of design composition in all design areas. They are found in art and design and applied in painting, sculpture, textiles, and pottery as well as in photography, graphic design, architecture, interior design, landscape architecture, and interior plantscaping. Design principles are used to manipulate design elements—line, form, texture, and color—in design composition. The actual selection and development of materials occurs after a design scheme is established. The selection decisions then strive to create a unified, harmonious, and attractive design composition. In interior landscape design, composition includes the space as it is defined by the architect, its furnishings and surfacing by the architect and/or interior designer, and plants by the landscape architect or plantscaper. Design composition should evaluate the project's visual and physical relationships in its development and its eventual use by people. In using design principles one should note that a single plant or design element can serve more than one design function. All of the design principles are crucial, but the most important visual aspect in a project's design is scale.

### Scale

Scale is the relative size of an object or objects within a space. Appropriateness of scale is essential to the success of a design (Figures 2.49–2.51). The scale of the parts of the design which define the various spaces—the floor, walls, and ceiling—is critical. Consistency of scale throughout a design is mandatory. A properly-scaled design appears normal and comfortable, while an area with scale conflict can generate uncomfortable visual tensions. One basis of measurement for determining appropriate scale is using the hu-

**Figure 2.49**

In this large exhibit hall, banners are suspended from the ceiling to help create more intimate subspaces for the displays and visitors at floor level. (McCormick Place, Chicago, Illinois.)

**Figures 2.50 and 2.51**

This large indoor garden is the Aviary Exhibit at the North Carolina Zoo. The plantings not only create a setting for the displays but provide shade, reduce glare, and scale the height of the space, thus creating a more pleasant environment for visitors. (Courtesy Tropical Plant Rentals Inc., Chicago, Illinois.)

2.50

2.51

**Figure 2.52**

In general, design schemes and scale factors are determined by the average height of an adult. The exception would be design situations specifically for children. The scale of this specimen *dracaena* is a large tree to this young child while to an adult the plant would be of average size.

**Figure 2.53**

In this atrium the architecture and plantings are scaled to create spaces for groups of people, while directing traffic through the court area. (Hyatt Regency, Indianapolis, Indiana.)

**Figure 2.54**

The concept of scale is defined as a visual and/or physical comparison of elements or spaces relative to a person or people. Human elements in a drawing are helpful to understand the size and scale of elements and spaces proposed or to be developed. In this diagram the perceived size of the vertical changes, as the size of the people used for scale change.

man body (Figures 2.52–2.54). In Figure 2.54 the vertical element shown is a graphic example of how scale is determined by a visual comparison of adjoining elements, assuming no written information about size is available. In each portion of the comparison sketch, the vertical element is shown in relation to the adjoining (human) elements, providing a basis for scale determination.

In design, the size and shape of a project area will determine the scale of the elements to be included. The spaces or areas within the space determine the use, possible activities, and plant opportunities. Proposed plants, and planters and containers as units, should be selected according to the scale relationship between the plant, the container, and the scale of the space they are to occupy. Other selection criteria are the grouping of design components, plants, and furnishings within the space and their locations relative to the room, the surroundings, and the movement of people (Figures 2.55–2.58).

In projects of smaller size or spaces, design proposals should utilize appropriately-scaled plantings and design elements. Selection of smaller-scale plants and flexible fixtures can help create functional, efficient, and attractive areas in the available areas. The installation of plants with potential "forest" proportions can be a frustrating experience in small areas. As larger species mature, they overwhelm the space and outgrow the project by extending beyond the area's or room's boundaries. But if the larger maturing plants are selected not as permanent plants but on a rental basis, they could be replaced when they grow too large for the space.

**Figures 2.55–2.58**

Two three-story atriums are included in this building complex at the University of Houston at Clear Lake City, Texas. *Figures 2.55 and 2.56:* The main entry of the building includes a permanent planting pocket. The plants collectively create a mass one-half the height of the atrium space. Within this permanent planting the north side of the planting is thin and less attractive due to shading by canopy plants. *Figures 2.57 and 2.58:* Another atrium in the building is used as a study and multi-use area. Cantilevered balconies, floor plants, and floor tables with umbrellas are used to scale the space. The movable tables, chairs, and plants allow the atrium to become an auditorium area when needed.

2.56

2.55

2.57

2.58

In expansive spaces, larger maturing plants and more varied and permanent site furnishings may be used. Project design should strive to adequately provide for physical use and visual scale. Through an understanding of a space, the areas within the space, its use, and its users these guides can serve to approximate the scale of design components to be proposed.

## Proportion

The concept of proportion is directly related to scale. Proportion is the relationship of design or compositional elements to each other. In interior planting design, proportion is the relative size of components in a room; its surfacings, furnishings, plants, and other elements. In Figures 2.59 and 2.60 the proportions of numbers and sizes of plants in relation to a plan–elevation and to containers are illustrated. When selecting plants and containers for an interior remember that physical sizes used in interior design have smaller proportions than those used in exterior spaces. This also holds true for constructed features. Exterior steps and edges are exaggerated to accomodate varying degrees of use and

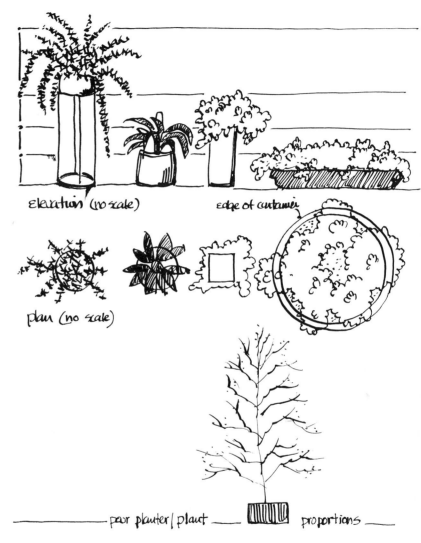

**Figure 2.59**

Interiorscape designers should consider the proportion of a plant to its container and the proportion of this unit to other furnishings. An overall evaluation of the space within which they are to be used should be made, to select plants and containers effectively.

47

**Figure 2.60**
In this interior scheme the permanent planting includes a tree form and
ground plants. The scale of the bonsai plant on the table and other
plants collectively are in proportion to the space, users, and uses.

climatic influences such as snow and ice. Interior areas and
spaces are smaller, in comparison to exterior spaces, for
efficiency in use. Thus plants, containers, planting beds,
and color selections need to be selected carefully. As for
color proportions, the use of accents and contrasts relative

to the simplicity or complexity of the project and site building are best. Remember that plant size and colors should
work with the size and color of the room and furnishings:
plantings should be subordinate to the space unless they are
the focal point of the area.

## Order

Order is the sense of organization and basic structure
within a design. Order may also be referred to as the project's theme or style—how the composition is arranged. A
design without order is simply a jumble of unrelated parts
working independently. Some examples of order are the
natural, formal, curvilinear, and symmetrical schemes—all
variations of a project's line.

The principle of order is based on visual and emotional
reactions to the overall organization and structure of existing buildings, room edges, lines, and forms within an area.
To evaluate order one may ask, "Does the space or room, its
furnishing and planting parts seem to fit together logically
and relate to the use?" It is probably easier to review already
developed proposals before applying this concept to a project in the planning stage. When evaluating an existing design or proposal, try to determine if an overall theme or
scheme has been developed. Straight, rectangular, diagonal, or curved lines can be the foundation of order in a
design proposal. Proposals that develop a design theme
through line need to either complement or contrast the inherent line of the architecture, the room–area configuration, or the use. Sight lines, views from inside and out, and
circulation ways are also design departures to consider in
creating a sense of order (Figures 2.61–2.64).

Since an interior project includes varied areas com-
prised of many different spaces and edges, the application
of order should strive to tie these separated areas together.
This sense of order is needed to unify the projects spaces so
that no single element or area stands out. Planning should
start at the floor plane and continue to the ceiling or top
enclosure with design components that enclose the space.
A sense of order may also extend exterior or entry areas into
interior spaces, as seen in the cover illustration of the Portside project.

**Figure 2.61**

In this mall seating area, visual and physical order is created through the aligned edges of the ground planters and pavement patterns. The focal point within this space is then the sculptural element.

**Figure 2.62**

In this mall, the pathways and plantings selected are logical and realistic for the context and situation within the mall. A feeling of order is achieved with the pavement and planter design edges aligned.

**Figure 2.63**

Order and organization are often achieved through the selection and repetition of construction materials. Here the brick floor surfacings accent and organize the floor areas.

**Figure 2.64**

In this seating area as in other seating courts in the mall the repetition of the seating type and design give the overall project a sense of order.

# Unity

Unity, closely related to order, is the harmonious relationship of elements or characteristics in a design. Unity is a perceived feeling of the visual quality considering the components of line, form, texture, color. More specifically, unity is the coordination of design elements appropriate for a specific area rather than a perception of the specific line and composition. In design proposals including many subspaces such as the corridor of a shopping mall, consistent floor and wall surfacings may provide unity to the space. Corridor accents include store fronts, plantings, and contrasting accessories to give a sense of place as well as unity to the megastructure. Unity within a defined area can be achieved by separating spaces and using transition zones to link diverse project areas together. Unity integrates details and reduces the number of competing components, thus creating a feeling of completeness rather than diversity between the parts (Figures 2.65–2.68). In design applications, unity is the harmonious relationship between line, form, texture, and color. When it is achieved, logical relationships are apparent and nothing seems out of place or inappropriate. Secondly, using the principle of unity becomes a way

2.66

**Figures 2.65–2.67**

These photos illustrate the sense of unity created by repeating the simple floor planters, benches, and trash receptacles throughout the mall. (Hawthorne Center, Vernon Hills, Illinois)

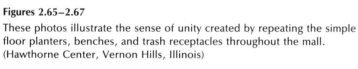

2.65

2.67

**Figure 2.68**

In this retail sales court, the pavement detailing and repetition of railing details help unify the space. The focus of the court planting is then movable floor planters, which add green and terra cotta colors to the basic tan background.

**Figure 2.69**

The water feature and rock outcropping seen in this atrium are dominant components in the design. By comparison, the material selection and form contrasts with the interior. Since it sets in a location central to the space, it is the dominant component within the atrium. (Embassy Suites, Indianapolis, Indiana.)

to simplify the number of differing elements within a given design, thus reducing any visual competition for attention.

Designers must be able to make the fine distinction between unity and monotony. Too much conformance from the repeated use of identical components is also undesirable. Design of a space such as an interior project should select a delicate balance between simplicity and complexity, similarity and difference, to achieve a sense of unity.

## Dominance

The total scheme within a composition may involve one or more accent elements. According to the project's size, shape, or location, some perceived dominance or emphasis within certain areas may be needed. Structures, lighting fixtures, sculpture, banners, fountains, paintings, or specimen plant materials can be the dominant elements within a space. These elements dominate by contrasting with surroundings. Varying sizes, forms, backgrounds, illumination, or other elements can complement these dominant elements within a space (Figures 2.69 and 2.70).

**Figure 2.70**

This fountain in this atrium corridor is (by its form, color, location, and staging) a dominant part of the space. By design it also can function as the focus for a brunch. (Opryland Hotel, Nashville, Tennessee.)

Dominance, used in composition, exhibits the importance of a single element. It is used to create interest or focal points of accent within a composition. When trying to determine what should have emphasis or be dominant within a design, the first step is to visually evaluate the space. When arriving at a project site the review of plans can identify the sequences that clients and/or users may take. This process helps you to assess the need for focal points within a specific area or space. For example, a reception area and desk may need a focal point or accent. In seating areas a low coffee table may need a design element such as a plant or flower arrangement as an accent. In either case, these added components strive for dominance in their surroundings, creating an accent within the user's view (See Figure 2.71).

## Repetition

A technique used to tie together or unify the various areas within a design is the repeated use of a particular element, such as a plant or construction material. As long as the concept of repetition is not carried out to an excessive degree, the appearance and reappearance of a consistently similar element is an effective means of stimulating "recall." In the perceiver's mind, it gives a sense of cohesion to the overall design composition (Figures 2.72–2.74). The concept of repetition in design generates negative feelings with many people. This is unfortunate because when it is used discreetly, repetition can be a very effective way of visually simplifying the overall design while reducing the total number of different components within a scheme. In a composi-

**Figure 2.71**
Temporary and/or varied focal points may also be part of an interiorscape scheme. In this hotel lobby seating area a dramatic live flower arrangement accents and dominates the space. (Hyatt Regency, Indianapolis, Indiana.)

**Figure 2.72**
In this sketch the repetition of the cactus in the two office areas helps to unify visually the separated office spaces.

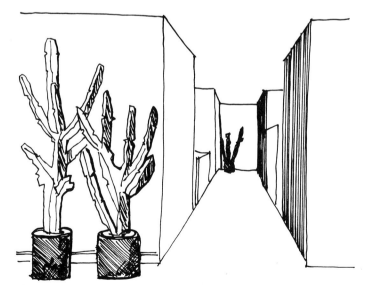

**Figure 2.73**

In this retail/commercial office atrium the repetition of planters on the ground and upper levels helps to tie the total atrium together visually. (The Galleria, Houston, Texas.)

room or office scale, repetition of carpeting, curtains, wall surfacings and plants is comparable to that of mulches, planting beds, and pavements in large scale interiorscape projects. In either case, repeated elements unify physically or visually separated areas.

**Rhythm.**   Rhythm is the establishment of a physical and/or visual pattern or movement within a project design. Rhythm within an interior space design may be used to move a visitor from the front door through a foyer to a receptionist. The visual recall of similar materials or plantings establishes movement through the foyer by a repetitive planting pattern, which reinforces the sequence of walking. In a larger interiorscape project rhythm may be used to help move shoppers in a mall from area to area, or visitors, clients, and workers through an office space or atrium (Figure 2.75).

**Figure 2.74**

The large floor planters repeated in this atrium help create a sense of scale and direct traffic, while unifying the space. (Hyatt Regency, Indianapolis, Indiana.)

tion using repetition, the use of fewer elements results in a refinement. Ground plantings, mulches, pavings, other plantings, site features, or colors may be repeated within a design to give unity and order. Repetition also establishes an emotional and visual link or pattern within the design, creating physical or visual movement within a scheme. In interior projects with multiple areas, repetition of recognizable materials such as floor surfacings or lighting fixtures helps tie separated or adjoining areas together. On the

**Figure 2.75**

In this photo, the asymmetrical rhythm of the planting pattern contrasts the symmetrical design of the building and atrium.

**Figure 2.76**

In this flower show exhibit garden, the space has been created around a central visual/physical axis with equal garden areas repeated on each side of the assumed axis. This type of balance is called symmetrical.

**Figure 2.77**

The equal size and placement of these fig trees within this atrium lobby reinforce the symmetrical nature of the building.

**Balance.**  Balance, the last of the design principles to be discussed, is the visual equilibrium or equalization of compositional elements within a composition. As mentioned earlier, most designs contain accents or dominant elements. Parallel to this requirement of a successful design is a need for the other elements to provide a subdued, neutral background. This means that much of the space within the composition should remain unfilled to create neutral areas. Designs in which no space has been left open appear cluttered and messy.

Basically, there are two types of balance—symmetrical and asymmetrical. *Symmetrical* designs have identical compositional arrangements on both sides of a perceived central axis (Figures 2.76 and 2.77). *Asymmetrical* designs are balanced by an implied equivalent counterbalance on opposite sides of the compositions; this balance is achieved without repetition (Figures 2.78 and 2.79). Achieving an effective balance between the positive features and open areas requires looking at a whole composition as an entity: the line of the architecture and shape of the spaces, the floor configuration

**Figure 2.78**
In this garden exhibit, the door is the central focus. With an unequal emphasis created by the plants and baskets to the right of the door an asymmetrical balance is created.

**Figure 2.79**
In this collected advertisement for Levolor blinds and ceilings, the vantage selected is unequal, or asymmetrical. This view allows framing by the plants and an off-center focal point at the corner of the room.

and areas relative to furniture and pathways, and the size and shape of areas for plant materials. The examples included illustrate several examples of balanced compositions. By planning planting masses in conjunction with the building and walls, windows and doors, designers–clients often develop compositions that are kinetic, or have visual movement. Balance as a design consideration helps create visual emphasis and physical direction in a project's development.

When identical plants or constructed features are placed on each side of the axis, a formal or symmetrical balance is established. This type of planting is often static; and problems result if one plant is damaged or dies. An asymmetrical composition is established by balancing one mass of varying but visually equal elements against another. In compositions such as this, the visual movement established makes the proposal more lively. Balance is often an individual preference, and is specific to the project and client. The feeling created in most interiorscapes is generally informal, thus asymmetrical.

Some of the design considerations that give direction to designers of interior landscapes, as well as other art forms, are included in this discussion of design principles.

Interior landscape designers should strive to use these design principles to create visually attractive and functional designs. The application of design principles must be done in a manner which exhibits a genuine understanding of and sensitivity to the building, the spaces within, and their use. Design influences may include client needs, plant cultural requirements, and space limits, as well as inherent construction materials. These principles of design are used by manipulating the elements of design—line, form, texture, and color. As concepts they are used in the communication of ideas as well as in the actual composing, drawing, and organization of project information.

After a design project has been drafted and presented, the next stage in achieving the desired effect is preparing for the actual implementation. No matter how much time and effort goes into planning and design of a proposal, if it is not installed or maintained with sensitivity to the anticipated design qualities, the desired effect can be lost. Sensitivity to design is just as important for the maintenance interiorscape professional as for the designer. Understanding the basics of design is a means to establishing and developing quality proposals. Remember that it is the attention to the overall scheme and "details" that marks a designed interior.

## SUMMARY

In composing an interior planting design proposal, the elements and principles of design are used to evaluate interior spaces and define their potential development. Evaluating, selecting, and combining the appropriate lines, forms, textures, and colors into well-defined and unified compositions are parts of the design sequence. Since interior landscape designs are three-dimensional spaces, designers must consider the potentials of everchanging viewing planes, level changes, and user perceptions within the space or spaces. The foreground, middleground, and background of rooms and interior landscapes—as well as exterior landscape designs—may be experienced by a constantly changing vantage point. Designers should understand these possible viewing points within a design so they can emphasize vistas or hesitation points accordingly. The visual and functional design of spaces should anticipate their uses and their most desirable views, coordinating all design considerations relevant to the project. With an understanding of the visual scheme of interiors in our daily lives and the desirability for seasonal change, any design should further enhance the dynamics of an interior and/or lifestyle. As we move through an interior or exterior environment, we experience a number of settings as opposed to the two-dimensional image of a painting or photograph. In the design, use, and appreciation of an interior landscape, specific plants and/or features are selected for a specific site, space, locale, client, and user. The visual and physical success of an interior planting result from a thorough background in planning, design, and plant culture. A planned and designed composition is only as successful as the underlying principles and elements used to achieve that environment.

# Chapter 3

# Planning Considerations and Design Processes

In the development of an interior landscape, the process of planning and design is a partnership between a client–owner and the designers. There are two distinct aspects of the proposal of a project's development: planning and design. *Planning* is the process of anticipating or formulating a project's future needs, activities, and developments. *Site planning,* the design process used in landscape architecture, is "a design process which explores the relationships between buildings, vehicular and pedestrian circulation, ground forms, vegetation, and site use in order to produce an aesthetic and functional development" (*A Technical Glossary of Horticultural and Landscape Terminology,* Horticultural Research Institute, 1971). In interior landscape design, the concepts of site planning and design process may be used as "umbrella" terms from the organization of your planning objectives through the selection of specific plantings and construction features. Since planning is a mental process applied to a physical place, you should also try to imply, through anticipation and role playing as a designer, installer, user, client advocate, and maintenance person, what may occur. The design process is directed by specific project goals and objectives defined by the client and designer. As designer you need to anticipate space, people, and plant possibilities and problems. Plants selected must be able to survive interior temperatures. Today's designers should take energy conservation measures into consideration, while providing for specialized project requirements as well.

The dictionary definition of the term *design* is (1) to plan, (2) make preliminary sketches, (3) to form in the mind, and (4) to propose (Webster's Dictionary, 1974). When discussed in relation to an interior landscape, design is the selection of appropriate project components, materials, plants, and plant combinations as solutions to limited and well-defined site problems. Interiorscaping is not plant decorating, just as landscape and interior design are different from landscape and interior decoration. Decoration in these cases is adding something as an accent without relating it to the space, user, or location. Common interior landscape design components may include planters, ground beds, plantings, water features, pavements, floor surfacings, and project furnishings. Design considerations may include establishing some sources of design incentive and including the functional uses of plants in an interior. These elements may be commonly included in small offices, or in larger mall or atrium developments. The design of larger interiorscapes may require more varied components: planters, drainage and irrigation systems, walls, bridges, decks, shelters, etc. The installation of these specialized features may be limited by law to specific design professionals. Please check local restrictions before embarking on an extensive project that includes such details. Some states do have registrations of design professionals such as architects and landscape architects that define the types of services and projects that they can be involved with.

The eventual proposal should result in an attractive and useful interior space including planned and design features. The space, floors, wall and ceiling details, as well as furnishings, accessories, and plantings are all included in an inte-

rior planting (Figure 3.1). To effectively create useful designs, include project inventories and evaluations, hold client interviews, and establish project priorities. Evaluation of a project or site conditions may include the space or area, its size, shape, and surfacings, existing HVAC systems, and services such as electric, water, drainage, etc. As an additional overall reference you may need to review and/or include the general layout of the building—relevant room locations, doors and their widths (for access of materials), windows, access drives—to put the project into perspective. You should also consider the architectural type, style, materials, colors, and details of the building for possible design implications (Figure 3.2).

At the start of the design process the designer is usually contacted by the prospective client or owner, or another design professional, as a consultant. Before the initial client–designer discussion it may be important to understand how and why the client has contacted you and exactly what services they are requesting. Some initial questions that you may ask yourself are: Are they being referred by an existing design client? Have they seen any of my installed work? Did they find my name in the phone book? By understanding how they have come to call on you for services you can determine the type of information needed in preparing for your initial meeting. If the prospective client has seen your work and/or knows other clients, they may be aware of what services you provide and the quality of your work, yet need to understand your fee structure. If you are talking with clients who are unfamiliar with your work, you will need to explain your procedures, show them examples of completed projects, and possibly give references.

In your initial client meeting it is important to establish yourself as a professional, define your services, and clarify the scope of the project, the work expected, and timing. You need a design portfolio at this time to visually communicate what you can do. After this introduction, you can further explain how the planning and design considerations relate to their specific project development. Clients often feel that design is something magical and assume that designers can guess their needs and expectations, thus keeping you uninformed in fear of "limiting" the designer's creativity. Since design is site and client specific, a design

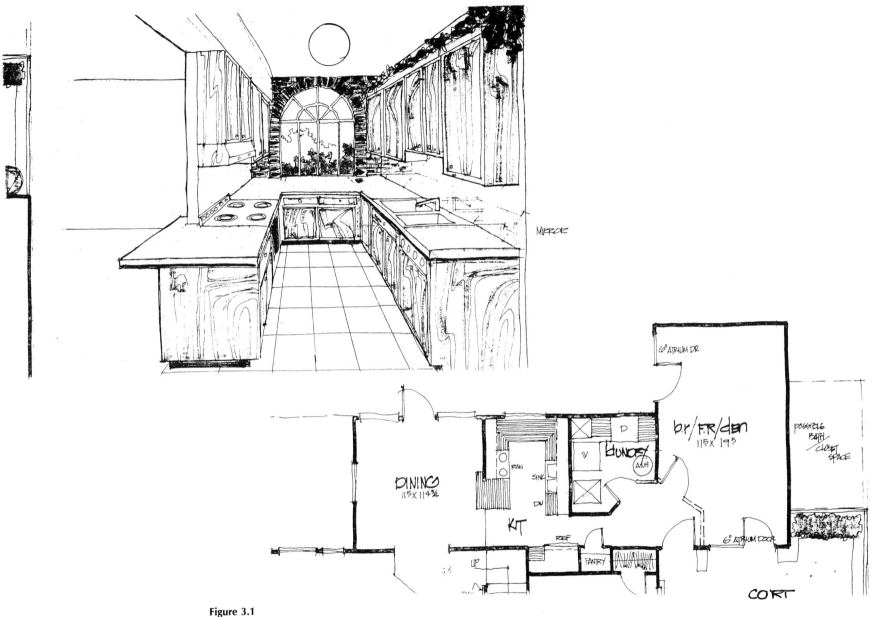

**Figure 3.1**

To adequately describe an interior space, floor plans, wall elevations, and ceiling plans are needed. In addition, electrical, plumbing, HVAC (heating, ventilation, air conditioning) and other construction details are also used to fully understand a space. (Designer: Wick Rimert.)

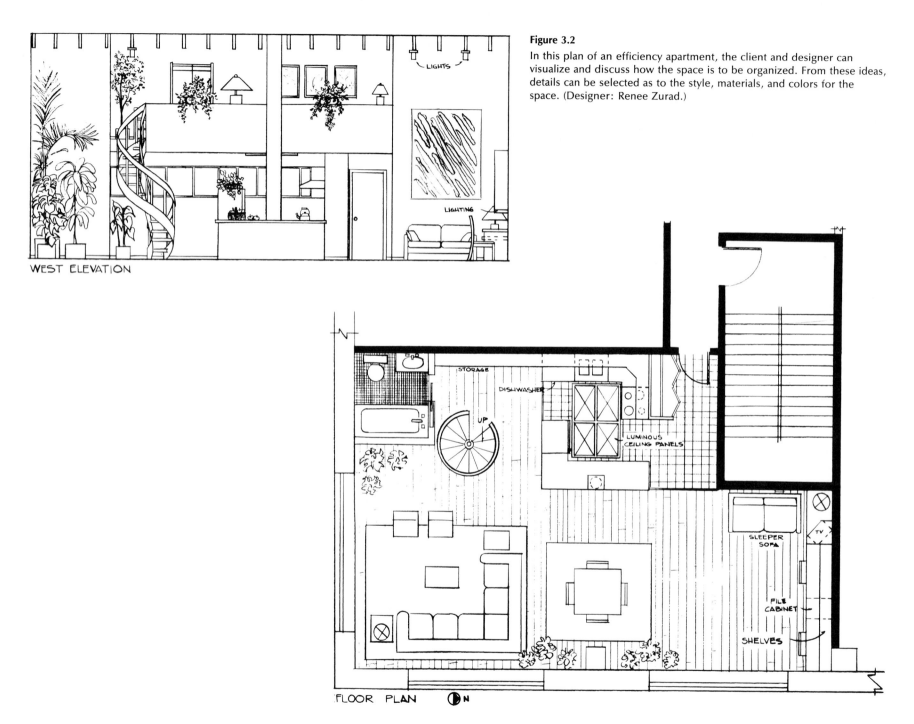

WEST ELEVATION

**Figure 3.2**
In this plan of an efficiency apartment, the client and designer can visualize and discuss how the space is to be organized. From these ideas, details can be selected as to the style, materials, and colors for the space. (Designer: Renee Zurad.)

LIGHTS

LIGHTING

STORAGE

DISHWASHER

UP

LUMINOUS CEILING PANELS

SLEEPER SOFA

TV

FILE CABINET

SHELVES

FLOOR PLAN    N

3.3

**Figures 3.3 and 3.4**

As a public relations and educational tool, the national Interior Plantscape Association (IPA) has developed this brochure as a point-of-sale guide for prospective interiorscape clients. *How to select and work with an interior plantscape specialist* explains the specialties and associated design processes involved in developing an interiorscape. (Courtesy of Interior Plantscape Association (IPA).)

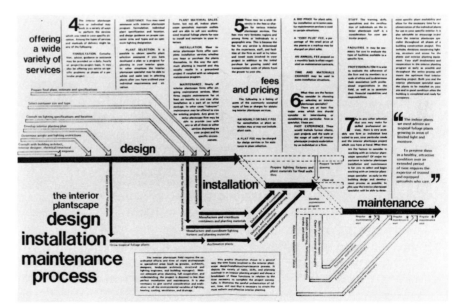

3.4

proposal can only be as realistic and relevant as the client information offered, or what the designer can anticipate.

Any initial client–designer discussion should include an explanation of what design is, the process used, and exactly what services can be expected. The design process provides for functional and aesthetic considerations first, then relates them to the specific project and needs.

It is the design professional's responsibility to accurately represent the client by proposing a scheme that is functional, attractive, and appropriate to the client–user's needs (Figures 3.3 and 3.4). Establishing client awareness and understanding of design, its benefits, and opportunities, is often the hardest part of the process. Other interiorscape, "green," and landscape industry publications are available to help you convey your design focus to clients. Some of these publications are seen in (Figures 3.5–3.14).

**Figure 3.5**
*Interiorscape Magazine* is published 6 times per year by Brantwood
Publications, Inc. 3023 Eastland Blvd., Suite 103, Clearwater, Florida
33519.

**Figure 3.6**
*Interior Landscape Industry* is published monthly by American
Nurseryman Publishing Company, 111 N. Canal Street, Suite 545,
Chicago, Illinois 60606.

**3.7**

**3.9**

**Figures 3.7–3.10**

These industry association publications are produced by the Associated Landscape Contractors of America, 405 N. Washington Street, Suite 104, Falls Church, Virginia 22046.

**3.8**

3.10

**Figure 3.11**
This industry advertisement provides consumer information as well as sales concerns. (W. R. Grace Company, 62 Whittemore Avenue, Cambridge, Massachusetts 02140.)

**SPECIAL ISSUE**

Tropical Ornamentals has had the opportunity to participate in many major interiorscape projects over the past 12 years. More than anything else, this involvement has given us valuable knowledge of our products in thoroughly creative interior settings and provided a close-up view of the responsibilities of the supporting partners in such ambitious endeavors.

TROPICAL TOPICS has a diversified audience of foliage and closely allied professionals. We believe the introduction of two of our recent interiorscape experiences in this Special Issue, along with the planning and particular considerations of other prominently involved parties, as viewed by them, would be of interest and value to our readers.

We are most pleased, therefore, to showcase the Opryland Hotel Conservatory and the ClayDesta National Bank Building Atrium, two different, yet dramatically similar projects that rank with the most creative, ambitious, beautiful and effective interiorscapes anywhere in the United States.

# Tropical Topics

**■ Vol. 4 No. 1 ■**

### OPRYLAND HOTEL CONSERVATORY

Nashville, Tennessee

The Conservatory is a 70,000 square foot addition to the popular Opryland Hotel. The unusual plant sizes and quantity (nearly 8,000 plants representing 57 families, 93 genera and 212 varieties) are located in a one acre planting area under a glass roof structure 110' high at its highest point. "Conservatory" is perhaps a misnomer for the foliage presents a tropical garden effect like one would expect to view, as it has been said, in a "plant museum."

### CLAYDESTA NATIONAL BANK BUILDING ATRIUM

Midland, Texas

The uncommonly spacious 44,000 square foot ClayDesta atrium easily accommodates a 53' Norfolk Island Pine and the other large, diverse specimens under its 77' high skylighted roof. The imaginative plant material includes 18 families, 31 genera and 57 varieties. The glass walled building itself is a huge six story commercial property with 500,000 square feet of office space overlooking the atrium.

As reported in **The Forbes Four Hundred 1983 Edition**, ...oilman Clayte Williams is busy erecting a mammoth commercial development north of town . . . This development . . . features a stunning atrium so filled with water and soaring trees it could pass for Big Sur. The Lord didn't use such natural beauty on Midland, so Clayte Williams is stepping in with the 50-foot pines.

**Figure 3.12**
*Tropical Topics* is published by Tropical Ornamentals, 5346 Woodland Drive, Delray Beach, Florida 33445-1198.

**Figure 3.13**
Many plant producers such as Southeast Growers, Inc., P. O. Box 2430, Boca Raton, Florida 33427 use brochures as information and sales tools.

**Figure 3.14**
*Florida Foliage* is a publication by the Florida Foliage Association, 114 E. Fifth Street, Apopka, Florida 32703.

# DEVELOPMENT CONSIDERATIONS

Designers use a design method or process to record, evaluate, and organize any background information needed for a design proposal. Through this organized sequence designers work towards a useable, attractive, and maintainable proposal. In your client–designer discussions you may find that clients—all too often—have more experience and knowledge of a specialty such as architecture, interiors, or plants than they have of the process involved in developing an interiorscape proposal. The design process to be described is a sequence often used in landscape architecture. Often projects designed by non-designers result in a collection of plants and materials used as decoration, not design. These projects are not as attractive or useful as they could have been if a unified scheme of space, furnishings, and plantings had been developed through the use of basic planning and design principles.

Site planning, long the focus of landscape architects, includes the process of evaluating the relationships between a site and its structures, people, and situations as the basis for any design proposal. Thomas Church, a prominent California landscape architect of the 1950s, advocated that landscape gardens surrounding a residence, as well as other design scales, should function as an extension of the interior space while being responsive to surrounding and climatic influences. Church developed three sources of design forms for site proposals that are also applicable to interiorscape design. His first design consideration included human needs and the specific personal requirements and characteristics of the client. The second consideration involved an awareness and knowledge of the technology of materials, construction, and plants, including maintenance and a whole range of form determinants desired from the site condition and quality. Lastly, Church had a concern for the spatial expression which would go beyond the mere satisfaction of requirements into the realm of fine art (Laurie 1985, p. 45). In interiorscaping these same considerations can be the basis of design proposals where the inside echoes the room, building, and site surroundings.

Today, the idea of extending indoor space out is being reversed to bringing the outdoors in with interior plantings, indoor courtyards, atriums, and conservatories. As buildings become larger and are constructed of starker building materials with simple lines, plants add a necessary human dimension. As new construction is developed, established projects remodeled, and new plant technologies introduced, the design opportunities for interior plants continues to expand. The image of outdoor life created by integrating interior plantings provides clients and users with a more pleasing and comfortable indoor environment. The use of plants within interior spaces has fostered new opportunities for all designers, professionals, and association practitioners (Figures 3.15–3.22).

Project design evaluation should include the client's needs, priorities, and preferences. To determine what the client expects of the completed project, a discussion or discussions between the designer and client is required. During these talks the designer tries, through selected questions and review of ideas, to determine the client's immediate and long-term needs. Other specific design elements and expectations may also be discussed regarding the phasing of the proposal. An outline of the planning and design processes often helps the designer explain to the client–owner how their needs, priorities, and preferences result in a design solution. When specific design details or questions arise, it is best to discuss them using project drawings and/or an actual site review, if possible. When the site review isn't possible, design drawings, sketches, and diagrams become the focus of discussion (Figure 3.23).

Off-site conditions or conditions outside the building can influence a project's use and design. Included in your evaluation should be the regional and local climatic influences of sun, winds, adjoining structures, surrounding land uses, and pedestrian and vehicular access to the project. After the basic project site and surrounding information is collected, the data should be evaluated in terms of the project use and the implementation of the design (Figures 3.24–3.26).

**Figures 3.15–3.22**

This series of photos illustrates the diversity of interior situations in which plants can be used. The opportunities for designers, plant specialists and associated professionals is only as limited as one's imagination. *Figure 3.15:* This simple corporation cafeteria is accented by planters that provide separation and color to the space. *Figure 3.16:* This Office Park Building includes a focal point of one specimen fig as its accent (Engledow Inc.). *Figure 3.17:* Department store sales displays as in this furniture display utilize plants to recreate home settings (D. G. Smith).

**3.16**

**3.15**

**3.17**

**3.18**

**3.20**

**3.19**

*Figure 3.18:* In the Hawthorne Center Mall permanent floor planters are used in combination with movable planters. *Figure 3.19:* This urban atrium creates the feeling of an exterior streetscape in Toronto, Canada (Victoria Willis). *Figure 3.20:* Holiday Inn Plaza Atrium restaurant and lounge area in the balcony, Matteson, Illinois. *Figure 3.21:* The University of Houston Atrium, Clear Lake City, Texas. *Figure 3.22:* The Opryland Hotel, Rhett's Restaurant, Nashville, Tennessee.

**3.21**

**3.22**

**Figure 3.23**

Simple line drawings can be the focus of client/designer discussions during the design process. These sketches are freehand ideas and can be traced. Copying drawings is one of the best ways to gain confidence in drawing as a beginner. (Designer: R. Mumaw.)

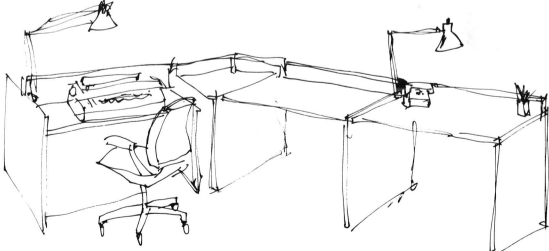

**Figures 3.24–3.26**

In today's urban settings, architecture and styles of site development ideas include mixed uses. These photos illustrate the Galleria Shopping Complex in Houston, Texas. The development is layered with high-rise hotels and a jogging track surrounds the central atrium area skylight. As an interiorscaper, an evaluation of the total project area and its surroundings is important to fully understand what can impact a planting proposal.

3.26

3.24

3.25

## FUNCTIONAL USES OF PLANTS

In considering the interior character and quality of a space and the related plants, interior planting designs should help provide a more functional and aesthetically pleasing interior setting. A few of the functional aspects that plants provide in our contemporary landscape are discussed in *Plants, People, and Environmental Quality* by G. Robinette (U.S. Gov't, 1972). The focus of this work is the exterior landscape environment, yet the concepts have parallels in the interior situations. Robinette writes that plants have always been considered aesthetic due to the appearance of their twigs, leaves, flowers, and fruit. However, the uses of plants in architecture, engineering, climatic control, and aesthetics are often dismissed because plants are living and growing things.

When plants are used as structural elements to create floors, walls, and/or ceilings, they are providing architectural functions. Tropical plantings used in an open office to create spaces through screening and separation are functioning architecturally. In atriums or shopping mall courts, plantings can subdivide larger areas into more intimate and

**Figure 3.27**
In this open office, movable screens and plants are used to create separated work areas.

scaled spaces (Figures 3.27 and 3.28). The plant selection process for an interior should consider optimal plant heights and densities for the space—its situation and function—and provide a focus within or beyond the project's limits. Plants in an interior landscape are usually kept at their installation size rather than encouraging extensive growth as in exterior landscape developments. Plant size and selection for interiors needs to be specific. Plants become elements of interest for use in project design through growth and response to cultural and environmental conditions.

In many ways, some of the plant functions considered by Robinette apply to current interior planting designs. Examples of the engineering uses of plants in exterior environments are: traffic control, soil stabilization, reduction of glare and noise. These uses can also be applied in some larger indoor planting situations. Plants in the interior and exterior fulfill an aesthetic function when they are selected and placed according to their inherent design elements: line, form, texture, and color. Appropriate species selection and placement may provide enframement, pattern, background, or sculptural accents within a design (Figures 3.29–3.32). It should be remembered that although specific and separate categories are identified, one plant can serve more than one of these functions.

In the determination of a plant's size, type, and location, designers should work within the project scale, the scheme, and functional needs as determined by the initial space review and design discussions with the client. With the listing of these potential functional plant uses, designers should specify what plants are available, evaluate spaces, and work towards appropriate plant selection.

The selection and location of plants in an interior landscape should reinforce the space's activities, provide functional benefits, and increase the physical and visual enjoyment of the space by the users. Plant selection should also consider the cultural limitations of the space. Light, temper-

**Figure 3.28**
In this shopping mall atrium permanent planters are used to help direct traffic and to provide some unity for benches and trash receptacles. These groupings visually link the two mall levels together.

**Figure 3.29**

Smaller plantings are often incorporated in sales areas as in this cosmetics display. Rental plants are used and cycled on a regular basis due to the low light within the store. Plant changes occur relative to the season and color accents desired. (Photo by D. G. Smith.)

**Figure 3.30**

In this greenhouse/patio display, unique plant forms such as the elephant foot palm, bromelias, and orchids are selected as sculptural accents. (Southern Living Show, Charlotte, North Carolina.)

**Figure 3.31**

In this garden display at the Indianapolis flower and patio show selected potted plants are included as accents and details around this garden gazebo form. (Photo by Michael Dana.)

**Figure 3.32**
This hotel lobby is accented by a creative display of poinsettias in a pyramidal frame. (Courtesy of Engledow Inc.)

**Figure 3.33**
In this mall atrium planting the selection of ground-level plantings reflect the reduced light. The lower light is a result of the canopy plant over the planting, as well as adjoining balcony areas.

ature, water, and nutrition are the basic plant necessities, but most important of all is light. Plant selection for design composition and light should include the plant layers—canopy, understory, and ground plane—as the basic plant size categories used in design. These categories are organized relative to the spaces they fill and to the scale of space and uses within the areas (Figure 3.33). Canopy trees, for example, provide a ceiling effect of enclosure for the space and plantings below. This feeling of a ceiling or enclosure may be solid, open, or a combination, depending on the canopy plant selected and light source available. The canopy plants selected should relate to the project space in which they are to be used. Smaller projects or spaces will need smaller maturing species, while larger maturing species should be used for large areas. Canopy trees should be identified prior to use, as the reduced light below will affect the understory plantings. Anticipate this reduction in light when lower layer plants are selected after the canopy layer.

Understory plants are individual plants or groupings of plants that are positioned at eye level and which fit within the cultural and physical limits defined by the ceiling or canopy planting. Understory plants can provide "wall-like" enclosure and create more space definition, scale, and/or visual interest (Figure 3.34). In smaller projects the ceiling may already be established, making understory and ground plane levels the only things to be identified. Visual interest may be provided by their overall forms, leaf texture and color, flowers or branches. These plants are most likely multi-trunked, and include a wide range of specimens to choose from.

The last category, ground plane plants, is used to define ground areas. These plants are waist-high and below in size. The plants may define spaces or areas physically or visually, depending on their height. Individual species with special leaf or flower characteristics may also provide visual interest to a scheme. These plantings may be used to reinforce or

**Figure 3.34**

The skylight shown provides light to the first and second floor areas of the mall. The railings and understory plantings then help define the court openings and mall seating areas.

**Figure 3.35**

In this permanent planter the selection of one plant species as a ground surfacing creates a unified understory for the canopy. Collectively these create a park-like setting for shoppers.

complement the understory focus and/or canopy plantings by defining the ground area below. Ground plantings can help to unify separated plantings areas within an area, just as a rug can unify the furnishings in a room. Ground plane plantings in combination with other ground surfaces and pavements define the project's ground area and related activities. In selecting ground plane plantings consider durability regarding light requirements and physical damages, as well as maintenance requirements and desired visual effect (Figure 3.35).

When choosing plants from these three categories remember that size is relative. Plants must be appropriate for the area or space in which they are to be used and for each other when grouped together; individual plants should relate to their containers (Figures 3.36–3.39).

Interior landscape plantings, constructed features, and furnishings are the basic design components used in developing and detailing an interiorscape project. Interior landscape development provides an extension of the outdoors,

indoors. Space limits, cultural conditions, the intensity of use, and construction components—rather than plantings—may often be used in project design to provide for some of the space's functional needs. Interior landscape design may then be the selection of plants, construction materials, and/or a combination of solutions to limited, site, or project design problems. If permanent plantings aren't realistic don't be scared to suggest design alternatives; these options may include plant rental, silk plants, or a combination of these options (Figures 3.40 and 3.41).

Durability and cost are also considerations in selecting furnishings, interior elements, and plantings to be used in an interior living space. Selection and definition of plant and construction materials are made after room areas have been defined, functional requirements listed, and relative forms, shapes, and sizes of the area outlined. Although implemented through the use of plants and construction materials, interior landscape design is made into functional and aesthetic compositions through the use of a design process.

**Figure 3.36**
In this restaurant the designer has selected planters and plant species that are appropriate for people when seated.

**Figures 3.37–3.39**
As a comparison of plant/planter size and shape relationships these photos illustrate that some plant species are more appropriate than others when planted in a mass.

3.38

3.39

3.37

75

**Figures 3.40 and 3.41**

In situations where existing light is too low for plant survival, plant rental options or silk plants may be the solution. In this conference room, the plant hanging in the corner is silk, while the planters under ceiling lights are live and used on a rental basis. In the hanging baskets, two silk plant options are shown.

3.40

3.41

After developing a feeling for the region and locale, the designer can better interpret the specific project considerations. Microclimate, a term used in landscape architecture to describe the climate near the ground, may have applications in interior situations. The exterior environment of sun, wind, and temperature may influence interior plant selection as well as the design, establishment, and maintenance of a proposal. The two climatic influences of sun and wind affect personal comfort and/or use of outdoor spaces as well as the amount of "conditioning" needed in an interior. Specifically, they affect the energy resources needed to heat and cool interior spaces, which influence the people and plants within.

## Solar Radiation

The sun takes a regular, cyclic path through the sky. Through an understanding of its movement we can anticipate the availability of natural light indoors for plant growth and potential plant locations. In temperate locales the sun rises in the east and sets in the west, with some seasonal height variations in this alignment. As the sun moves from east to west seasonal differences relative to the movement of the earth on its axis occur, influencing the sun's alignment as well as its height in the sky. The latitude of the project and the season influence the sun's height above the horizon. The summer sun in the more temperate regions of the U.S. rises early in the northeastern sky and sets late in the northwestern sky. In its summer cycle the sun is high overhead, which produces shadows almost directly beneath objects and plantings. The winter sun, in contrast, rises in the southeast and sets in the southwest. This variation caused by the rotation of the earth on its axis affects the angle at which the sun's rays strike the earth's surface. These more acute sun angles, resulting in long shadows during the winter, also provide passive solar gain to interior-spaces, if appropriate openings are available (Figure 3.42).

In a project analysis, solar angle information can be used to locate the sun in relation to a skylight and/or windows for plant growth and planter placement. The available sun and shadow patterns vary according to how a building or other structural feature is established in the landscape. Each eleva-

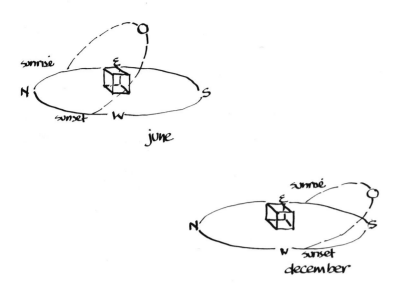

june

december

**Figure 3.42**

The variation in sun angles is a design consideration when developing an interiorscape proposal. In this simplistic sketch, the general height and path of the sun in the northern hemisphere is shown in summer and winter, the yearly extremes. The sun is highest in the sky in June, whereas in December the sun's angle is at its lowest point. In summer, short shadows result from the sun being almost directly overhead, while winter shadows are long due to the almost horizontal aspect.

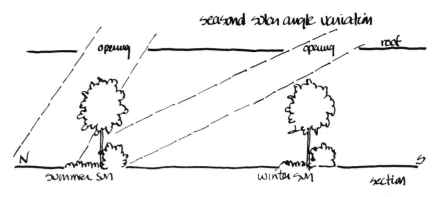

**Figure 3.43**

Due to the seasonal change in the earth's axis the angle at which sun enters a skylight varies. In a building with skylights, an on-site review is best to determine plant selection and placement relative to available light.

**Figure 3.44**

This plan drawing represents a section drawing of Figure 3.43. It illustrates that permanent planters under skylights may not receive the light one might think, due to the varied altitude of the location and height of the sun. The orientation of the building also affects light as well as skylight size and shape in evaluating potential plant options.

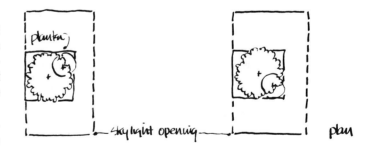

tion of a building has a different orientation, thus a different interface with the sun's heat, light, and resulting shadows. A building's orientation can influence the placement of skylights and plants or planters as well as the amount of light and heat penetrating into interior spaces if openings are available (Figure 3.43).

As the sun's patterns are regular and predictable, designers should realize that they can include this information in proposals design and development. Modifying both exterior and interior spaces with respect to the amounts of heat, light, and shade that result are desirable design opportunities to consider. Each space or room has a different exposure to the sun depending on its window or skylight opportunities. Plant establishment of a permanent basis should reflect the available light sources and the minimum light areas. There are three factors to evaluate when considering natural light in an interior: first, the size, shape, and orienta-

tion of the roof opening or skylight; secondly, the exterior surfacing and interior ceiling buffering or covering; and lastly, the height of the ceiling (Figure 3.44). After an evaluation of section and plan the optimal floor locations for plantings or planters can be selected. As a general rule of thumb, select the plant location according to the afternoon sun, rather than morning sun.

# THE DESIGN PROCESS FOR INTERIOR LANDSCAPE DESIGNS

Interiorscape design, as landscape architecture, is a problem-solving activity that strives to develop functional yet attractive spaces. The project's functional and aesthetic goals are achieved through the application of the design process in coordinating the area, its surroundings, plantings, and constructed features. Interior landscape design deals with existing and proposed interior spaces. The interior is defined by floors, walls, windows, doors, ceilings, as well as room furnishings and appurtenances. Interior landscape designs should also reflect the project's surroundings, the interior controlled environment, and climatic influences. These in combination with the basic cultural requirements of plants and the use of the space are coordinated to influence the design and eventual installation. With basic functional considerations and design concepts in mind, the designer must take inventory of, evaluate, and interpret all these project and client–user concerns. The final solution attempts to coordinate the building, its spaces and uses, into a compatible composition that is functional and attractive and serves the client needs while maintaining a positive plant environment. The shape of the building, its interior spaces, its orientation and resulting light are all necessary considerations for plant growth (Figures 3.45–3.49). While there are other cultural requirements—water, temperature, and soil—the most crucial for plant growth, establishment, and selection is light.

The process of design uses guidelines rather than rules in the development of solutions. In design disciplines such as architecture, landscape architecture, and interior design there are numerous "design processes." Design process is a designer's guide and an educational tool for clients in understanding the route to functional and aesthetic solutions to specific design problems. It is important to remember that application of design process varies with the design situation. Basic to any design process is a logical, systematic approach. The sequence should identify and define problems, outline data collection procedures, evaluate information, and utilize existing and proposed concerns in working towards design alternatives.

**Figure 3.45**
In the urban situation showing Indianapolis, Indiana, new and old architecture alike provide opportunities for the development of interiorscapes.

**Figure 3.46**
The Arcade in downtown Cleveland, Ohio, built in the early 1900s, is a historic atrium filled with sun which provides a great retail and commercial area for the patrons of shops, eateries, and office spaces.

**Figure 3.47**
If plants are to be a permanent part of an interior space, skylights (to provide adequate light) or plant cycle options are needed. Light is the most limiting factor in the design and management of any interior planting. These corridor skylights provide adequate light for the floor plantings of fig trees to grow and develop. (St. Clair Square, Fairview Heights, Illinois.)

**Figure 3.48**
This vaulted skylight provides an accent to a conference center lobby. The built-in ceiling planter and floor plants add attractive accents to the space.

**Figure 3.49**
In this urban atrium, plants help provide human scale and add a living component to the massive structure, all of which creates a street-like setting. (Photo by Victoria Willis.)

Out of the review of these basic ideas and interrelationships comes a conceptual design and the selection of specific forms, materials, and details relative to the site, client, and surrounding conditions. The early schematic developments of the concepts help to identify the various project areas, uses and/or circulation interrelationships independent of the proposed plantings and design features. Both planning and design considerations are needed to conceptualize and detail a design proposal. An example of an interiorscape design process is identified in the following paragraphs. The example uses general terms in order to communicate the concepts and steps of the process. The overall process of designing an interiorscaping parallels this case study description.

Case Study—Office Interiorscape

## Problem

The client/owner occupies this professional office, and has requested some interiorscaping services. Figures 3.50–3.52 are drawings of the interior and illustrate a great opportunity for the addition of plants to serve both aesthetic and functional objectives. The main areas of the office have adequate natural light, thus plant selections should include moderate to low light species. It has not yet been decided whether the plants will be rental or permanent elements, or what their cultural requirements will be. This is stage one.

## Research

The basic considerations for stage two include the collection of physical and client data:

### Physical Environment

1. Architectural information (see drawings for details).
2. Environmental data: baseboard heating; cooling vents overhead; closed system; artificial and natural light; winter relative humidity maintained at about 30%.
3. Furnishings: few textures (patterns); neutral color scheme.

### Client Needs

1. Lease arrangement for plantings, including maintenance.
2. Image to convey: efficient and organized.
3. Plant preferences: to be specified by interiorscaper and to include some seasonal flowering specimens as accents.
4. Clientele: primarily adults.
5. Moderate budget.

## Analysis

### Constraints

1. Lighting: limited; client approves of supplemental lighting as needed.

2. Water source: necessary to install tap in storage room.
3. Floor surface: carpet; nonporous saucer or waterproof containers needed.
4. Air vents overhead; place plants to avoid cool drafts or heat blasts.

### Resources

1. Moderate budget, adequate for size of space.
2. Leasing plan with professional maintenance possible.
3. Ample room for plants.
4. Storage space available for supplies.
5. Window orientation: south and west, good for plant selection.
6. No window treatment, thus no reduced light.
7. Few textures and neutral color permit greater emphasis on plants.
8. No adjoining structures outside to reduce light in winter.
9. Building overhang provides shade in summer.
10. The clerestory and upper windows should provide adequate light for loft area plantings.

## Synthesis

The following design objectives have been chosen for this case study:

- Direct traffic from the entry, past lounge, to receptionist (functional)
- Screen secretarial work station from lounge (functional)
- Block passage under stairwell because of low clearance (functional)
- Provide transitional elements between levels (aesthetic/architectural)
- Soften appearance of spaces by adding textural interest (aesthetic)
- Establish focal points throughout the office where needed (aesthetic)
- Design objectives for specific areas are noted in Figure 3.50.

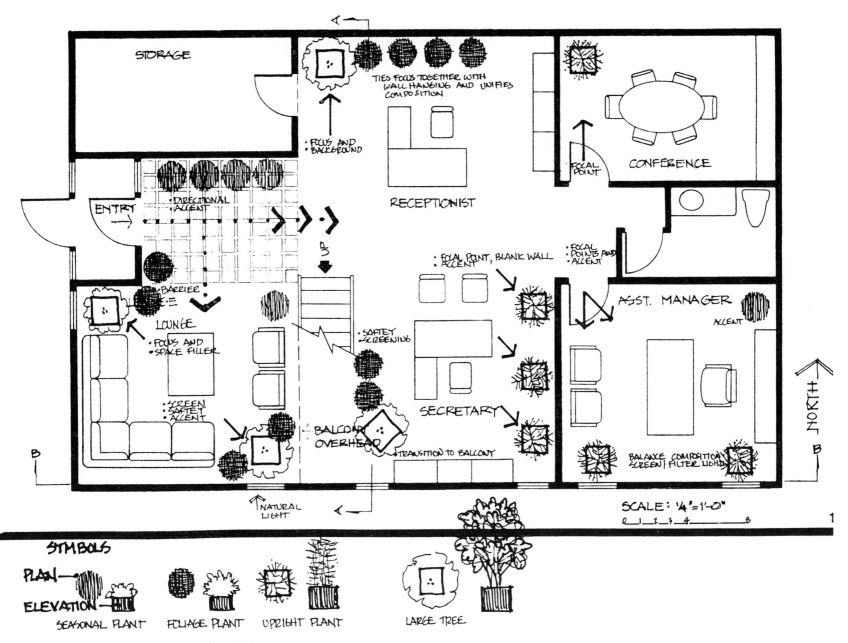

STORAGE

TIES FOCUS TOGETHER WITH WALL HANGING AND UNIFIES COMPOSITION

· FOCUS AND
· BACKGROUND

RECEPTIONIST

CONFERENCE

· DIRECTIONAL
· ACCENT

ENTRY

FOCAL POINT

· FOCAL POINT, BLANK WALL
· ACCENT

· FOCAL POINTS AND
· ACCENT

UP

ASST. MANAGER

ACCENT

· BARRIER

LOUNGE

· FOCUS AND
· SPACE FILLER

· SAFTEY
· SCREENING

SECRETARY

· SCREEN
· SAFTEY
· ACCENT

BALCONY OVERHEAD

·TRANSITION TO BALCONY

BALANCE COMPOSITION SCREEN / FILTER LIGHTS

B

B

NORTH

↑ NATURAL LIGHT

SCALE: ¼"=1'-0"

0  1  2  3  4        8

1

SYMBOLS

PLAN

ELEVATION

SEASONAL PLANT    FOLIAGE PLANT    UPRIGHT PLANT    LARGE TREE

**Figure 3.50**

This proposed floor plan and planting for a small office space includes the room layout, proposed furniture, and plants. Symbols are used to represent these elements because a description in words would be lengthy. (Judy Watson and G. M. Pierceall.)

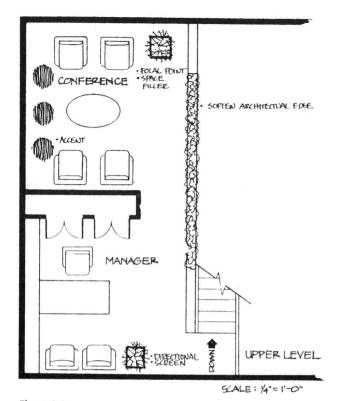

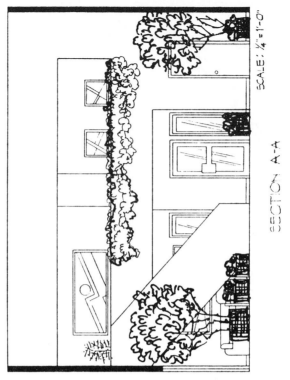

**CONFERENCE**

- FOCAL POINT
- SPACE FILLER

SOFTEN ARCHITECTURAL EDGE

- ACCENT

**MANAGER**

- DIRECTIONAL
- SCREEN

DOWN

**UPPER LEVEL**

SCALE: ¼" = 1'-0"

SECTION A-A

SCALE: ¼" = 1'-0"

**Figure 3.51**

The second floor plan and section drawings of the space help explain the vertical dimensions of the proposal. (Judy Watson and G. M. Pierceall.)

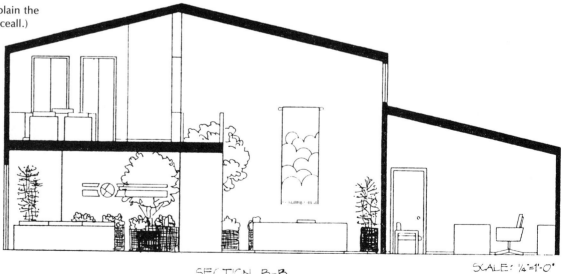

SECTION B-B

SCALE: ¼" = 1'-0"

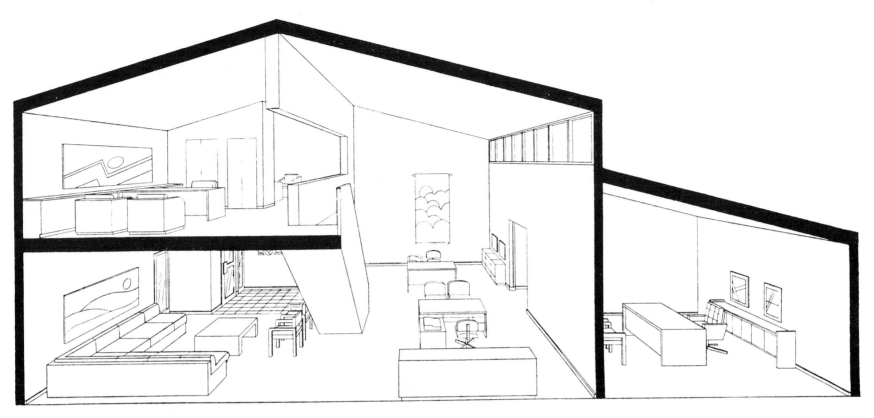

**Figure 3.52**
This section/perspective helps to describe the office areas prior to plant
selection and placement. (Designer: Judy Watson.)

The design objectives should be integrated when alternatives for each area are considered. As an example, two options for the balcony ledge are compared here:

**Option 1, Hanging Baskets.** Hanging baskets in the
opening above the ledge could interfere with views, disrupt
the architectural line, and create a closed environment
which conflicts with the intended openness of the architecture. This option was discarded in favor of Option 2.

**Option 2, Recessed Ledge Planter.** A ledge planter would
permit hanging plants to hug the ledge and grow downward, complementing the architectural line. The plants

would not interfere with the view between levels and would
break the monotony of the balcony wall by adding textural
interest.

## Solution and Proposal

Figures 3.50–3.52 are typical drawings which would be included in a professional solution. Figure 3.52 is a drawing of
the space before the plants were proposed. Figure 3.50 is
the floor plan of the first level and includes the interiorscaping design. Figure 3.51 shows the balcony and floor plan and
two interior sections. These views illustrate the height,
shape, and physical characteristics of some of the plantings.

## DESIGN DOCUMENTS

As mentioned, the presentation of ideas, concepts, and planning for project plantings and construction in the design process normally includes plans, drawings, sketches, or other graphics. These presentation drawings are used to detail and communicate information that cannot be written in words. Graphics and drawings, while representing a project, its spaces, and proposed ideas, are abstract and pictorial: designers and clients use them not as photographic representations but as an expression of the essence and character of existing conditions and proposed changes.

As ideas are formalized and presentation drawings are completed, reviewed and accepted, these sketches, plans, elevations, and perspectives become design documents. Design documents thus can be divided into two groups, presentation drawings and construction or working drawings. Both kinds of drawings are used to present ideas (Figure 3.53). *Presentation drawings* use graphics to communicate preliminary design inventory and analysis, conceptual ideas, and final illustrative master plans. *Construction* or *working drawings* are legal documents used to actually build the project, and thus are exactly scaled with directions and instructions for development. These design documents are called "working" because on-site changes are often made during construction (Figure 3.54).

In the average interiorscape situation, the scope and scale of a planting proposal may not require working drawings. The important point to be made is that the drawings produced to propose ideas should be complete enough so that someone other than the designer can understand and implement them. Sometimes you may be reading another's drawing rather than designing. When reviewing or drafting design drawings, make sure adequate labels, directions, and instructions are included so that the completed proposal results in the quality that the client and you, as designer or contractor, have envisioned.

Design documents used in preliminary design stages may include a basic building footprint, a plan of rooms, and a description of the project (Figure 3.55). If an architectural plan or other plans are not available, or if the scale of the plan is too small, the designer may have to generate another drawing prior to any graphic presentation of ideas and/or design. Rough survey, analysis, and preliminary design ideas are sketched out on graph paper or on a base plan prior to the development of any formal or final presentations. After the designer has a good understanding of the given project elements, surrounding influences, and client needs, then design solutions and selection of presentation formats can proceed.

Graphic presentation of design documents may be simple or detailed. The methods used and the information presented should relate to the scale of project as well as the audience or client for which the project is being developed. When a coordinator is installing the project, more descriptive information may be necessary to ensure adequate installation and achieve the intended design character. In the case of a large, contracted project, many different professionals may be involved in the installation, requiring a varied format to communicate the design proposal (Figure 3.56).

For a project to be implemented basic concepts need to be identified with written information as further explanation for a homeowner or contractor. Typical larger scale working drawing packages include layout plans, grading plans, planting plans (for larger planting projects), and constructional details in addition to specific information concerning pavements, steps, walls, and other constructed features. Descriptions of typically used design documents are as follows:

*Master plans* show the development of a comprehensive proposal by illustrating existing and proposed features. The base of this proposal may also be called a site plan (Figure 3.57), which includes the basic project limits and existing conditions. *Layout plans* are working drawings that identify the location of buildings, rooms, walls, walks, and planting areas by specific measurements and dimensions. This drawing (or drawings) may include the entire project or may be an enlargement of specific areas within a master plan. *Planting plans,* probably the most commonly recognized landscape design drawings, locate and identify all plant materials to be proposed and any existing on-site plantings to be preserved or removed. *Grading plans* show existing and proposed landform elements and elevations. These may be

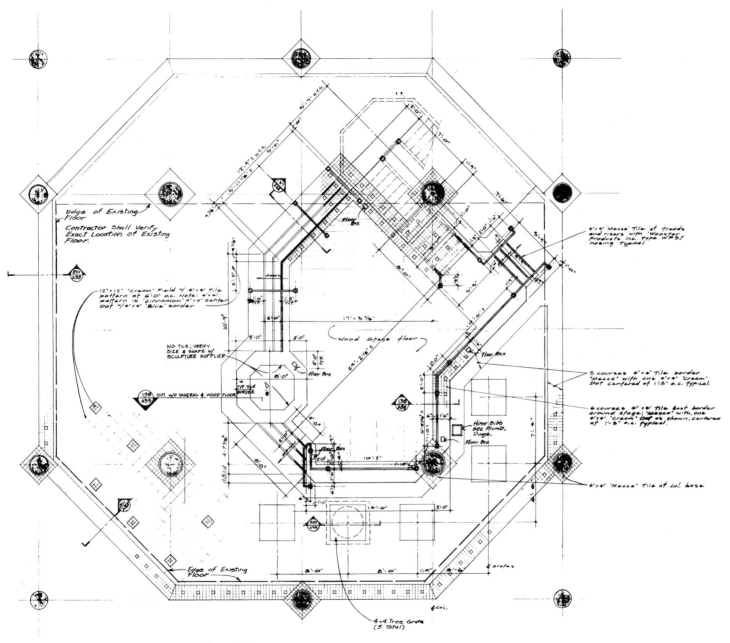

**Figure 3.53**

Construction drawings, like this floor plan, communicate what is proposed before development occurs. (Designer: The Collaborative, Inc., Toledo, Ohio.)

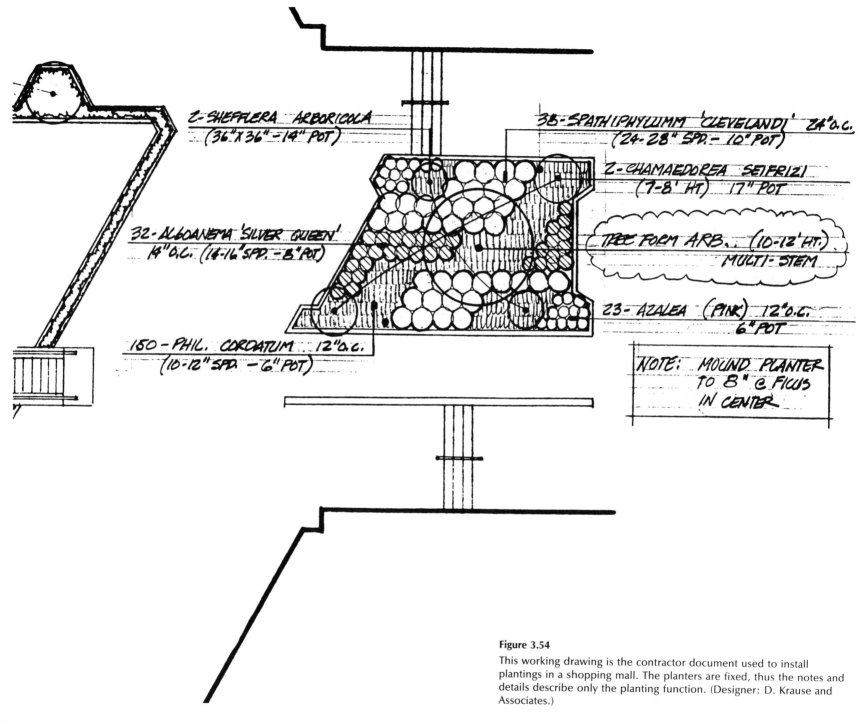

2-SHEFFLERA ARBORICOLA
(36"X36" - 14" POT)

32-AGLOANEMA 'SILVER QUEEN'
14" O.C. (14-16" SPD. - 8" POT)

150 - PHIL. CORDATUM 12" O.C.
(10-12" SPD. - 6" POT)

38-SPATHIPHYLLUMM 'CLEVELAND' 24" O.C.
(24-28" SPD. - 10" POT)

2-CHAMAEDOREA SEIFRIZI
(7-8' HT) 17" POT

TREE FORM ARB.. (10-12' HT.)
MULTI-STEM

23- AZALEA (PINK) 12" O.C.
6" POT

NOTE: MOUND PLANTER
TO 8" @ FICUS
IN CENTER

**Figure 3.54**
This working drawing is the contractor document used to install
plantings in a shopping mall. The planters are fixed, thus the notes and
details describe only the planting function. (Designer: D. Krause and
Associates.)

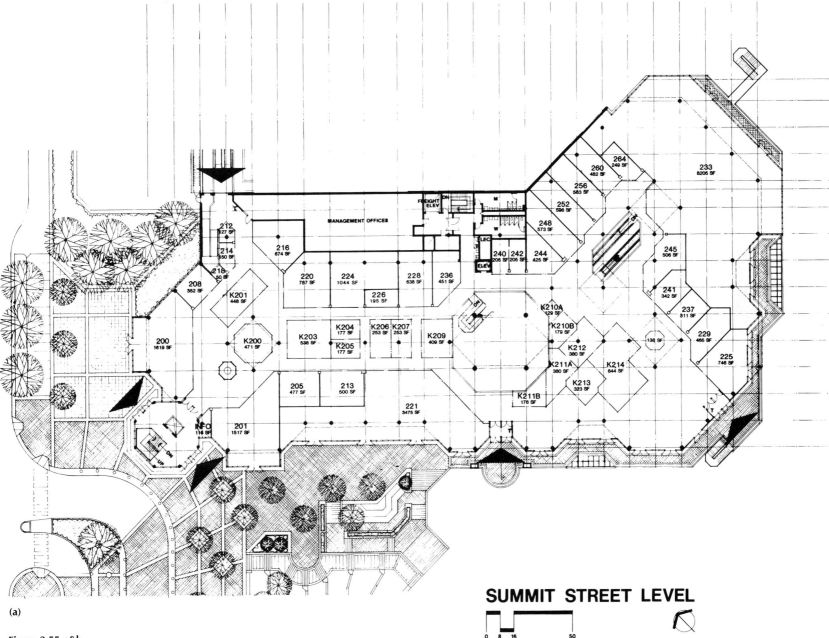

(a)

**SUMMIT STREET LEVEL**

0   8  16                    50

**Figure 3.55 a&b**

Design documents may include floor plans, as is illustrated here for an
urban commercial area called Portside in Toledo, Ohio. (Developed by
The Enterprise Development Company, The Collaborative, Inc.,
architects and landscape architects, Toledo, Ohio.)

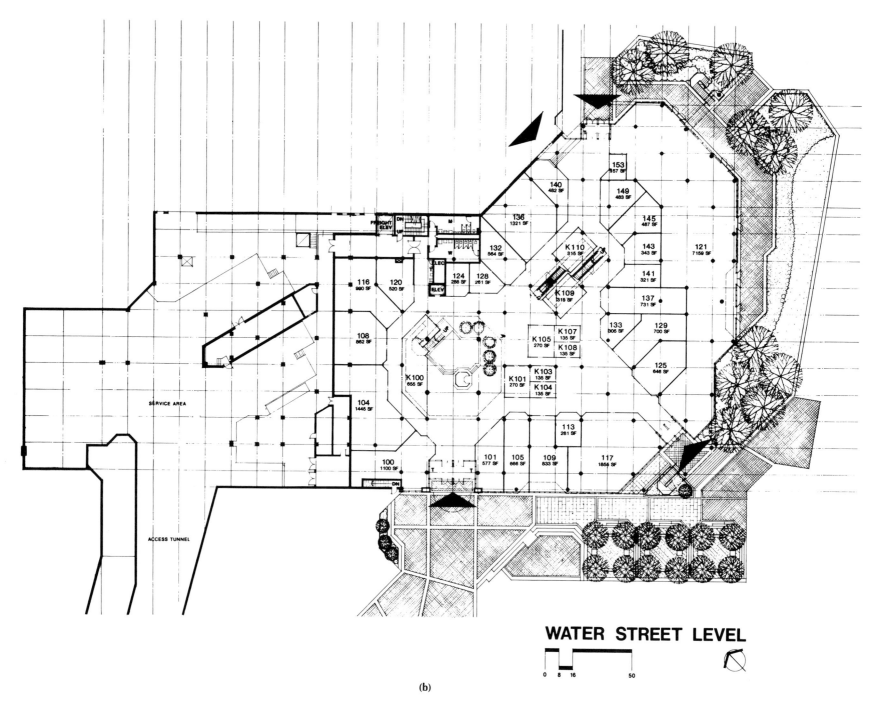

**WATER STREET LEVEL**

0 8 16     50

(b)

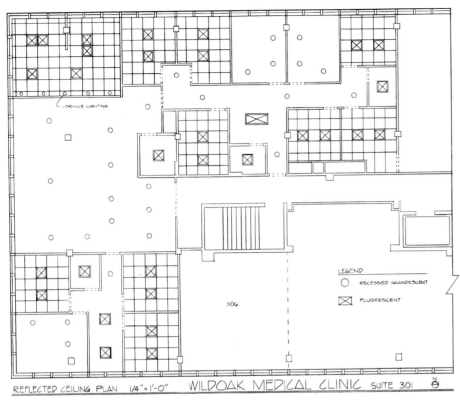

REFLECTED CEILING PLAN  1/4"=1'-0"  WILDOAK MEDICAL CLINIC SUITE 301

**Figure 3.56**

This detailed plan for a medical complex defines the floor and ceiling plans, as well as furniture and planting details. (Designer: Renee Zurad.)

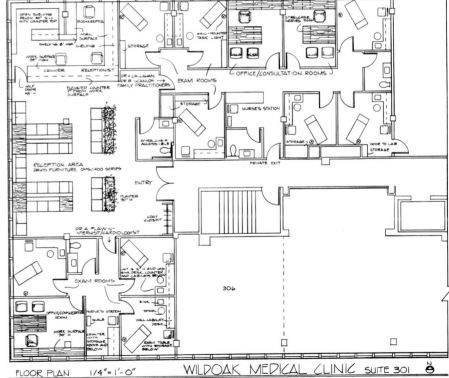

FLOOR PLAN  1/4"=1'-0"  WILDOAK MEDICAL CLINIC SUITE 301

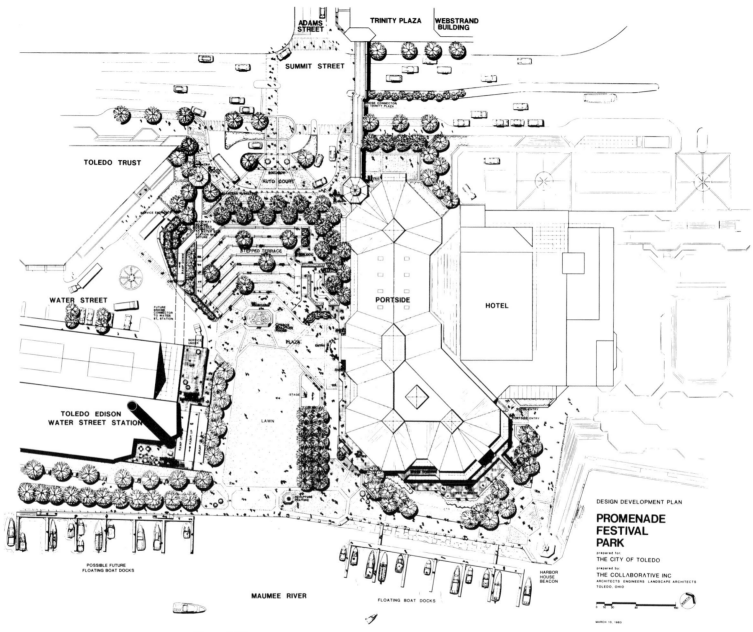

**Figure 3.57**

This illustrative master plan communicates Portside in downtown Toledo, Ohio. (Developed by The Enterprise Development Company, The Collaborative, Inc., architects and landscape architects, Toledo, Ohio.)

used in larger atrium or conservatory proposals, as were seen in Figures 1.6 and 1.7. They are used to determine appropriate soil levels, prior to development, for planting beds, retaining walls, steps, ramps, and drainage locations. Lastly, *construction details* are drawings of plans, sections, and elevations concerning individual elements of the site or master plan such as plantings, steps, walks, walls, drains, and paving or floor surfaces. As can be seen from these brief descriptions and illustrations, an interior landscape design proposal entails much more than a single sheet planting plan. The following generalized outline discusses the concepts of design process as applied to the previously discussed office interiorscape.

## DESIGN PROCESS

Design process is a systematic approach used by design professionals to plan and develop project proposals. First, a design problem or situation is established as a focus of the process. The problem could be the development of an entry space and office interior, or a temporary display at a flower show. Either of these would include both plant placement and species selection and possible constructed features. Other design problems could be the interior planting for an atrium or an open office complex. In the development of design proposals the designer should strive to maximize the desirable while minimizing the adverse factors influencing the situation. The design process may be organized in several ways; the following is a suggested approach. The detailed process discussion is the same sequence used in the case study of a professional office plantscape.

The first design step is to define the necessary final results of the project (Figure 3.58). The designer and client start to identify exactly what exists and what possibilities or opportunities are available (Figures 3.59–3.62). After a "wants" or shopping list is established, the designer can start to expand on this list to fully understand all the parts. Details concerning the sizes, shapes, types of materials, etc. are collected. This stage is the program research. The next and/or parallel step is the project survey or inventory. Here the designer does a physical inventory of what exists or is

**Figure 3.58**
In this interior situation, a court space and rock outcropping with plantings was the client's intent. (The finished project is seen in Figures 3.63 and 3.64.) This illustrates the basic framing out of the base elements of pavement and rock forms. (Courtesy of Tropical Plant Rentals, Chicago, Illinois.)

**Figure 3.59**
Selection of textures are important within interiors. These massed spider plants and palms may be the feeling desired in an interior that has stark surfacings.

**Figure 3.60**

Selected specimen plants such as these may be the accents desired in other interiorscape situations. (Greenhouses, North Carolina State University, Raleigh, North Carolina.)

**Figure 3.61**

Custom displays such as this bromeliad tree may serve as a focus for a specialized interiorscape situation. (Greenhouses, North Carolina State University, Raleigh, North Carolina.)

**Figure 3.62**

Simplicity and flexibility are design considerations in this shopping mall corridor.

going to be developed, making sure to evaluate everything of possible relevance to the design proposal. After the given conditions have been accurately recorded they are evaluated in relation to the anticipated uses. At this stage the designer can role play to better understand the functional and visual aesthetics of what exists and what could be. Role playing can be from the perspective of the owner, user, contractor and/or maintenance professional. After the designer has completed the program list, established as a checklist, and a survey and analysis, the actual design development begins. This combining of the analysis and wants list (program) may be called the synthesis stage. Using the elements and principles of design, the designer at this point composes functional options for the space. By sketching out ideas you can modify them in the process of developing a final solution. At this conceptual or preliminary stage the designer and client review and evaluate the options for the final design. After a scheme is selected the final detailing and drafting occurs. Then development options are selected and phasing and budgets are planned in working towards implementation (Figure 3.63). During the installation stage the designer, as client's representative, should be available to review both technical and design related details. After the installation a post designer evaluation can occur to see if what had been envisioned is actually attractive and functional. This review helps not only the client and project but also the designer's perspective for future projects (Figure 3.64). The following is a discussion of the development of ideas in a design process for an interiorscape.

## The Problem

As an introduction to the process of design and basic design considerations an office interior landscape design is included. The initial step is to define the project including the purposes for which it will be used or modified. A survey or inventory of existing project conditions called a site survey or site inventory is then developed. In conjunction with this step, a listing of client–user needs called a program is developed. After these pieces of information concerning the site, use, and client needs are established, the process

**Figures 3.63 and 3.64**

This is the completed project that was begun in Figure 3.58, and it satisfies the client's needs. Design considerations include functional aspects of traffic, views, use, and aesthetics. (Courtesy of Tropical Plant Rentals, Chicago, Illinois.)

3.63

3.64

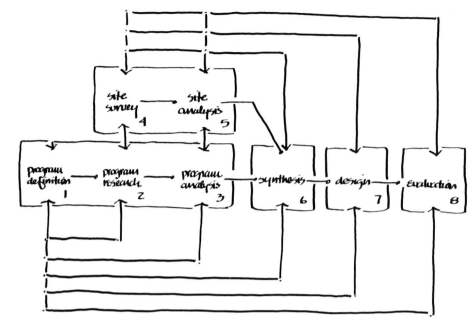

**Figure 3.65**

This basic flow diagram illustrates the design process as described in the text.

focus shifts to combining the site and client data into functional schemes. The details and interrelationships between these project elements are refined and eventually composed into a master plan. From this a phasing schedule, cost estimates and the eventual implementation occurs. The flow diagram in Figure 3.65 illustrates a design process.

## Phase One

**Step One: Program Establishment.** A design program or checklist outlines ideal elements, objectives and project before the actual proposal is developed. The elements are selected according to the project's use, users, character size, materials, and components. These elements may be identified or suggested by the designer, the client, or both through design dialog and discussion.

Initial project objectives are established to describe the character and quality of the proposal or areas within the project. Typical objectives are concerned with visual image, safety, security, flexibility, or the opportunity for change and convenience. Other interior considerations such as environmental ranges, budget, maintenance levels, legal re-

strictions, priorities, responsibilities, and historical data may also be included in the program and used throughout the design process. At this initial stage the services the client is requesting and the expected results are defined.

There are several design possibilities and services in interiorscaping that can be provided: 1) new plantings—selecting plant materials for free-standing planter, units, or built-in planters in a new or existing interior; 2) renovation—replacing or reorganizing existing plant materials; 3) permanent planting design—creating a specific planting effect during the developmental stages of an interior project; or 4) plant rental options. Other design opportunities combine these options.

Typical program objectives for an office interiorscape design proposal may be as follows:

1. Create a sense of separation between the entry door and other office areas.
2. Propose plants or planting options that are tolerant of interior light and conditions.
3. Provide an opportunity for flexibility within the space by providing office circulation yet separating use areas.

4. Select some plant materials that provide seasonal interest.
5. Propose plantings and support components that can be maintained by the clients or at reasonable rates.

**Step Two: Program Research.** After all the basic design elements and objectives have been defined, all the design program elements must be thoroughly understood. Of particular importance are the owner's requirements and whatever they translate into in terms of minimum and maximum size, types of areas, numbers, connections between areas and so forth. In this research effort, one always considers the three umbrella requirements—image, function, aesthetics—as well as structure or constructibility. In most cases, the client's request is straightforward: "add plants to improve the overall quality of the space." This brings us to the second stage of the design process, researching problem parameters and analyzing possibilities. Designers investigate two primary considerations as sources of information: First, the physical features of the interior, and secondly, the client's needs and preferences. You may begin by gathering pertinent data on the interior environment. This includes architectural information such as location and size and the wall, floor, and ceiling surface materials of the project. Dimensions of walks, walls, doors and windows, locations (from sketches of floor plans and elevations), and environmental data are other possibilities. Note the type of heating and cooling systems, day and night temperature ranges and weekday vs. weekend temperature cycles. Also to be identified are the location of vents and artificial light sources, the orientation of skylights in relation to natural light, and local climatic conditions. Other characteristics of interiors such as style, furniture, color scheme, and window treatments as well as traffic patterns, etc. are also necessary.

The needs and preferences of the client are best determined in a personal interview and discussion. Budget is the concern most mentioned by clients. General prices should be discussed, but not as the sole factor in the overall design. If you design only for the funds immediately available, once it is complete they don't know where to go. Part of the budgeting may be discussion of available options: plant purchasing, plant leasing, and maintenance contracts. Determine as early as possible the client's plant preferences as well as his ideas about seasonal and permanent plantings. Information on the type of business, clientele, and company image is helpful in making plant choices and establishing a design theme in conjunction with the architectural and interior schemes. A general review of operational procedures and office schedules also helps to understand interior traffic patterns and activity areas. Actual observation of the space is desirable if possible.

From a list of program requirements established by the client and designer in Step One research would define the following relative to the general objectives:

1. Is "separation" as defined in the program to be physical, visual, or both? Where are the room's lighting sources? Is natural light available or, if artificial, what are the hours of duration?
2. In what areas can plantings be proposed to work with use and furniture arrangements? How will space limitations due to doors, windows, drawers, vents, etc. affect plant locations?
3. What exactly is meant by color or seasonal interest; leaves, stems, flowers, or all of these?
4. What skills or capabilities do the clients have with respect to plant care and establishment?

**Step Three: Program Analysis.** The various design requirements are grouped so that compatible elements, functions, and influences are brought together. After information has been gathered, it is time to analyze the data in Steps One and Two. This determines the design implications by evaluating the basic needs and given conditions. List the information according to resources and constraints imposed by the client's needs or space limitations. At the same time, add notes on how these will affect the selection of plant material.

This analysis or combination of program elements can be called a functional diagram. The ideal relationships between program and space are defined and combined. In general design situations, the functional diagram can be drawn directly over the base survey. In more complex design situations, functional diagrams may be developed separately and later applied to the base plan.

A compatibility matrix and/or a bubble diagram may be employed to express graphically the many relationships which usually become too complex to store in one's head. Based on these interrelationships, an abstract plan is developed. The concepts developed and communicated through this general plan show the arrangement of the design parts and/or functions to be introduced into the space. This step is begun without scale to consider these elements independent of the project. As a final scheme develops, scale is incorporated to determine the relative sizes and shapes of the various interrelated parts.

## Phase Two

**Step Four: The Project Survey.** As an independent step (parallel to Steps One, Two, and Three) a space survey is developed. This survey or inventory gathers together project data including natural, cultural, and perceptual information about the area, the building, access, skylights, and illumination as well as furnishings and any influences that may affect the design proposal.

**Step Five: The Site Analysis.** The collected survey information is then analyzed to determine inherent opportunities and limitations relative to the anticipated project functions (use). This is accomplished by graphics, diagrams, tone and color, or patterns drawn on the survey or presented in an additional drawing. The analysis may be set up to determine how the project can best serve the intended use(s), or how the site should be used based on its inherent qualities. With the inventory of existing conditions the design evaluates the situation relative to the desired changes. In the design program, plant conditions may have been identified. Here an assessment is needed to prevent inherent conflicts. The existing conditions versus the other program elements are reviewed by this same process.

## Phase Three

**Step Six: Synthesis.** As the "mid" or "pivot" stage of the design process, the synthesis generates and evaluates alternatives by combining the project constraints and resources with design objectives and client uses. This is probably the most challenging stage, where design principles are applied

to the proposal using collected data to determine how the plants can best be used in the interior and what plants will grow within the *interior conditions*. Be sure the design proposal developed relates to the design objectives. Both aesthetic and functional contributions of plants should be considered.

Implementation of these initial goals is best explored through sketches. Listing alternatives and indicating the advantages and disadvantages of each possibility is also useful. This is the critical "putting it all together" stage. A plan starts to appear when the program concepts (functional diagrams) are superimposed over the analysis drawing, using an overlay process. The revision of scale, alignment of spaces, and stretching, warping, raising, and lowering of design program elements relates them to site specific situations. At this synthesis stage it is often helpful to project existing edges inherent in the project. The corners of buildings, rooms, windows, doors, and other fixed features help establish edges and spaces for development of program requirements.

Although some site or schematic compromise may be necessary to develop site alternatives, the plan should exhibit a "fine fit" between the site analysis and program. Care should be taken not to sacrifice client priorities and the schematic relationships established in the earlier stages of planning.

A great deal of adjustment and refinement are usually required to achieve this fine fit. Although adjustments have been made regarding function, visual image, and structure throughout the process, continued refinement now insures that the project is realistic and can be constructed in accordance with the three umbrella considerations—function, aesthetics, and constructibility.

## Phase Four

**Step Seven: Problem Solution Communication.** The plan or problem solution selected must now be communicated. In the final stage of the design process, the best alternatives to an interiorscaping problem are presented as solutions. The client must be provided with the drawings and documents necessary for the eventual construction, and should be able to understand the proposal. Drawings may include a master plan, furniture plan, detailed planting plan, electrical plan, construction details, specifications, and detailing through sketches. Some of these drawings or documents may be drawn up during the master plan development or after review, when construction is impending. It should be mentioned that the types of drawings and services provided may be regulated by local registration laws according to the designer's status as a landscape architect, landscape designer, interior designer or plantscaper.

### Phase Five

**Step Eight: Evaluation.** The last step, which in one sense could be considered the first, is the evaluation of the master plan and design solution. No one definable evaluation technique can adapt to every project. As least two points should be considered in any evaluation:

1. The degree to which the stated objectives were met in the design developed.
2. The validity of the objectives as determined by the user and site situations.

Design changes considered after evaluation may be used in the project development as project drawings are revised. The knowledge gained through this evaluation can also be applied to subsequent projects. Through post-design review one achieves a better understanding of design process and what decisions must be made to achieve functional and aesthetic design proposals.

## DESIGN PROCESS: SUMMARY

The process as presented reads as if one were to follow a step-by-step path in one direction—forward—yet at any point in the process it may be necessary to circle back and reevaluate, reexamine, or gather more information. The design process in application is a cyclic sequence of definition, analysis, conceptualization and detailing working towards a unified and functional proposal.

## SUMMARY

Interior landscape design is a professional design area that strives to create functional and aesthetic settings for building interiors which reinforce their uses and activities. Interior landscape designers need to develop an understanding of the functional and aesthetic considerations concerning a project's development. As an interior landscape designer or other design professional the technical skills of delineation, design, and construction combined with a plant background help to combine these specific concepts and ideas in the use of the design process. For the design professional, graphics provide a means of proposing concepts, ideas, and philosophies to clients relative to site specific situations. It is necessary for the interior landscape designer to understand planning and design in order to communicate with other design professionals—architects, landscape architects, interior designers—and with all clients involved in the interiorscape industry.

# Chapter 4

# Graphic Materials and Processes

Skillful communication of ideas and concepts through graphics results from a designer's understanding of and proficiency with available tools, materials, and processes. The equipment, supplies, and processes used in the production of drawings are only as effective as an individual designer's understanding, skill, and creativity. Designers need to understand basic graphic skills and their individual capacities, and evaluate the project at hand to determine the appropriate graphics. Another graphic selection criteria is the person to whom you are communicating (Figures 4.1 and 4.2).

From the beginning to the end of a design problem, designers use equipment, materials, and techniques to record, evaluate, and develop design proposals. Early design ideas are often sketched out using soft pencils, inexpensive paper, and color markers. These inexpensive and informal materials provide the designer with maximum flexibility and creativity. As ideas crystallize and are refined, the tech-

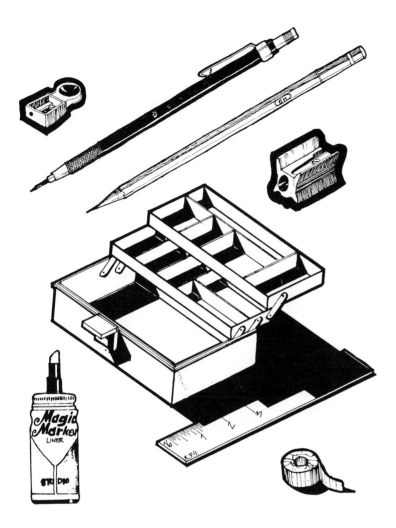

**Figure 4.1**
Some of the graphics equipment used to communicate design ideas are pencils, sharpeners, markers, and rulers. A tackle box can be used to hold these and other supplies. (Designer: R. P. Strychalski.)

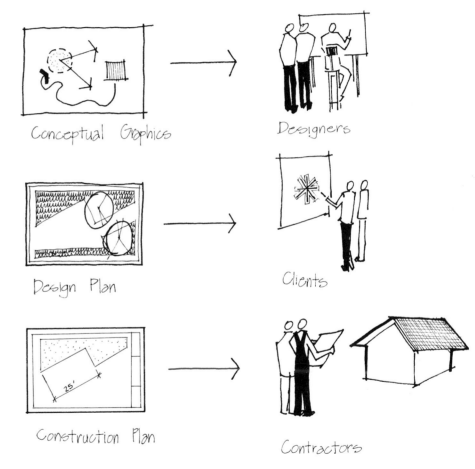

Conceptual Graphics

Designers

Design Plan

Clients

Construction Plan

Contractors

**Figure 4.2**
The type of drawings used to communicate ideas often depends on to whom you are communicating. Varied drawings are used between designers, from designer to clients, and from designer to contractors. (Designer: T. Kramer.)

# OFFICE ATRIUM Case Study #101

## LANDSCAPE ARCHITECTS
## GRAHAM
### DESIGN GROUP

100 CATHEDRAL STREET
ANNAPOLIS, MARYLAND 21401
BALTIMORE (301) 269-5886
WASHINGTON (301) 858-5330

**DEVELOPER**
Spaulding & Slye

**ARCHITECT**
Clarke, Tribble, Harris & Li

**CONTRACTOR**
Creative Plantings, Inc.

**DESCRIPTION**
Office Atrium, four stories, 1800 square feet. Shady Grove Executive Center, Rockville, MD. Balanced sunlight and electric light.

**OBJECTIVE**
To create a distinctive interior landscape with visual strength that will continue the exterior landscape into the building and provide a "soft" counterpoint to the "hard" architecture.

**RESULT**
A dramatic and aesthetically appealing space that gives the building a competitive edge in the marketplace. The space is a focus for casual meetings and a sense of office community.

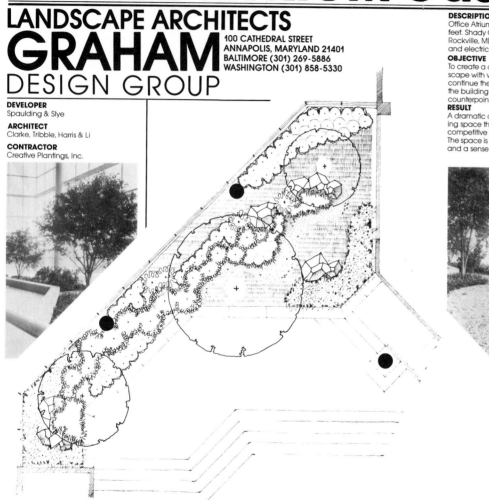

**APPROACH**
An illusion of expansiveness accomplished by the arrangement of plants in layers, according to size. Tall trees overhang the public areas and are underplanted by numerous textures of groundcover. Medium size plant material forms a washing of green foliage that is a foil for the architecture.

The supporting details include non-plant features that complete the effect of a landscape. For example, the boulders provide a juxtaposition of contrasts for the plants while the washed river gravel recalls a dry river bed offering a strong geometric organization to the ground plane as seen from the upper floors.

The final spark to the design is the red and yellow colors in the bromeliads. Because the color is in the foliage rather than the flowers, there are not the frequent and costly changes of floral materials, just the benefit of color.

**Figure 4.3**

This professional interiorscape project communicates design details through a plan and actual project photos. While graphics are good to communicate design ideas, written information is also used to fully convey the designer and project concepts. (Designer: Jay Graham.)

niques and materials used to illustrate them can become more controlled and defined. Final colored presentations result from many layers of ideas and refinements of design, having utilized a wide range of media and techniques. As you review the equipment, materials, techniques, and processes described in this section please be aware that the resources used in presenting a proposal should be selected relative to individual project requirements and the individual skills of the designer (Figure 4.3).

## EQUIPMENT AND MATERIALS

### Pencils

Pencils are one of the basic drawing tools used by all designers. To start with the basics, the component parts of a pencil are the lead, casing or shell, and the cap which may or may not include an eraser. A variety of leads are available: graphite, plastic, and plastic–graphite. The hardness or softness of the lead selected should produce the line qualities desired. Generally lead hardness ranges from 9H to 6B; H is harder and B is softer (Figure 4.4). Pencils can be used for sketching ideas, guidelines, and layouts before hard lining with pencils or ink occurs to produce finished drawings. Construction drawings are normally drafted in pencil since the information included is routinely changed during specific revisions and/or redesigns. Harder leads for drawing produces thin sharp lines and is often used in drawing or lettering guidelines and construction drawings where line quality is important. Harder leads produce thin, crisp lines and do not smear, but are not as easily erased. Softer leads are used to produce thicker, darker lines for primary drawing lines, sketching, and lettering. Designers should be aware that softer leads, while producing thicker, darker lines, also smear more easily and thus require careful presentation and drafting techniques.

The types of pencils used in design are often identified by the casing or mechanics that enclose and protect the lead. Commonly used pencil casings include wooden, lead holders, or mechanical pencils. The most traditional and

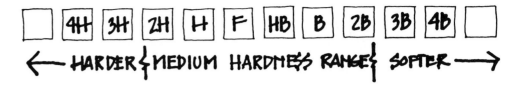

**Figure 4.4**
Lead hardness chart. (Designer: R. P. Strychalski.)

**Figure 4.5**
Wooden pencil and lead holder. (Designer: R. P. Strychalski.)

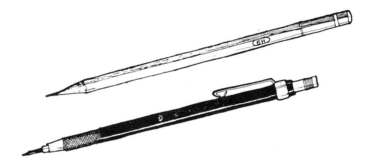

least expensive is the wooden pencil. Its light weight and low cost makes it a popular choice. Wooden pencils are sharpened with a knife or sharpener and have a simple casing with no breakable "mechanical parts." (Figure 4.5). The lead holder has a plastic, metal, or combination casing with interchangeable leads inside. Lead holders allow the flexibility of changing lead hardnesses easily and sharpening without wooden shavings. They are sharpened by lead pointers rather than pencil sharpeners (Figure 4.6). Lead holders may be heavier in weight and are more expensive than wooden pencils. Again, the flexibility of a lead holder lies in its interchangeable lead hardness and the availability of specialty leads such as nonprint or nonphoto leads. Nonprint leads are purplish in color and are used as guidelines for the layout of information before lettering or final drafting is added in ink or pencil. When original drawings are duplicated, the blueprinting process does not recognize this purple color on the paper, thus the nonprint lines do not "print" while

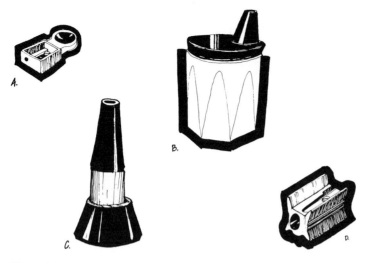

**Figure 4.6**
Lead sharpeners A, B, and C are used to point lead in a leadholder. Sharpener D is typically used with wooden pencils. (Designer: R. P. Strychalski.)

**Figure 4.7**
Mechanical pencils can be purchased with a specific lead diameter from .5 to .9 mm, and need no sharpening. (Designer: R. P. Strychalski.)

the ink or pencil portions of the drawing do. Thus no erasing is required before duplication. Nonphoto leads are similar to nonprint leads except they are used in the photographic process rather than in the duplication of information on a print machine. Caution should be taken when using nonphoto lead for lettering guidelines or layout lines on vellum drawings to be printed. Due to its color, the nonphoto lead does print in the blueprint process, resulting in undesirable lines on the final copy. Overall, designers will probably use all three types of pencils in the course of producing a variety of design drawings.

The mechanical pencil is similar to the lead holder in construction, cost, and flexibility, yet requires no sharpening due to the predetermined sizes of leads used (Figure 4.7). Mechanical pencils are available in .3 mm to .9 mm sizes whereas wooden pencils and the leads used in lead holders come in only one diameter size. While the variation in lead thickness is desirable, it limits the opportunity of interchanging the leads among mechanical pencils. Selection of the correct lead diameter for your drafting needs is important. To help with pencil lead selection, smaller lead

sizes, .3 to .5 mm, are often used for lettering guidelines, whereas larger leads, .5 to .9 mm, can be used for the final lettering and heavier line work. Mechanical pencils are chosen for their consistent lines and ease of use. Graphite and plastic leads are available for use in these mechanical pencils. Since no sharpening is required, they save time and lower overall costs. Pencil line quality depends on the hardness of the lead and the drafting technique used. To draft a concise quality line, the designer's pencil is pulled and rotated with consistent pressure. Both hard and soft leads must be pulled and rotated while scoring a line with a straight-edge to maintain a sharp point and consistent line. Figure 4.8 shows the pulling and rotating motion used to develop consistent lines. Harder leads retain their point longer and require less sharpening than softer leads, which require constant sharpening for maintenance of line quality. Line darkness or opaqueness also results from lead hardness: the softer the lead the darker the line.

Other factors influencing pencil line quality are the drawing surface and the drafting surface. Smoother papers are used for harder leads while rougher papers are used for softer leads. The surface texture of paper is often referred to as its "tooth." More tooth means a rougher surface, less tooth means a smoother paper. When using pencils, the graphite or lead material is rubbed onto the paper. Harder leads wear down slower with less graphite, thus are better applied to smoother papers. Softer leads wear quickly and so need more tooth for the graphite particles to attach to. The resiliency of the drafting table or surface also influences pencil line quality. Softer surfaces allow flexibility between the paper and pencil. Harder surfaces may cause more scoring of the paper instead of a clear graphite line.

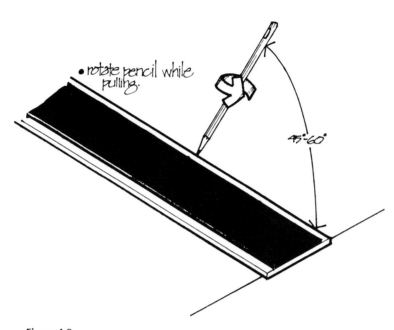

**Figure 4.8**
Technical skills are needed to produce a clean, consistent pencil line. While the pencil is pulled it is also rotated to keep an even point and uniform line. (Designer: R. P. Strychalski.)

**Figure 4.9**
This technical pen diagram illustrates the various pen parts. (Designer: R. P. Strychalski.)

## Ink

Ink as a medium is used for final drawings such as sketches, illustrative plans, and other permanent information. Titles, sheet, borders, scales, and north arrows may be drawn in ink as they do not change as often as design information during the design process.

For optimum contrast and quality in line, inking or technical pens are used for their consistency, accuracy, and ease of reproduction (Figure 4.9). Drawings produced with technical pens result in clear, consistent lines because ink flows through a manufactured point of specific width. This consistency of line width may also be called line weight. Line weights vary from fine to thick and are identified by metric or other measures (Figure 4.10). There are numerous brands of technical pen available; they should be selected only after individual features, uses, and costs are understood. When using technical pens, make sure the ink selected is waterproof and nonclogging. Ink pens often clog due to neglect, poor maintenance, or dormancy; a primary disadvantage and a major cause of dissatisfaction. Reading the instructions and understanding the pen's mechanics, care, and use help reduce the clogs and frustrations. Illustrative plans may be done in ink, pencil, or a combination while sheet titles, borders, and other permanent, nonchanging

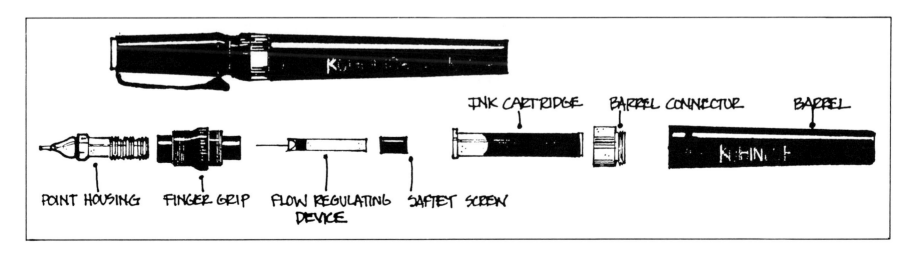

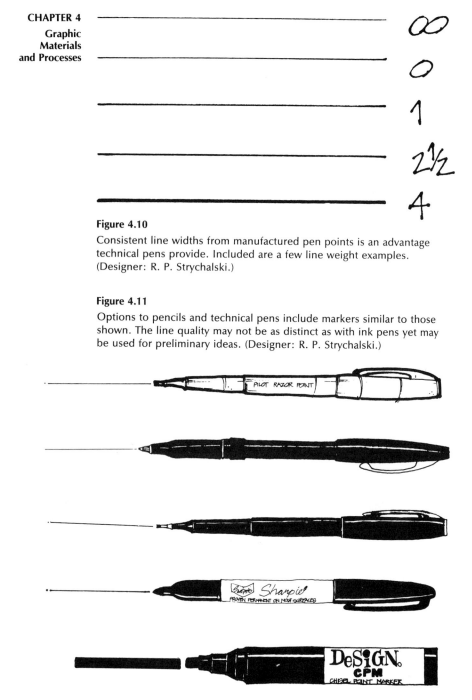

**Figure 4.10**

Consistent line widths from manufactured pen points is an advantage technical pens provide. Included are a few line weight examples. (Designer: R. P. Strychalski.)

**Figure 4.11**

Options to pencils and technical pens include markers similar to those shown. The line quality may not be as distinct as with ink pens yet may be used for preliminary ideas. (Designer: R. P. Strychalski.)

information are normally inked. Sketches, construction drawings, and drawing guidelines are usually completed in pencil.

### Optional Drawing Tools

If an alternative to the exclusive use of pencils or pens is needed due to costs or the need for variety, many options are available. Commercial brands such as the Pilot, Sharpie, Markette, and Design chisel point marker (CPM) are all good graphics alternatives. These less expensive graphic tools also produce a variety of line weights and line contrasts (Figure 4.11). While similar to rendering dry markers, these drawing tools use a chisel-shaped plastic or felt tip to distribute ink in a fine line or broad stroke. The basic advantage of these drawing tools is the variety of points available and their ease of use. When used on vellum, their line quality and darkness are similar to ink, yet they have less line weight contrast which can produce lower quality prints. As a drawing ages over 6 months these materials do separate and leave a halo type of line. As drawing tools they can be used in conjunction with colored markers. Dry markers are used to add color to presentation prints; this is also called rendering. These color markers also have a variety of felt tips to distribute colored inks for highlighting design drawings. Marker tips also range from a fine point to a broad chisel.

### LINE WEIGHT, CONTRAST, AND LINE QUALITY

In presenting design ideas, designers use lines, textures, and colors to represent ideas. Basic to any graphic presentation of information is the line drawing, which uses line and line variations of width and style to define objects and compositions. Line weight, line contrast, and line quality are the main aspects to be considered in the production of line drawings.

### Line Weight

A line's width and darkness is its line weight. When a line drawing is composed of varied line weights a hierarchy

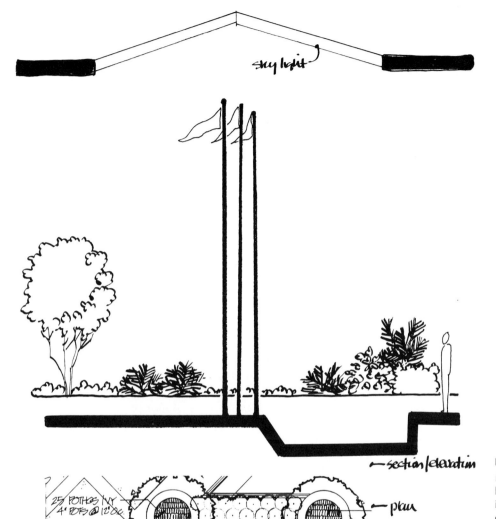

*stay light*

*section/elevation*

*plan*

*25 POTHOS IVY
4" POTS @ 12"OC*

**Figure 4.12**

In plan view and other drawings, varied line weights help to establish a visual priority among the illustrated parts. In this plan, the important ground edges and canopy of the plants use heavier line weights to make accented lines darker than other parts of the illustration. In the section drawing, the roof and floor areas are bolder than other parts of the drawing, indicating their importance.

or contrast of dark, wide lines to light, thin lines should be developed. The heavier the line weight, the more important the element being defined. Wide lines are used to outline the edges of major forms such as buildings or rooms. These lines may also be used to define elements closest to the viewer in a sketch or plan. Lighter lines in drawings should be used for secondary elements and to add textural detail. Thinner lines are also used to define the edges of lesser forms and to present objects further away from the viewer in plan or sketch (Figure 4.12).

## Line Quality

Line quality in a drawing refers to the regularity and clarity of a line. Just as a drawing should include a consistent line hierarchy or contrast, so line quality also needs to be consistent. Line weights and line quality in drawing depend on the designer's drafting technique and skill in the use of the tools.

Ink line quality is achieved by holding the pen perpendicular to the paper or drawing surface, as shown in Figure 4.13. As mentioned previously, line sharpness or clarity is affected by the drawing surface. When using ink pens, smoother toothed papers or plastic-type drawing surfaces (mylar) should be used. Drawing surfaces are included in the next section of text.

## DRAWING SURFACES

Directly related to the media of leads and ink are drawing surfaces. Graphic ideas can be presented on thin tracing papers, sketching grade papers, quality grade vellums, film

**Figure 4.13**
When technical pens or other pens are used with a ruling edge such as a T-square or triangle, make sure the pen is perpendicular to the ruling edge. This helps to reduce wet ink being drawn under the ruling edge. Since a ruling edge often has a bevel or raised edge on its underside this helps reduce ink blotting problems. (Designer: R. P. Strychalski.)

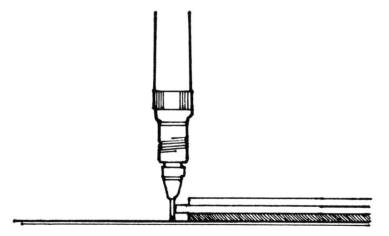

(plastic), and illustration boards. In selecting a drawing surface one should consider the type of drawing, the presentation format (informal vs. formal), sheet size needed, drawing permanence, costs, and the reproduction process—if any is to be used.

## Tracing Papers

Preliminary thoughts, diagrams, or initial design ideas are often conceptualized on thin tracing papers. Their relatively inexpensive cost and transparency allows the freedom of developing many variations by tracing ideas from one sheet to the next. Revisions and final ideas can then be traced on to a more permanent drawing surface. The benefits of thin tracing paper are its low cost, transparency, and ease of use throughout the design proposal phase. The papers are available in a variety of roll widths and lengths including 12", 24", and 36" widths. These papers are ideal for preliminary design because of their minimal cost, compared to quality tracing papers. The main disadvantage is that they are brittle and sheared; they are sometimes called "trash" paper or "bum wad" as some preliminary ideas are thrown away. Soft pencils and colored markers are the media most used with these papers to conceptualize ideas. Thin tracing papers can be duplicated in a blueprint machine, but extreme care and caution must be exercised because of their brittleness. The slightest tear becomes major when trash papers are run through the printer. Taking photos of preliminary design ideas is probably the best means of recording and storing drawing information when this less permanent paper is used.

Sketching grade papers include sketchbooks, sketch pads, and marker papers. All of these are good for original drawings in ink, black marker, or pencil that do not require reproduction. Sketching paper and marker papers both have a rough-toothed surface that accepts pencil and markers easily. Marker paper comes in pads of 9" by 12" or 18" by 24" which include a waxed backing to prevent markers from bleeding through the sheets on to desk surfaces or other sheets. These papers are normally used for preliminary sketches or presentation information that does not require reproduction. Xerox or other means of duplicating these originals is often the best means of recording and storing this information. An inexpensive option to marker paper which comes in a roll rather than a pad is waxed freezer paper. Normally used to wrap frozen foods, this paper has a toothed surface and waxed backing similar to marker paper. The 18" by 50' roll is an available alternative to the marker paper pads.

For designers brainstorming on a coffee break the illustration of preliminary ideas on paper towels or napkins, while suitable not for formal presentation, are another inexpensive media. Marker-type media work best on these surfaces to "sketch out" early design concepts. Due to their usual small size they are best used for individual ideas relating to a project. Later, these sketched ideas can be refined and drawn on more permanent paper if necessary.

## Vellum

Quality grade tracing vellums are the papers used in final presentation drawings. The term "vellum" was originally used to describe a type of parchment made from calfskin and used as a writing surface or for book bindings. Today paper vellums are normally 100 percent rag paper and they provide a quality transparent surface for finished line work.

When selecting vellums one should consider the proper paper surface in relation to the drafting materials to be used. Smooth-toothed papers are best for ink or hard lead drawings, while rougher-toothed surfaces are best for softer pencil presentations or sketches. Vellum whiteness and transparency are also important qualities to consider when selecting quality papers. Transparency and whiteness will affect the quality of prints produced. The size of vellum paper ranges from individual sheets of $8\frac{1}{2}$" by 11", 9" by 12", 11" by 17", and 12" by 18", to rolls of 18", 24", 36", and 48" in width with varying lengths. Pencil and ink used on vellum surfaces are the most permanent for original drawings. Markers used on vellum often separate and disperse into the paper over time, leaving a faded line and halo effect which destroys the drawing. If a marker has been used, a general recommendation would be to get a sepia print of the work before line problems occur.

This other available drawing surface is a sepia print. A sepia is a piece of vellum which has an emulsion applied to its surface to produce, in essence, another original of a drawing. Sepias are produced as part of the blueprint process and are used when multiple drawings are needed in a presentation. The blueprint process is covered later in this chapter. The sepia or sepias produced can then be used, just as an original drawing, to produce prints. Sepias will be discussed further in the section involving blueprint process.

To provide clearer drawings that accept pencil or ink more evenly, designers may use pounce as a surface preparation. A fine granular powder, pounce, is sifted into the paper tooth to produce a smoother drafting surface.

## Plastic or Film Drafting Surfaces

Drawing surfaces of film, plastic, or mylar are the most permanent and durable. These synthetic surfaces accept pencil and ink readily and are waterproof and harder to damage, thus assuring permanence and durability. However, there are disadvantages to plastic or film drawing surfaces. They cost much more than paper and the surface can be damaged if objects are dropped or drawn across them, causing dents or scratches. In the selection and use of plastic drawing surfaces, the ratio of costs to benefits relative to the project and the need for permanence must be considered and compared to those of other drawing surfaces.

## Boards

Illustration board can also be used as a drawing surface. It is available in either a toothed surface (cold press) or a smooth surface (hot press) for original line work and drawings. The range of colors and thicknesses provides an excellent surface for durable presentations. If original work is drafted on boards, it cannot be duplicated or revised as easily as when drafted on transparent drawing surfaces. Corrections or revisions are almost impossible because erasing would alter the colored board surface. Illustration boards provide a quality base for drawings, yet require precise and accurate drafting skills. They can also be used to mount or mat drafts or other presentations.

# DRAFTING EQUIPMENT

In combination with the large selection of pencils, inking pens, and papers, designers use a wide range of other equipment to control, organize, and remove lines in scale drawings. Typical supportive drawing equipment includes a drawing table or board, T-square or parallel-rule, triangles, templates, erasure shields, electric erasers, scales, and lettering guides.

## Drawing Boards and Tools

The drawing table or board is a squared surface that allows designers to align papers squarely and securely so as to produce drawings and lines that are parallel and perpendicular to the paper's edges. Drawing boards are normally wooden with metal edges machined to maintain a "square" drawing base. Often a resilient plastic surface covers the wooden surface to protect it from mechanical injury and to provide a flexible surface for drafting. Some board covers also have a grid that provides a scale and guidelines for drawings. A T-square or parallel-rule is used to draft lines parallel to the board's square edges. The T-square, as a drafting tool, is used off the left or right square edges of the board to provide perpendicular guides for paper alignment or drafted lines. The left side of the drawing board is used for right-handed people and the right edge for left-handed people. The parallel-rule produces similar line guides yet is permanently attached to the board, whereas T-squares are removable (Figure 4.14).

T-squares and parallel-rules are primarily used for horizontal lines, while triangles are used for vertical and diagonal lines. The most frequently used triangles are the 30 degree, 45 degree, 60 degree, and 90 degree. Selection of a triangle and its size should reflect the types of angles used in drafting to satisfy the range of project involvements. Triangles come in 6″, 8″, and 10″ lengths and larger, all of which are appropriate for most drawings. When selecting a triangle consider the following: (1) colored triangles are easier to see on desks than clear ones; (2) triangle edges with "cut

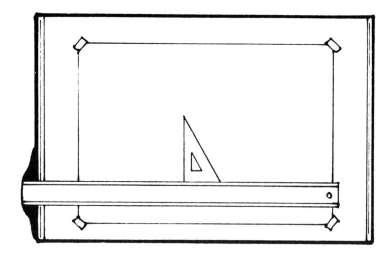

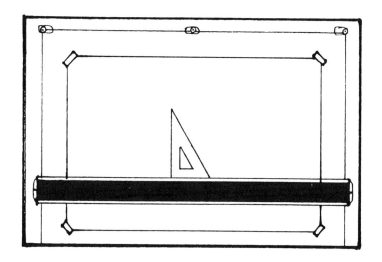

**Figure 4.14**

The top illustration shows the use of a T-square and a triangle by a right-handed person. The drafting instrument should be used on the opposite side that they draw with. The bottom illustrates the use of a parallel rule, which is affixed to the drawing board, and a triangle. (Designer: R. P. Strychalski.)

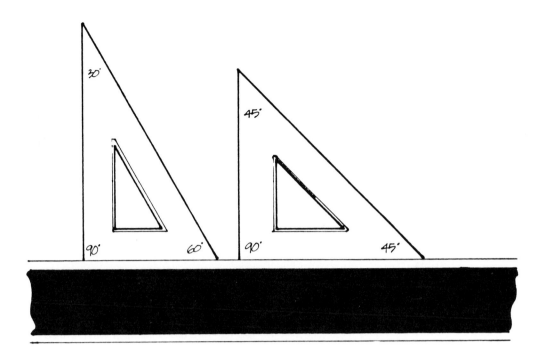

**Figure 4.15**
The use of triangles allows lines to be drawn perpendicular or diagonal
to the drafting straight edge. The "L" and "R" indicate the usual edges
used by right- or left-handed persons. (Designer: R. P. Strychalski.)

areas" can be picked up more easily; (3) an inking edge is
desirable to prevent ink from running under the plastic
edge. See Figure 4.15 for an example of triangles and their
use in conjunction with a T-square or parallel-rule.

Templates are used in design to draw commonly used
shapes quickly. For example, circular templates are used by
some designers to establish the outlines of trees and shrubs
before the plant symbol is established and drawn in ink or
final pencil (Figure 4.16). If ink is to be the presentation
medium it is used over the lead guidelines, since templates
often do not have inking edges. An inking edge is the variation in a ruling edge that reduces the ink blots which often
occur under a template or triangle.

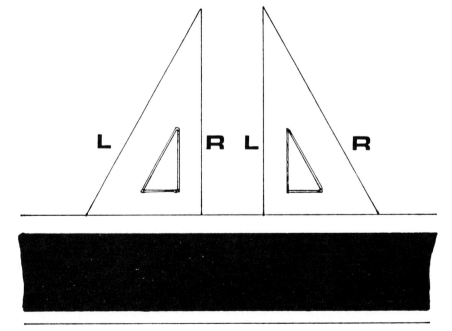

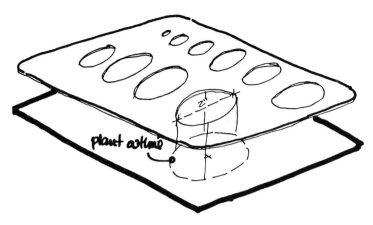

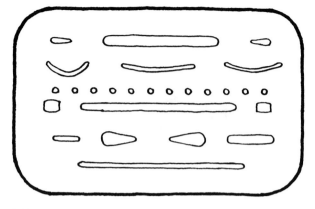

**Figure 4.17**

Erasure shields are used to clean up drawings. They mask the areas to be kept, leaving the exposed area in the template to be erased. (Designer: R. P. Strychalski.)

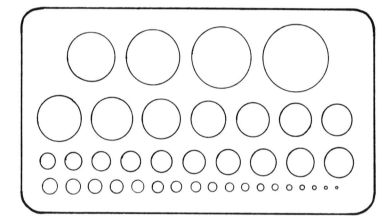

**Figure 4.16**

A circle template can be used as a scaled guideline for the spread of proposed plants in plan view. At a scale of 1″=1/8′ a 1″ circle represents an 8′ spread. (Designer: R. P. Strychalski.)

A variation of the template is an erasure shield. Erasure shields are used to control the area that needs to be erased in pencil or ink drawings. The shield, as you might assume, masks desirable lines and exposes the line areas to be erased (Figure 4.17).

A very helpful tool to use in conjunction with an erasure shield and sepia drawing is an electric eraser. This uses an eraser shaft to "peel off" lines much more easily, efficiently, and quickly than a common eraser (Figure 4.18). While efficient, electric erasers are expensive: They are most beneficial when used for their time savings value but not as a necessity.

## Scales

Since scaled drawings are representations of actual spaces, designers use a tool called a scale to accurately draw plans. Three scales are commonly used in design. An architect's scale is a rule, one foot in length, including scales of 1/16″=1′0″, 1/8″=1′0, 1/4″=1′0, 1/2″=1′0, 3/8″=1′, 3/4″=1′0, 1″=1′, 3/16″=1′, 3/32″=1′, 1½″=1′, and 3″=1′. This scale range is most often used for architecture, interior design projects and construction drawings. A drawing using 1/8″=1′ shows the contractor or workman that 1/8″ represents one foot in size of the actual project to be constructed. The engineer's scale commonly used in landscape architecture is also one foot in length. It is divided into six scales on the individual scale faces, which are subdivided into 10, 20, 30, 40, 50, or 60 parts to the inch. This scale is commonly used on plans which represent larger site areas. When using an engineer's scale, each equal segment can be interpreted as one foot or more depending on the scale drawing needed. As an exam-

**Figure 4.18**
Electric erasers, when used to erase large drawing areas, are often used with an erasure shield. (Designer: R. P. Strychalski.)

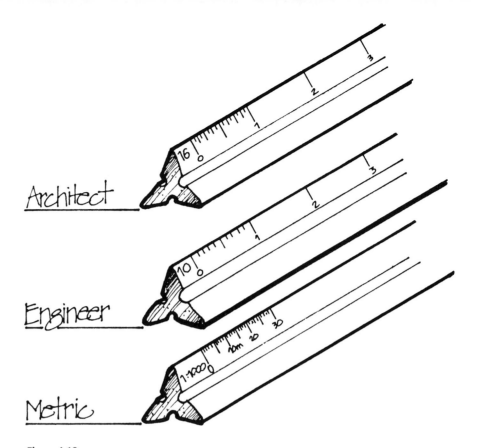

**Figure 4.19**
Architectural, engineering, and metric scales can be used to produce scaled drawings. These triangular scales offer six or more scales on their edges. Architectural scales usually include 1″=16′, 1″=8′, 1″=4′, 1″=2′, and so on.

ple, when using the 10 scale, one segment can be read as one foot, thus a scale of 1″=10′ or each ten units representing 1″=100′. The metric scale, similar to the engineer's scale, includes ratios of 1 : 100, 1 : 125, 1 : 200, 1 : 500, 1 : 750, 1 : 1,000. The ratios on a metric scale relate to a meter. Thus a scale of 1 : 100 represents graduations in the length of a meter totaling 100 equal parts. A scale of 1 : 500 represents a division of 500 equal parts to the meter, and so on.

Figure 4.19 shows an architect's scale, an engineer's scale, and a metric scale. These triangular scales can include as many as eleven different scales. For example, eleven are included on the architect's scale, six on the engineer's scale, and six on the metric scale. It is important to mention that scales are precision tools with exact graduations and should never be used as a straight-edge for drafting. Scales may be constructed from wood or plastic, but plastic scales are most common. They are easily cracked or broken and so should be handled with care. To help conceptualize the concept of scale it is often desirable to measure a drawing area and then relate it to the space in which you are drawing. Floor tiles are often one foot square, which helps you to visualize the actual space you are reviewing in the plan.

## MISCELLANEOUS EQUIPMENT

Another tool that helps designers present sheet information better and more efficiently is a lettering guide. This guide is used in conjunction with a T-square to draw horizontal guidelines for lettering and for organizing words to form notes. Figure 4.20 shows the use of a lettering guide.

Other tools that designers may use are exacto knives and burnishers. An exacto knife is used to cut paper and illustration boards to the proper dimensions. They are also used for constructing models, matting presentations, and sharpening wooden pencils. Exacto knives come in a variety of sizes and blade shapes. Burnishers are used in design for applying "press-on" lettering and zip-a-lines, or for manufacturing visual textures or surfaces. Their hard, blunt end is used when transferring lettering, lines, or textures from manufactured sheets to design proposals.

Other pieces of equipment and/or tools may be helpful in design. Awareness of new products and resources available to make your job easier and more effective is a skill that must be developed. If you have questions about the application of products, ask your local drafting supply or art dealer. Figure 4.21 shows examples of various other drafting tools and equipment.

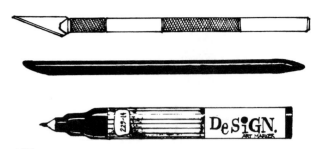

**Figure 4.21**

Miscellaneous graphic tools include an exacto knife, burnishers to apply pressure-sensitive lettering or textures, and markers for adding color to drawings. (Designer: R. P. Strychalski.)

## DRAFTING SEQUENCE AND DUPLICATING PROCESSES

### Drawing Sequence

To prepare finished drawings, designers normally follow a procedure or routine in setting up paper, guidelines, inking steps, and so forth. A typical sequence of steps is as follows (see Figure 4.22 as an illustration of this process):

**Figure 4.20**

Lettering guides can be used to establish guidelines for written areas in drawings. (Designer: R. P. Strychalski.)

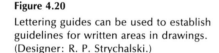

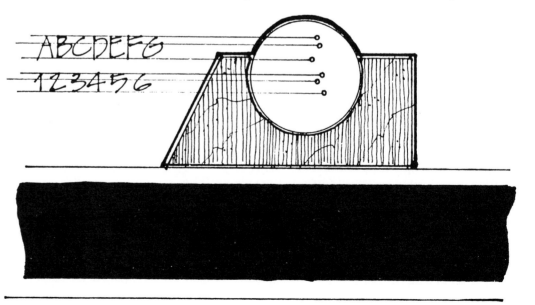

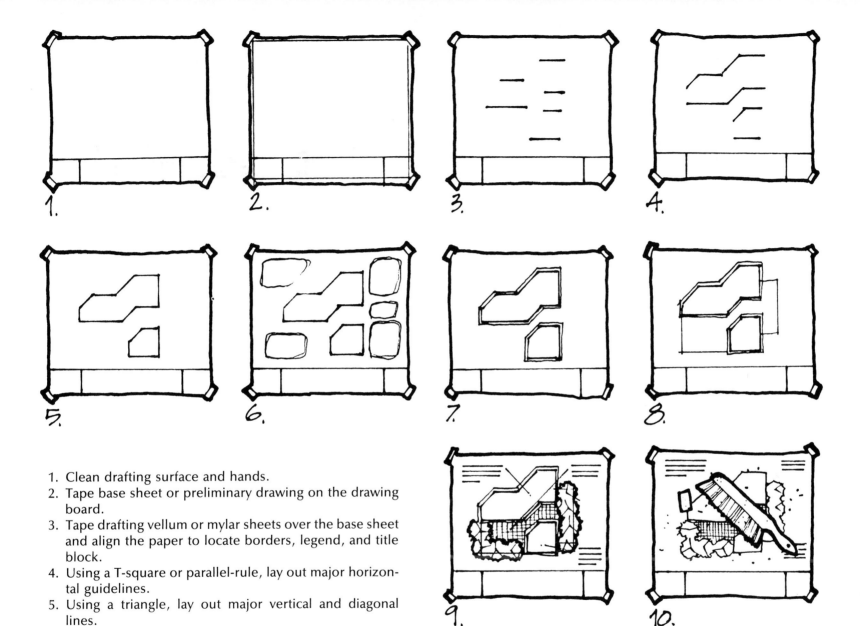

1. Clean drafting surface and hands.
2. Tape base sheet or preliminary drawing on the drawing board.
3. Tape drafting vellum or mylar sheets over the base sheet and align the paper to locate borders, legend, and title block.
4. Using a T-square or parallel-rule, lay out major horizontal guidelines.
5. Using a triangle, lay out major vertical and diagonal lines.
6. Lay out secondary horizontal and vertical lines.
7. Organize areas for support information such as lettering, labels, and legend.
8. Hard line in ink or pencil major horizontal and vertical lines.
9. Add secondary lines in ink or pencil.

**Figure 4.22**

A drawing sequence is identified through this sequence of drawings. While this is an example of a possible process each designer often uses his or her own method and techniques in developing design drawings. (Designer: R. P. Strychalski.)

10. Add textures, surfaces, lettering, labels, and legend information.
11. Erase pencil guidelines, if using ink, and clean up sheet for reproduction.

After this sequence of steps, the designer takes the original drawing to a blueprinter for duplication. After duplication the designer may render, that is, add color, to the plans before presenting the design package to the client for review.

## Blueprint Process

Duplication of original vellum drawings is required because a designer never gives original drawings to clients. Original tracings should also be retained as part of the designer's records and in case future revisions are needed. The blueprint, sometimes called the diazo process, was traditionally used for duplication of tracings. The ozalid process has now replaced the diazo process for reproduction of drawings. Basic to both ozalid and diazo processes is the use of a reproduction paper coated with a light-sensitive emulsion, usually a chemical compound. When these reproduction papers, in combination with original tracings, are exposed to high intensity light, the areas on the print paper covered by lines of the drawing are not exposed. When the chemical coating on these unexposed areas is exposed to light it is burned off the surface, resulting in a white area when developed. Development of these lines occurs when the print paper and remaining emulsion areas are exposed to ammonia compounds. Figure 4.23 shows the basic printing process.

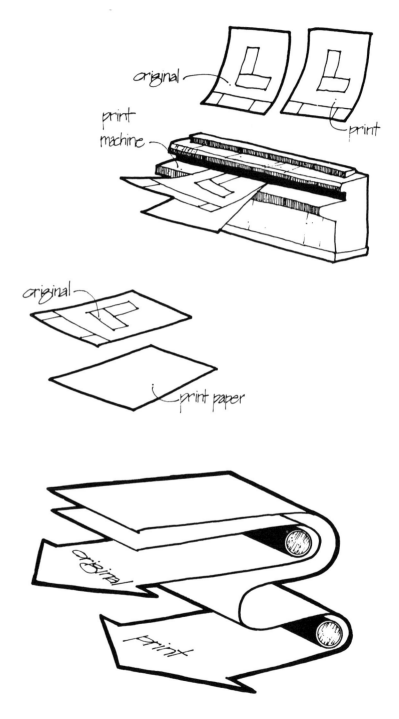

**Figure 4.23**

In the blueprint process, an original drawing on a transparent surface such as vellum or mylar is laid over ozalid paper with an emulsion on one side. The two sheets are pulled through the roller and exposed to a light source. The light showing through the transparent original burns off the emulsion on the ozalid paper. As the sheets separate, the ozalid paper is exposed to ammonia compounds which develop the lines resulting in a print. (Designer: R. P. Strychalski.)

The emulsion and paper used will determine if the duplicate drawing is a blackline, blueline, brownline, or sepia. Blackline and blueline prints are made of an opaque, toothed paper ideal for colored markers and colored pencil presentations. A sepia, unlike the blacklines or bluelines, is a copy made on transparent or translucent vellum that can then be used for making additional direct copies, either prints or sepias. Sepias are often called intermediate drawings and can be made for additive information based on the original drawing. If a sepia will involve erasing information as well as adding new data, a reverse sepia can be used. This allows removal of information on the back and addition of new data to a clear drafting surface (Figure 4.24). Sepia lines can be easily erased with an electric eraser or sepia eradicator, a chemical solvent. It should be noted that original drawings and print paper age quickly and deteriorate when exposed to strong sunlight. Originals and prints should be stored away from direct sources of light to reduce the yellowing and disintegration of these papers. Plan files or plan tubes are available and desirable storage options.

## Other Reproduction Methods

Other duplication processes that might be helpful to designers are photographic methods of reducing and enlarging drawings. Original drawings, maps, and plans can be photographically enlarged or reduced onto print paper or film. In the case of topographic maps, enlargement or reduction can save time and ensure accuracy.

The PMT, or photographic mechanical transfer, is a method of reducing large line drawings to 10″ by 12″ or 12″ by 18″ print sizes. Prints photographed at a 10″ by 12″ print size can have an image area of 8½ by 11″. Thus, they can be used in page-size portfolios and are easy to handle and store (Figure 4.25). These reduced drawings convey the overall effects of the project and may even look more attractive, as the detail is reduced. Most of the examples in the text are PMTs.

Another method of reducing drawings for portfolios or storage is a contact negative. Projects are photographically reduced using an 8″ by 10″ contact negative. This creates a

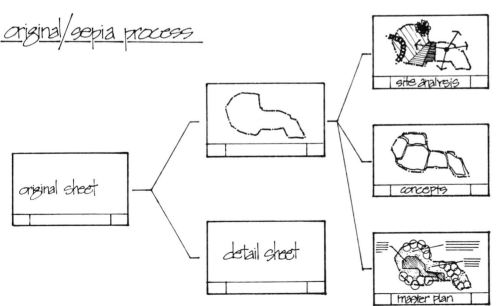

original/sepia process

original sheet

detail sheet

site analysis

concepts

master plan

**Figure 4.24**
Sepia prints (also called intermediate drawings) are used as originals. Sepia prints are produced by using ozalid papers that are transparent rather than opaque, as are blackline, blueline, or brownline papers (Designer: R. P. Strychalski.)

(a)

**Figure 4.25 a&b**
These photos illustrate the potential of PMTs (photographic mechanical transfers). The first illustration is the center portion of an original line drawing 18 × 24″. The second illustration is a PMT of this original, photographically reducing the 18 × 24″ drawing to a 8 1/2 × 11″ format. (Designer: K. Fry.)

**(b)**

117

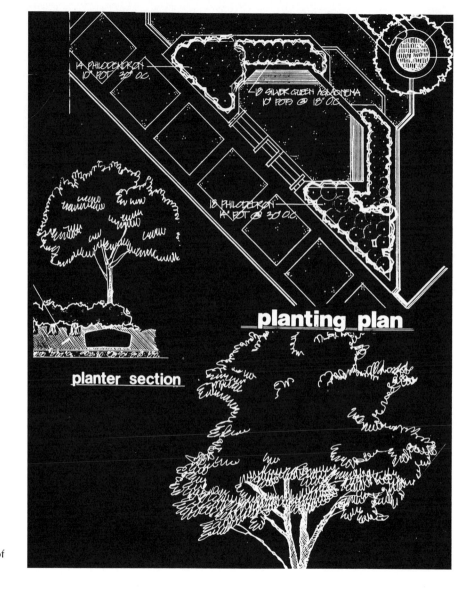

**Figure 4.26**
Oversized photographic negatives, 8 × 10″ or 10 × 12″ can be used to create a reverse image for presentation. When the negatives are produced they can be run through an ozalid machine using ozalid papers to achieve the reverse of the original.

reverse image of the original drawing, with black lines now white and white areas black. These negatives can then be put through a blueprint machine, the resulting ozalid prints are white lines on dark backgrounds. Figure 4.26 shows a blackline of a PMT reduction in comparison to the same project presented using the contact negative process.

## SUMMARY

Graphic production of drawings requires an understanding of the equipment, materials, procedures, and processes used to communicate design ideas. Designers should experiment with a wide range of materials and methods to discover those that are most applicable to the project. Designers should also practice with new techniques and materials to ensure proficiency. The basic requirements of any drawing are accuracy, neatness, and reproducibility. The procedures and techniques used to achieve the drawings depend on the drawing required and the style and preference of the designer.

# Chapter 5

# Graphic Communications

In the process of design and development, planning and design graphics is the language used to describe and present a visual record of our thoughts. The design elements of line, form, texture, and color are often used in the same way that an author uses words to stimulate our imagination and thinking. As ideas arise, graphics are used to record, sketch, and revise them as solutions for and alternatives to design problems and situations. Graphics are the most convenient, efficient, economical, and flexible means designers have to communicate and present information. Drawings are not an end unto themselves but a means to communicate our design intentions. The type of graphics developed depends on what is being presented, and to whom (Figure 5.1). Successful graphic communications result from a working understanding of the various techniques, concepts, and drawing styles used in presenting design information.

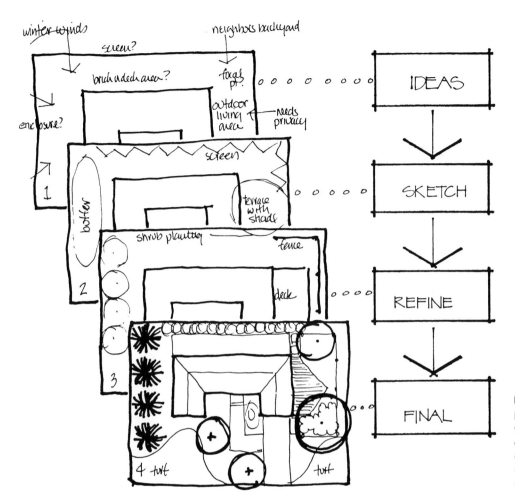

**Figure 5.1**
Design ideas, while they are communicated
through drawings, are the result of many layers
of ideas, evaluations, and revisions. At the start
of the design process ideas are often loose and
quick. Progressively, these ideas are refined until
a final hardline drawing is completed.

In the recording of information and the presentation of
ideas designers often use specific graphics. Successful use
of graphics as a tool requires an understanding of the language (terms) and practice (application), just as we work to
refine any skill or activity. Graphic plans and sketches are an
efficient, convenient, and flexible means of "planning before planting." The term "planting" in this case means the
actual implementation of a project, not just plantings of
plants.

## Graphic Presentations

Designers use graphic techniques that, through lines,
textures, symbols, and often color suggest the likenesses of
objects or scenes in the design proposal. In the presentation
of drawings one must understand that design graphics, although not photographic, use photographic techniques in
the composition and presentation of images and ideas on
flat, two-dimensional surfaces (Figure 5.2). While planning a

**Figure 5.2**

Design drawings should be representational, not photographic. One of the easiest ways to practice your drawing skills is to copy published images. Shown is a freehand sketch of an advertisement. (Designer: R. Mumaw; Advertisement: Kirsch Co.)

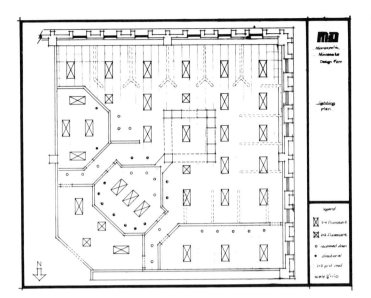

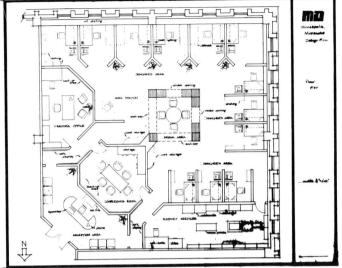

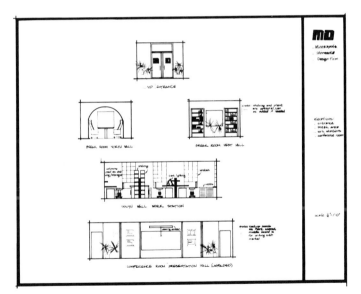

**Figure 5.3**
Architectural and interior design drawings are used to develop functional and attractive spaces. Drawings allow review, revision, and refinement before construction occurs. (Designer: R. Mumaw.)

proposal designers select the vantage and frame through which one can view an existing or proposed image or scene. The basic difference between drawings and the photographic reproduction of images is that the designer interprets and abstracts the image in addition to adding proposed elements to a drawing; while a photograph reproduces the scene exactly as it exists.

Typical design drawings and illustrations include plans, sections, elevations, and perspectives. Through the use of these drawings, design proposals can be presented, reviewed, revised, and laid out on paper long before any actual development occurs (Figure 5.3).

123

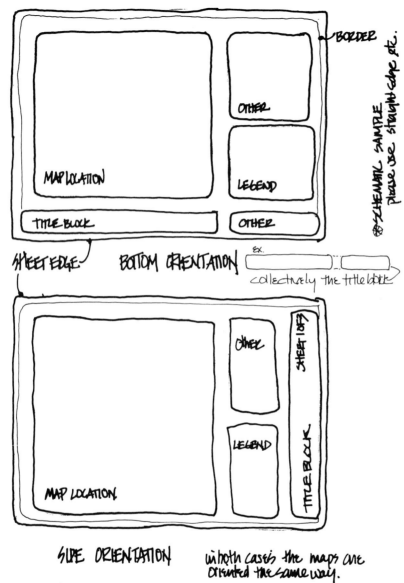

Labels in figure:
BORDER
@ SCHEMATIC SAMPLE please use straight edge etc.
OTHER
LEGEND
MAP LOCATION
TITLE BLOCK
OTHER
SHEET EDGE
BOTTOM ORIENTATION
EX.
collectively the title block
OTHER
LEGEND
MAP LOCATION
SHEET 1 OF 3
TITLE BLOCK
SIDE ORIENTATION
in both cases the maps are oriented the same way.

**Figure 5.4**

Sheet organization and composition include the selection of a sheet size and drawing orientation, either vertical or horizontal. Within the sheet a title block, legend, drawing area, and other components are usually organized.

## DRAWING CONCEPTS

When preparing to present a design project, always understand the project's focus and the client's needs before selecting graphic techniques. Understanding the project and being aware of what drawings are needed, such as plans or sections, can help in choosing sheet organization, graphic techniques, and styles to use. Always select a sheet size large enough to present the necessary information as well as support data such as title blocks, legend, and labels. Figure 5.4 shows examples of typical title blocks and sheet information, and their organization with a sheet. If the initial design drawings are to be preliminary, the graphic techniques used should concentrate less on refinement and more on creativity and planning ideas. Ideas and details can be refined in the final stages of the design process.

To present ideas graphically, the first criteria used to develop drawings should address the question, What is to be presented? Will the drawing present planting plans, construction details, or other design information? Second, To whom are you communicating the information? Is the drawing for other designers, clients, or contractors? Third, How is the information to be used? Are the ideas just preliminary, will they be presented to the client or to a contractor, or are they for yourself? And fourth, What is the expected, accepted, or necessary format? Are they, for example, illustrations or construction drawings? With these questions answered you can develop a drawing relative to the project and client needs.

Drawing techniques and styles are often individualized; they relate to a designer's skills and the character of the design problem. As a design professional, a time vs. benefit equilibrium should be established; that is, the techniques and styles selected should be appropriate and realistic for the scale of the problem in conjunction with the time and fee framework defined. Remember, more lines drawn require more time and thus money. The progressive refinement of design ideas resulting in final design proposals can be seen in the illustrations included (Figures 5.5–5.8).

**Figure 5.5**

Initial design drawings are often simple outlines with basic forms and edges defined.

Artist's rendition of the new SAF headquarters

**Figure 5.6**

As presentation drawings are refined, forms, textures, line hierarchy or weights, and human elements are included. (Courtesy of Society of American Florists.)

**Figure 5.7**

As the detail in drawings increases, so does the use of lines and textures. Remember that the more lines you include, the more time the drawing requires. (Drawing courtesy of Hart Marx Inc., Chicago, Illinois.)

## GRAPHIC PRESENTATIONS

Designers show how the built proposals will eventually look through a variety of illustrations, design drawings, and graphics. The most widely used drawings include the plan, section, elevation, and perspective. In a plan view, the drawing is developed from the vantage of a plane above the project. Plans allow a designer to work with the entire project, which often cannot be seen otherwise. Horizontal distances (widths) can be easily recognized, but vertical dimensions (height) of objects are only represented if shadows are included. Shadows in plan, elevation, and perspective drawings help create depth and define the vertical aspects and configuration of the project elements. Without shadows and shading, drawings look flat and unrealistic (Figure 5.9). To communicate a feeling of realism in plan, elevation, and perspective drawings, an assumed light source should be established. A generally accepted rule of thumb is to draw shadows to the bottom and/or right edges of a sheet, rather than to the top or left. This is because plans are read from left to right and top to bottom. Thus shadowing and plan orientation place the "visual weight" to the bottom of the drawing, where it appears to be more at ease. Sections do not use shading and shadows because they are technical drawings used primarily to express heights and widths in design proposals. An exception to this rule is the section–elevation drawing discussed in the following discussion.

### Section Drawings

Since many project features shown in a plan drawing have both width and height, section drawings are used to help communicate details of the vertical aspects of objects or areas. A section is a specific vertical plane cut through a site plan. It is a scaled drawing of "a slice" of the project plan, drawn to the same horizontal and vertical scale as the plan drawing. The designer selects a section line across the base plan that best explains major site features. This line is eventually highlighted on the plan as a section reference. Compare Figure 5.9, the plan, and Figure 5.10.

**Figure 5.8**
In these sketches line, texture, and tone are used to create depth and detail to the sketches. (Drawing courtesy of Crown Center Shops, Kansas City, Missouri.)

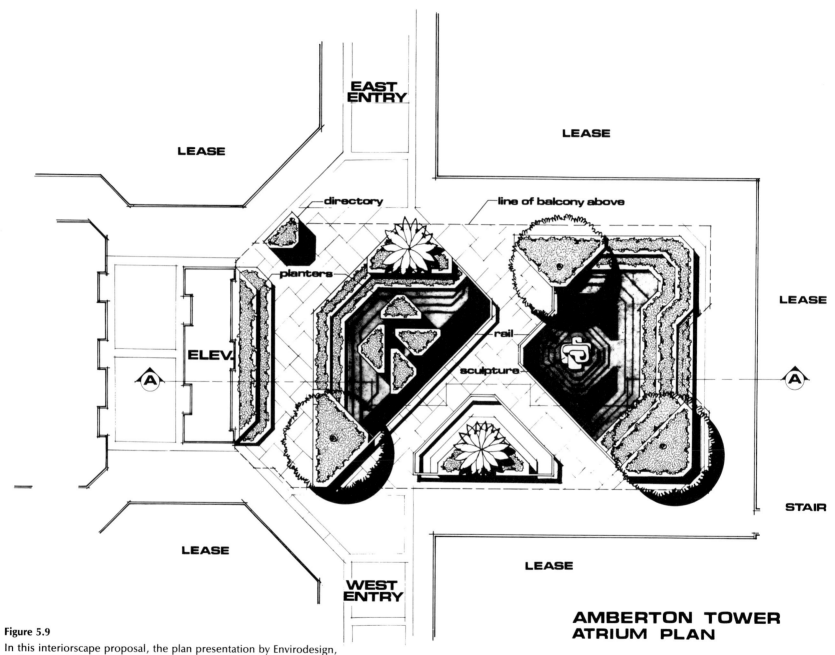

EAST ENTRY

LEASE

LEASE

directory

line of balcony above

LEASE

planters

ELEV.

rail

Ⓐ

sculpture

Ⓐ

STAIR

LEASE

LEASE

WEST ENTRY

AMBERTON TOWER
ATRIUM PLAN

**Figure 5.9**

In this interiorscape proposal, the plan presentation by Envirodesign, Dallas, Texas includes a fountain, planters, pavements, and plantings. (Courtesy of A. L. David and Dick Author.)

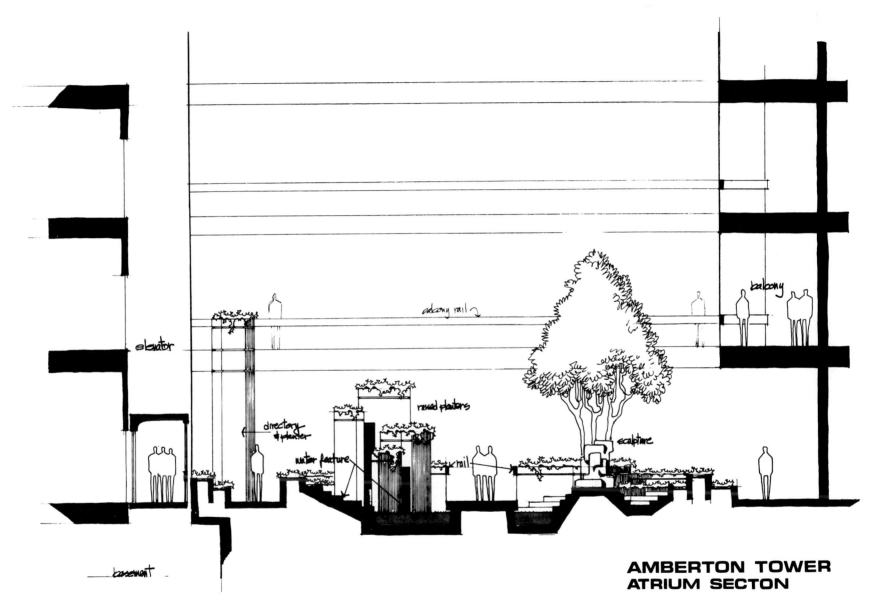

Labels within image: basement, elevator, directory & planter, water feature, raised planters, rail, sculpture, balcony rail, balcony

**AMBERTON TOWER
ATRIUM SECTON**

**Figure 5.10**

A section of the plan shown in Figure 5.9 helps convey the vertical dimensions of the plan by Envirodesign, Dallas, Texas. The varied floor configuration, related balcony, and walking areas all can be seen in this drawing.

Section drawings usually show any level changes that may occur on the project, offering a view of the project above and below ground levels if necessary. Section drawings are also selected to explain existing or proposed level changes in the master plan proposals or floor level variations.

A variation of the section drawing is the section–elevation, seen in Figure 5.10. This drawing shows depth behind the primary drawing object and may include shading and/or shadows. Figure 5.10 shows a typical section–elevation, and Figure 5.11–5.14 are selected photographs of the actual installation developed from the plan (Figure 5.9) and section-elevation (Figure 5.10). Section drawings provide a view of horizontal and vertical dimensions together, further reinforcing the plan and its dimensions. Figure 5.15 shows a typical section–drawing of an overhead planter.

5.12

**Figures 5.11–5.14**

These photos represent the completed Amberton Tower Atrium initially seen in illustrations 5.9 and 5.10. (Courtesy of Envirodesign, Dallas, Texas.)

5.11

5.13

5.14

## Elevation Drawings

Elevations are like sections in that they are drawn from the vantage of the base plan. They represent a side view of an area within the master plan as opposed to a slice through the proposal, as in a section. Elements above the ground or floor surface are drawn from the vantage of a person looking directly at the scene with no perspective other than foreground, middleground, and background (Figure 5.16). This view of the project assumes the vantage of an average person standing at the site's ground level. Surface details of elements—glass reflections, the forms of buildings, construction materials, and surfaces—are shown in these drawings. Elevations show more depth and surface detailing of objects and forms than sections, and thus seem more realistic. The design elements in the foreground are larger and more detailed than those in the middle and background planes. Thus the usual emphasis of the drawing is the area between the foreground and middleground planes (Figure 5.17).

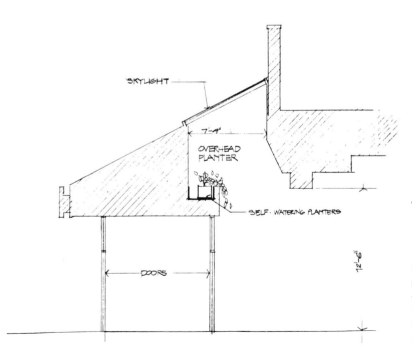

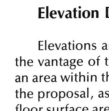

**Figure 5.15**

Often plan and section drawings are combined to communicate what is to be constructed and planted. In this illustration the entry detail plan includes a detail reference F/4, an overhead planter. This is then seen in the section drawing above. (Courtesy of Melvin-Simon Associates, Indianapolis, Indiana.)

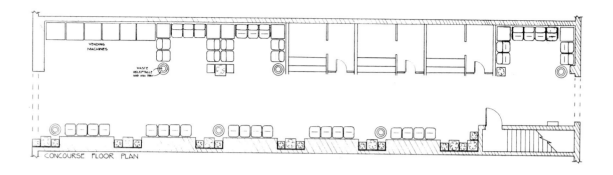

CONCOURSE FLOOR PLAN

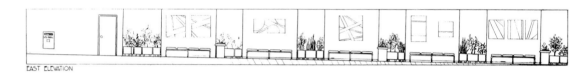

EAST ELEVATION

**Figure 5.16**
Elevation drawings, like section drawings, communicate the vertical and side view that plan drawings don't communicate. (Designer: Renee Zurad.)

**Figure 5.17**
Foreground, middleground, and background are normal planes in all sketches and drawings. The general emphasis of a drawing should be in the fore and middleground areas of a drawing. (Courtesy of T. Brickman Company, Long Grove, Illinois.)

## Perspective Drawings

Perspective drawings present images pictorially, as they would be seen by the naked eye looking through a camera lens or at a photograph. The scene is represented as if the viewer were actually standing in the plan or design. Depth, proportion, and relative distances are included in these drawings to fully convey the volume of a space. Line, texture, and color are added to reinforce the feeling of realism. Objects closest to the viewer are larger and more detailed than those in the background. Thus, the emphasis is on depth and the foreground and middleground elements. Figures 5.18 and 5.19 are examples of perspective drawings. In the development of plan, section, elevation and perspective drawings designers use the basic elements of design, line, form, texture and color to convey existing project details and other design ideas.

## Graphic Communications Using Design Elements

In the composition and presentation of drawings, lines, textures, shadows, and colors must be coordinated to fully communicate the proposed design concepts. Line is the first element used to establish the form or framework for textures, shadows, and color. Line is initially used to define or outline areas and forms. Using line or tone, textures are added to forms to indicate surfaces, show details, and often to show shading. Shadows are used to create depth and reinforce the realism of forms and shapes in the drawing. Color is often used to further complement the line, textures, and shadows already drawn. Since clients are often not familiar with plans or sketches, color helps add the contrast needed to represent the planes and components within a scene. Using color at the start of the design process helps us to visualize design components. If duplication or photographic reproductions are to be used, note that black and white reproductions are less costly than color. Make sure to have a strong black and white drawing to facilitate this duplication if needed.

5.18

5.19

**Figures 5.18 and 5.19**

Perspective drawings help convey the width, length, and depth of project proposals. Here a one- and two-point perspective are illustrated. (Designer: R. Mumaw and Technical Graphics Department, Purdue University.)

133

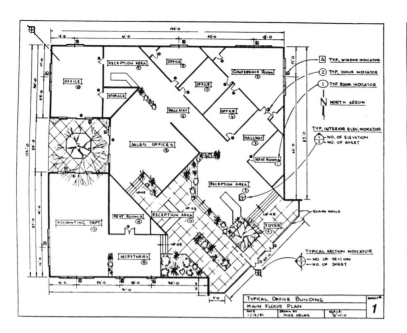

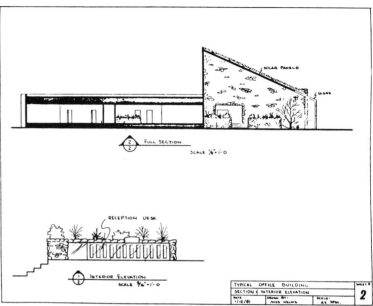

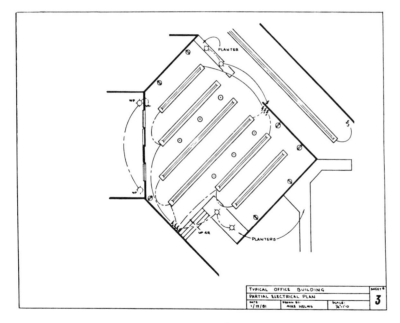

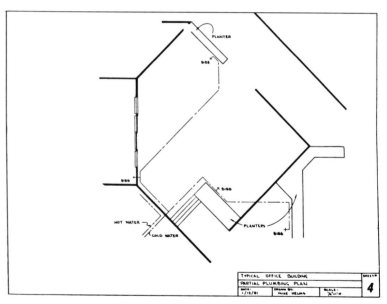

**Figure 5.20**

These drawings help convey the design concepts for a small office space. Included is a floor plan, section/elevation, and ceiling and plumbing plans. (Designer: Mike Helms.)

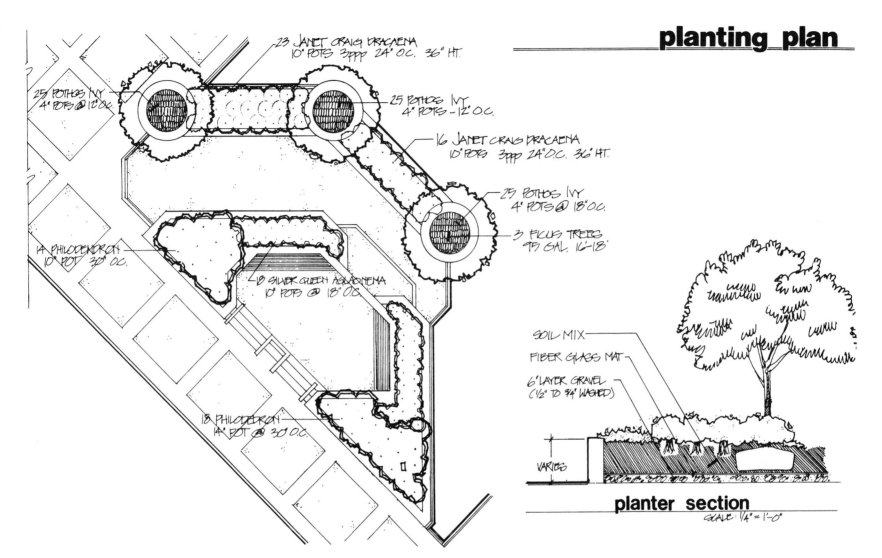

23 JANET CRAIG DRACAENA
10" POTS 3ppp 24" O.C. 36" HT.

25 POTHOS IVY
4" POTS @ 12" O.C.

25 POTHOS IVY
4" POTS - 12" O.C.

16 JANET CRAIG DRACAENA
10" POTS 3ppp 24" O.C. 36" HT.

25 POTHOS IVY
4" POTS @ 18" O.C.

3 FICUS TREES
95 GAL. 16'-18'

14 PHILODENDRON
10" POT 30" O.C.

18 SILVER QUEEN AGLAONEMA
10" POTS @ 18" O.C.

18 PHILODENDRON
14" POT @ 30" O.C.

SOIL MIX
FIBER GLASS MAT
6" LAYER GRAVEL
(1/2" TO 3/4" WASHED)

VARIES

**planter section**
SCALE: 1/4" = 1'-0"

**Figure 5.21**
Line hierarchy and profile lines are important in the development of plan and section drawings. In this drawing the tree canopy and planter edges are highlighted. (Courtesy of Melvin-Simon Associates, Indianapolis, Indiana.)

In plan, elevation, and perspective drawings, the primary or tallest objects or edges such as buildings, balconies, pavements, or ground beds and edges are presented with a heavier line weight, often called a profile line. These heavier lines indicate the importance of the objects they represent.

Smaller objects or secondary elements such as furniture, pavement patterns, or accessories are normally drawn with thinner line weights and values, as they recede into the background relative to the profile lines. Plan drawings and elevation presentations of plants are shown in Figure 5.20. Note that objects closest to the viewer are drawn with darker line weights and values which decrease as the eye moves within the drawing towards the ground plane. The same concept may be used for its plane contrast as seen in Figure 5.21 of plan and section drawings.

**Figure 5.22**

This perspective line drawing traced from a slide shows a mall interiorscape. (Designer: Kevin Fry.)

**Figures 5.23–5.27**

This sequence of illustrations shows the need for consistency in design drawing and the graphics used to convey an interiorscape. Included are a plan, multiple sections, and perspective views. (Designer: Kevin Fry.) *Figure 5.23:* Plan view with section drawing references; *Figure 5.24:* Section A view; *Figure 5.25:* Section B view; *Figure 5.26:* Section C view; *Figure 5.27:* Aerial perspective view.

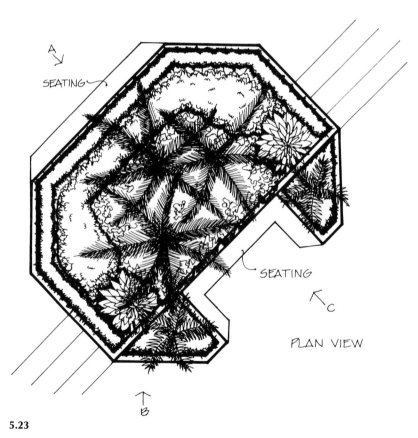

5.23

ELEVATION / SECTION A

5.24

In section drawings, the primary line weights and contrasts are again the outline of major objects and the ground line. Sections not showing textures and secondary elements use less secondary lines. Figures 5.10 and 5.15 compare typical sections and a section–elevation drawing.

In elevation drawings, primary lines are used to emphasize middleground elements and the outline of objects. Secondary lines are used for surfaces, textures, and so forth.

Perspective drawings use a variety of line weights, values, and contrasts to give depth and proportion to the objects presented. Again, objects closest to the viewer have greater line contrast, detail, and shading than receding elements in the perspective. Figure 5.22 is a perspective showing an interior landscape design proposal.

When drawing multiple views of the same area or proposal, remember that all drawings should work together in supporting the design concept. Plan, section, elevation, and perspective should use consistent drawing techniques and styles, line weights, and contrasts to best present the primary components in the design. Figures 5.23–5.27 show consistency of drawing styles and graphic presentation.

SECTION B

5.25

5.26                          SECTION   C

5.27                                    PERSPECTIVE   VIEW

## Line Types and Materials

The basic line qualities that can be selected, used, and manipulated are line weight, line contrast, and line style. Line can be produced by pencils, pens, or markers and is one of the basic elements of any design proposal or drawing. It establishes the skeleton which defines existing and proposed component and material edges, areas, and shapes. Line also defines surfaces by including textures, shading with line and shadows.

## Freehand and Drafted Drawing Styles

Drafting styles are often determined by what is being drawn. The graphics and line style selected may use freehand or drafted techniques. Drafted styles use exact pencil guidelines drawn with a straight-edge for accuracy and clarity. Drafted lines are used for their exactness in defining design elements to be constructed. Building outlines, walls, windows, and other structural features in presentation drawings are drafted lines. All construction drawings use drafted lines because the actual element being built will be defined from these drawings. These design documents are used as guides for the estimating and bidding processes prior to the project's actual implementation.

The freehand style of drafting may use lightly ruled pencil guidelines, with all final lines drawn without a straight-edge using ink or a heavier pencil weight. Freehand drafting lends itself to representation of the more natural elements in a site plan: plant materials, surfaces such as mulch, and ground planes. Realistic textures and time savings are probably the main advantages of freehand drafting. Freehand graphics also results in a more informal format than other drafted presentation styles, is also less time consuming, and can be used if the project is only to communicate the design concepts in a presentation drawing. Figure 5.28 compares drafted and freehand techniques for the same plan.

**Figure 5.28**
A comparison of drafted versus freehand drawing techniques. (Designer: T. Kramer.)

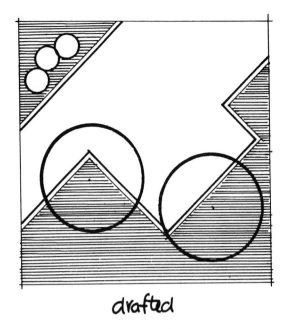

drafted

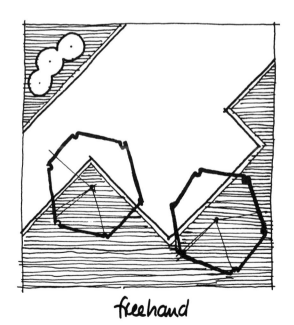

freehand

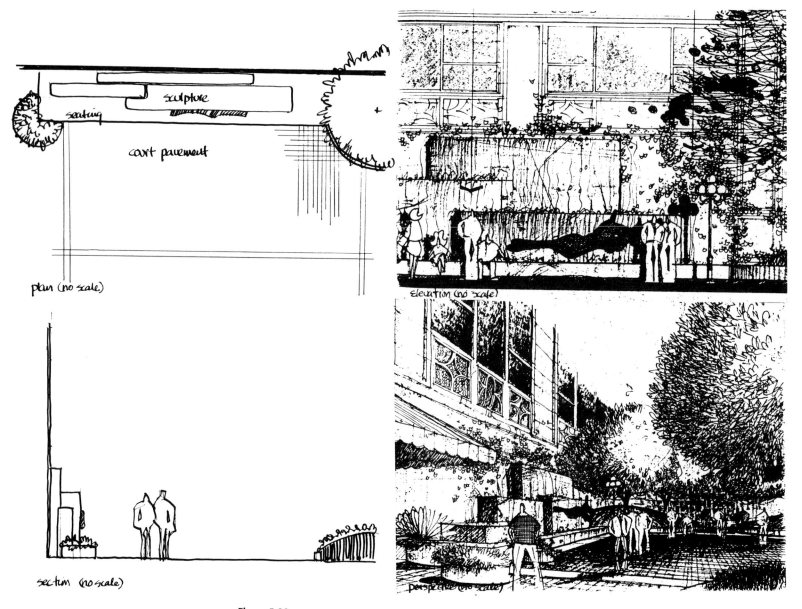

plan (no scale)

sculpture

seating

cart pavement

section (no scale)

elevation (no scale)

perspective (no scale)

**Figure 5.29**

In plan, section, elevation, and perspective drawings, symbols composed of line, forms, textures, and shading represent existing and proposed project features. (Courtesy of T. Brickman Company, Long Grove, Illinois.)

## SYMBOLS

Symbols are like abbreviations and are used to represent what the design elements in a composition will look like in plan, section, elevation, and perspective presentations before the project is actually developed. Graphic styles and techniques should convey the "essence" or what is being symbolized and should be easily differentiated. Symbols should be consistent throughout a project, especially when multiple drawings are used. Designers use combinations of line, form, textures, and shading as symbols to illustrate existing information and proposed ideas. These symbols represent plant materials and surfaces more accurately than simple lines, forms, and textures (Figure 5.29). Remember that they represent surfaces, textures, forms of plant, and construction materials; they may not duplicate the actual forms these design elements take. Design symbols are found throughout the text; please evaluate their potential for you in projects you're involved with. (See Chapter 6 for specific examples of plant and interior design symbols.)

## PRESENTATION MEDIA

After original drawings are completed and blackline ozalid prints produced, color can be added to enhance the line textures, shadows, and shading techniques used in drafting the drawing. Blackline prints are usually used for rendering the application of color by pencil, chalk, or markers. Blueline prints are not as easy to read when rendered because of their blue tone. Blueprints or blue lines are usually made for construction type drawings. The addition of color, or rendering, can be accomplished by a variety of single media including markers, color pencils, pastel chalks, or combinations of these.

The addition of color enhances the realism of a proposal and helps clients to better visualize the ideas. Like line weight, color is layered in a hierarchy relative to the drawing being presented. Rendering all ground plane elements and allowing the lines of understory and canopy elements to "read" through is one presentation option for color and basic drawing styles. This technique makes it easy to per-

ceive the various layers of plants and features proposed. Another technique to consider is rendering the canopy elements, thus covering over components under this "overstory" layer. This method provides a realistic plan view yet often eliminates many of the underlying details.

Realism is not the sole criteria of color selection for a presentation. Value contrasts—the relative light and darkness within the drawings and shadows—are important to define the various areas within the proposal. The depth or vertical layers in a drawing may be shown by having a light ground plane and dark canopy or a dark ground and lighter canopy. When selecting colors for projects consider the client and presentation uses. For example, selecting a purple ground plane with orange and green trees may provide high value contrast and readability, yet may not be realistic enough to present to a "traditionally" minded client. The best way to gain skill and proficiency in color presentations is through experimentation and practice. Explore the resources, techniques, and references available and try duplicating illustrations to develop your own technique and style.

### Markers

Markers are a popular rendering media for presentations because of their range of colors, relative neatness, boldness of presentation, and ease in use: they are easy to work with, fast drying, and convenient. Markers are expensive and do take practice before they can be used with any proficiency. Often the best way to learn how to use them skillfully is to see them demonstrated.

Colored markers are produced in a variety of tips including a wide tip, pointed nib, and fine point (Figure 5.30). Wide-tip markers have a soft felt-tip approximately 1/8" wide and 1/4" long. The widest edge is used to render large areas, while the opposing edge provides a narrower line. The pointed nib markers have a cone-like tip that produces a thin, constant line similar to an ink pen. Two reference books available on marker techniques are *Landscape Painting with Markers,* by Harry Borgman (Watson Guptill Publishing, N.Y., 1977), and *Sketching with Markers,* by T. C. Wang (Van Nostrand Reinhold Co., 1981). Both cover the equipment, techniques, and products involving markers.

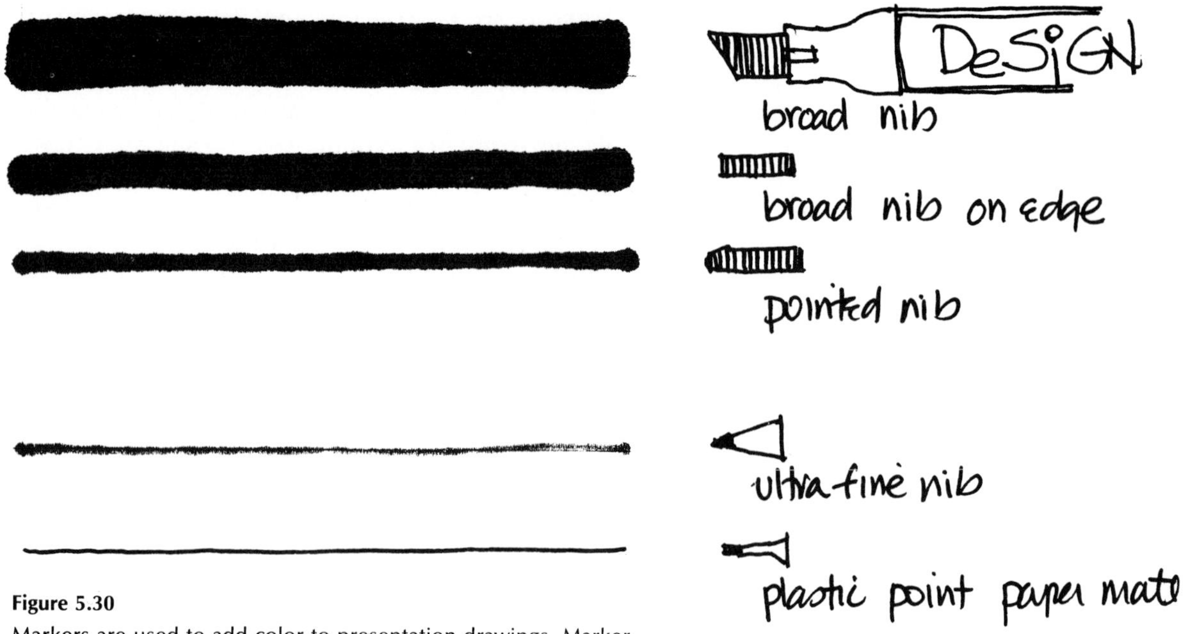

broad nib

broad nib on edge

pointed nib

ultra-fine nib

plastic point paper mate

**Figure 5.30**
Markers are used to add color to presentation drawings. Marker manufacturers produce a variety of types to fit a variety of design situations.

More comprehensive yet expensive references which include extensive discussions of markers and colored pencils are *Color Drawing,* by Michael Doyle (Van Nostrand Reinhold Co., 1982), and *The Sketch in Color,* by Robert S. Oliver (Van Nostrand Reinhold Co., 1984).

## Colored Pencils and Chalks

Colored pencils, another rendering media, are available in a wide range of colors and are neat and convenient. They can be used effectively in combination with markers to add details and/or textures to flat-looking drawings. Colored pencils have a more pastel color range and, if used alone, do not read as well at large group meetings.

Chalk, while offering similar coloring as pencils, can be pale and messier than both pencils and markers. If chalk is used a fixative may be applied to keep colors from smearing. While an entire drawing cannot be done in chalk, accents and elements such as sky and water may be done more

effectively in chalk than other media. This material is also discussed in *Color Drawing* and *The Sketch in Color.*

## Pressure-Sensitive Media

Other materials that can be used to save time and create striking presentations are press-on lettering, symbols, and textures. These press-on or pressure-sensitive materials are used in the graphic production of drawings before prints are made. Many commercial brands of preprinted, stick-on type graphics are available; they are appropriate for a range of drawing situations. Note that these press-on media should not be used as a crutch for individual design or lettering skills. Effective use of pressure-sensitive materials requires an understanding of their advantage as a time-saver, and not as a substitute for composition presentation skills. While they save time, these materials are generally expensive. Figures 5.31 and 5.32 show the diversity and availability of press-on media.

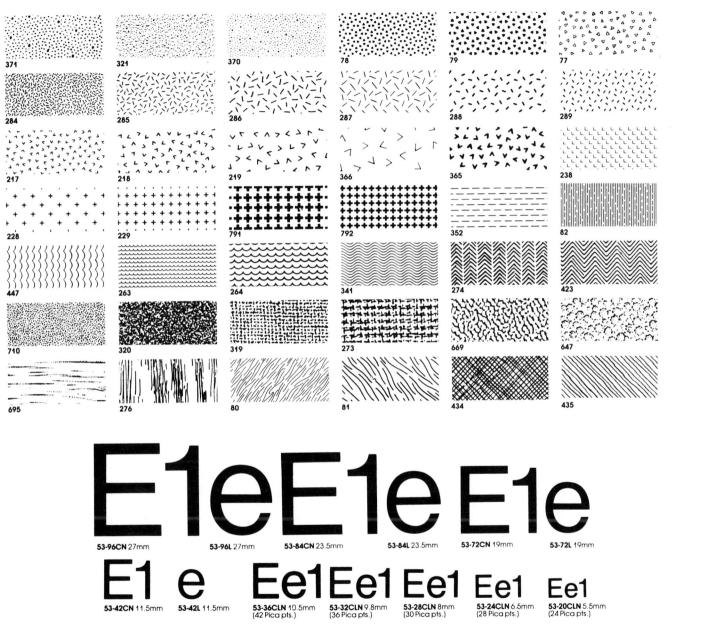

371  321  370  78  79  77
284  285  286  287  288  289
217  218  219  366  365  238
228  229  791  792  352  82
447  263  264  341  274  423
710  320  319  273  669  647
695  276  80  81  434  435

E1eE1e E1e

**53-96CN** 27mm  **53-96L** 27mm  **53-84CN** 23.5mm  **53-84L** 23.5mm  **53-72CN** 19mm  **53-72L** 19mm

E1 e  Ee1Ee1 Ee1 Ee1  Ee1

**53-42CN** 11.5mm  **53-42L** 11.5mm  **53-36CLN** 10.5mm (42 Pica pts.)  **53-32CLN** 9.8mm (36 Pica pts.)  **53-28CLN** 8mm (30 Pica pts.)  **53-24CLN** 6.5mm (28 Pica pts.)  **53-20CLN** 5.5mm (24 Pica pts.)

**Figure 5.31**
Pressure-sensitive material can help convey furniture, textures, and
lettering. (Courtesy of Zip-a-Tone Inc.)

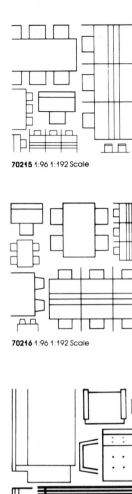

70215 1:96 1:192 Scale

70216 1:96 1:192 Scale

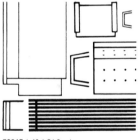

70217 1:48 1:96 Scale

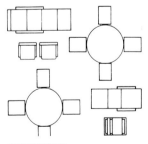

70218 1:96 Scale

ACTUAL SIZE

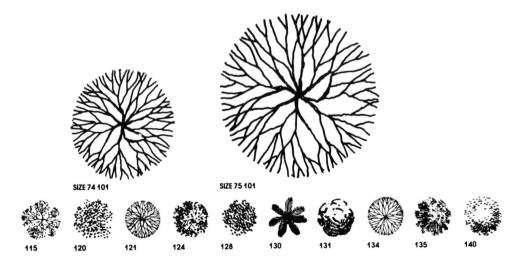

SIZE 74 101    SIZE 75 101

115    120    121    124    128    130    131    134    135    140

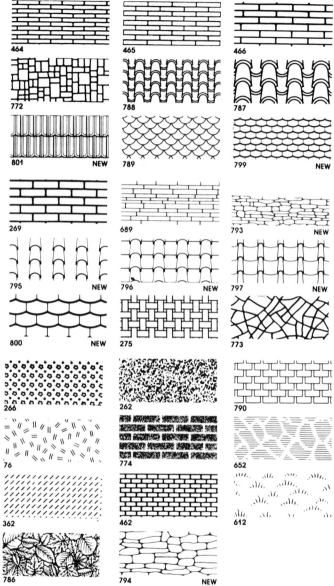

464    465    466
772    788    787
801    NEW    789    799    NEW
269    689    793    NEW
795    NEW    796    NEW    797    NEW
800    NEW    275    773
266    262    790
76    774    652
362    462    612
786    794    NEW

**Figure 5.32**

Plants, construction materials, and symbols are also available in pressure-sensitive materials (Courtesy of Zip-a-Tone Inc.)

144

## SUMMARY

The styles or techniques used in graphic communications should express ideas clearly; and their application should fit within the time frame available for their presentation. Early in the design process ideas and drawings may be loose and free, using color to define the design components. As ideas are reviewed and selected they should be refined as necessary for presentation and installation. A common mistake among beginning designers is finishing drawings too early rather than later in the design process.

The presentation of ideas is a learning process for any designer. Through studying examples and illustrations one learns to think and communicate graphically. The best way to gain graphic skills and develop self-confidence is to become technically proficient with paper, pens, pencils, and other materials used in graphic communications. As you observe new techniques or ideas, try to employ them, when appropriate. This practice of observing and applying ideas or techniques improves and sharpens your skills, giving you the background needed for further presentations. Tracing graphic examples is often the best way to gain confidence in graphics.

Collecting graphic ideas, composition methods, and techniques in a notebook or file can help to stimulate ideas for future projects. Collected graphics can include images from newspapers, magazines, advertisements, or design project work. They will serve as a reference for lettering, lines, symbols, forms, textures, colors, and combinations. Collected graphics also provide you with individual examples of composition. Additional practice in design and graphics can be achieved by tracing objects or using ideas from a variety of sources and "creating" new compositions. Both experiments exercise your composition thought process and drawing skills.

Graphic communication requires an understanding of the vocabulary and applications available to the designer. Graphic proficiency is as good as the designer's skills and use of available techniques in expressing ideas for specific design situations. Much of graphics is trial and error, thus learning often results from your successes and failures. Observe, collect, compose, and practice—these are the guidelines to success and proficiency in graphic communications.

# Chapter 6

# Design Symbols

When starting to develop an interior landscape design proposal, a portion of your time is spent in design development and the remainder is spent trying to decide how to communicate your ideas. As a reference and as a means of stimulating your imagination and your observation and collection skills, examples of plan, section, elevation, and perspective drawings are included in this Chapter. Review the individual symbols or symbol combinations in these examples. Whether you use the symbols shown here or draw your own, make sure it is representative of what you want to illustrate and is scaled properly. One of the most common errors is to draw symbols too complex, too simple, too small, or too large for what they represent.

Symbols are used to represent the sizes, shapes, textures, and details of plant and construction materials. Individual symbols and their compositions should relate to the project need, considering the simplicity or complexity of the proposal and the person to whom you are communicating.

When reviewing the examples be aware of the differences between canopy, understory, and ground plane plant symbols. These major categories of symbols are usually used in all plans. Different symbols may also be used to distinguish fine, medium, and coarse plant textures. The use of symbols is only as limited as the minds of designers and the materials to be represented. The selection of techniques and styles depends on your individual skills, drafting style, and the project's need for detail or simplicity. Remember, the more detailed the symbols and plan presentation, the more time it takes to present.

When presenting plants in plan view, a general rule of thumb is to draw them to the desired size for the space. With this rule, plant sizes should represent the actual spread in plan and height in elevation at installation. By using this concept the planting reinforces the anticipated functions of screening, enclosure, etc. more easily than if undersized symbols are used, which is often the case. When drawing

the ground plane or large plant masses, lightly pencil in the anticipated plant spreads before defining the mass's edge with a heavier pencil or ink line. Individual plant centers should then be indicated within the planting mass. If planting masses are drawn showing individual plants, the overlapping of edges often clutters the drawing and distracts from the sheet (Figure 6.1). Errors of plant scaling are one of the biggest problems for beginning designers. Including human elements in your drawings helps give a relative scale: a table and chairs could serve this purpose.

A rule of thumb when presenting canopy plants may be to draw them as simple outlines so that proposed plantings and/or construction features under these plants can be shown. Open tree symbols provide no line conflicts with other understory or ground plane elements. Detailed branch symbols are very effective if specimen plants are being proposed, yet can obscure proposed ground elements.

**Figure 6.1**

In these plan graphic examples, lower or ground levels, medium or shrubbery layers, and larger or canopy plantings are shown. While no drawing scale is indicated, the symbol sizes, line hierarchy, and textures help establish a differentiation in plant levels and their relative sizes.

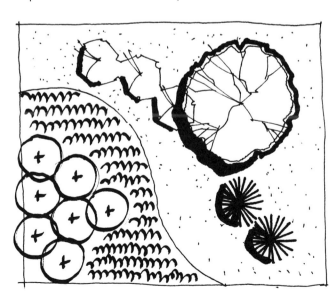

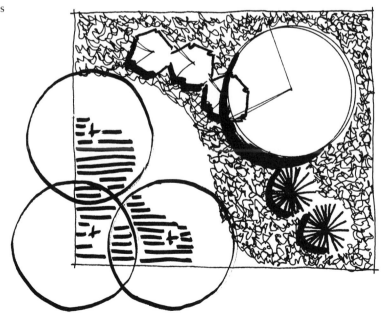

**Figure 6.2**
These plant sketches are drawn to illustrate basic plant forms. The basic outline and trunk/stem-to-crown relationships are included as well as a hint of the leaf textures.

In both plan and sketching presentations, plant and construction material symbols only represent the forms, textures, and lines of the elements. After having outlined the plan, elevation, or sketch forms of elements, select a line weight and type that is representative enough to communicate the materials' texture and essence and add detail to these. In an elevation view, plants and materials should be drawn in the same style as the closely related plan view

(Figure 6.2). Graphic presentations, like handwriting, require rhythm and flow to be consistent and effective. When trying to develop varied plant sketches why not use some of the writing or lettering "strokes" you have already mastered as a means of developing abstract textures and forms? Figures 6.3–6.6 show an example of plant forms developed in plan and elevation by abstracting the strokes used in writing particular alphabet letters. If you'd like to try the technique,

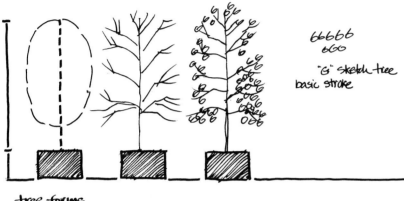

6666b
660

"G" sketch tree
basic stroke

tree forms

m m m
ฟ ฟ ฟ
modified m stroke

shrub type forms

iii        m           w w      abstract     x         .·        oo3

ground plantings

**Figure 6.3**

In this illustration, tree or canopy forms, shrub or understory, and ground plantings are shown in elevation. The ground or trailing symbols at the bottom of the sheet illustrate seven potential symbolic representations. In the shrub and tree form diagrams, the drawing sequence should read left to right. In these cases the designer defines the basic plant size and form in pencil as a guide then detailing out the symbol as needed.

LOW-FAN            IRREGULAR            ROUNDED

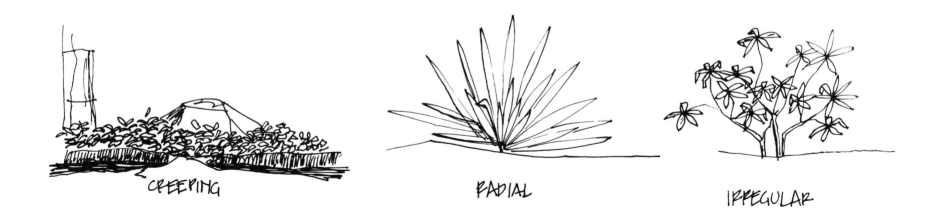

CREEPING            RADIAL            IRREGULAR

BASIC SHRUB FORMS

**Figure 6.4**
Plant form symbols in elevation. (Designer: Don Staley.)

LOW-FAN                IRREGULAR                ROUNDED

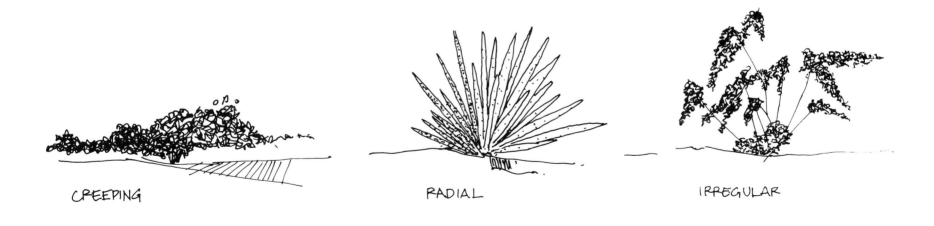

CREEPING                RADIAL                IRREGULAR

BASIC SHRUB FORMS

**Figure 6.5**
Plant form symbols in elevation. (Designer: Don Staley.)

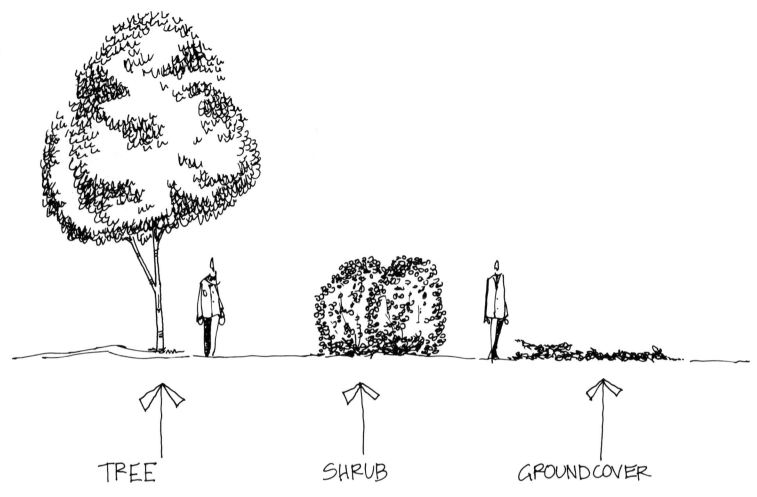

TREE          SHRUB          GROUNDCOVER

**Figure 6.6**

Plants in elevation are given scale by including human elements. Here a figure is used to help define canopy, understory, and ground plane plantings. (Designer: Don Staley.)

sketch out in pencil the outline of a canopy, understory, or ground cover in plan or elevation. Then use a letter from your name as a basis of the "texture" you develop. Try to not be precise in the lettering formation as quick and often incomplete strokes help give a looser character and form (Figures 6.7 and 6.8).

The graphics now included (Figures 6.9–6.21) are di-

vided into examples of plan view, sections, elevations, perspectives, and sketching. Some of them are full scale while others have been photographically reduced. Please be aware of the scale if noted, and if you are transposing any of the examples in projects you may develop make sure the scale is appropriate. The sketching examples have been included to illustrate freehand and drafted styles used in the presentation of design proposals. Sketching techniques are important tools in the development of survey information and in the preliminary stages of design. If you sketch out your ideas early in the design process, you can better visualize the proposal at the end of the design process.

**Figure 6.7**
Plant form elevation examples. (Designer: Don Staley.)

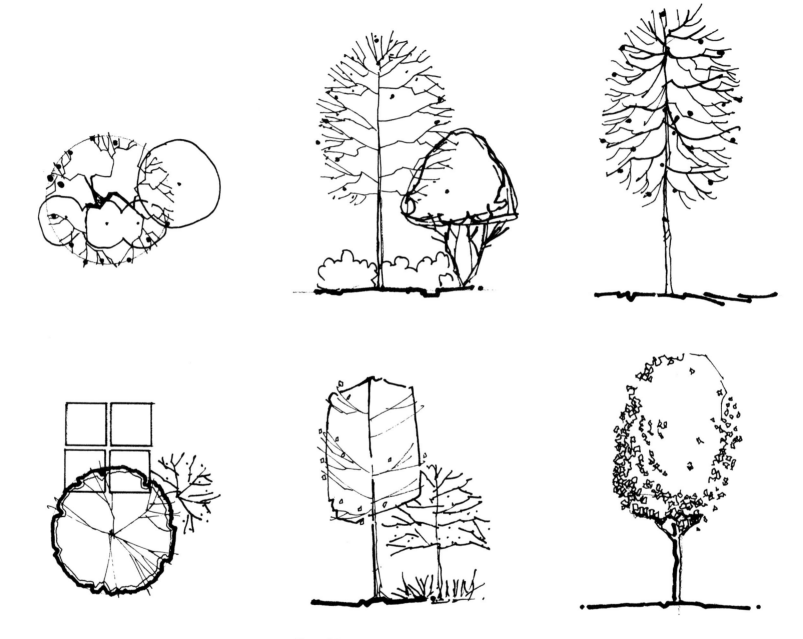

**Figure 6.8**
Plan/elevation symbols. (Designer: T. Kramer.)

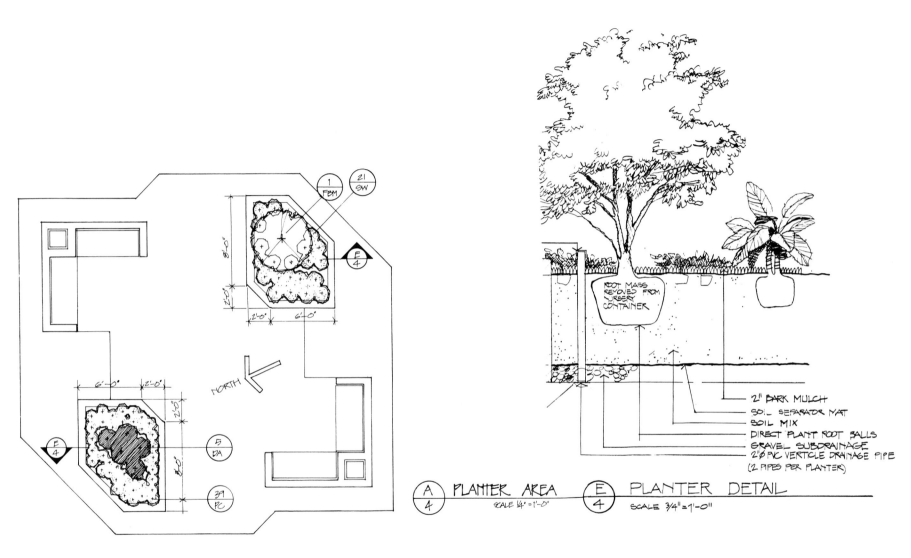

(A/4) PLANTER AREA
SCALE ¼" = 1'-0"

(E/4) PLANTER DETAIL
SCALE ¾" = 1'-0"

**Figure 6.9**
Seating area planting plan and planter detail. (Courtesy of Melvin-Simon Associates.)

155

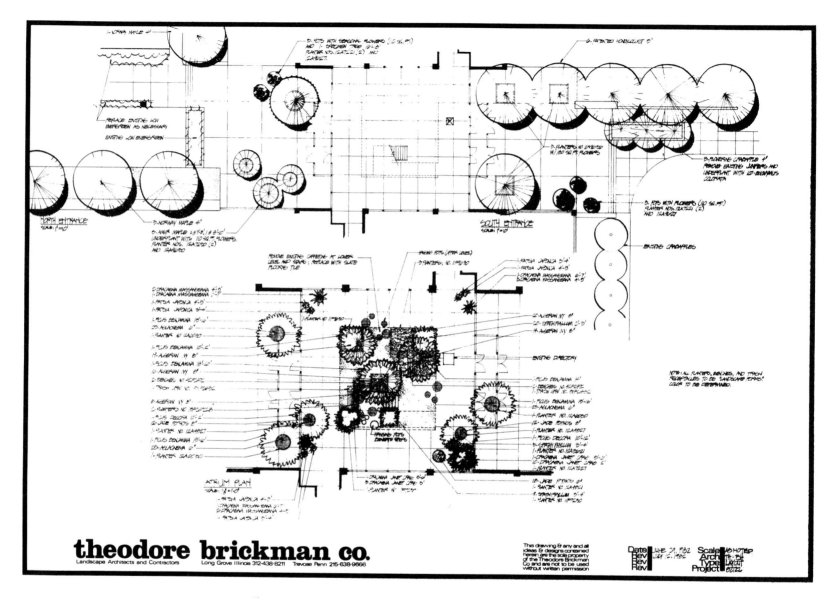

**Figure 6.10**

Site design for an entry, including the exterior and enlargement of the interiorscape atrium. (Courtesy of Theodore Brickman Co., Chicago, Illinois.)

**Figure 6.11**
An outline sketch of a shopping mall staircase and related planting
traced from a slide. (Designer: Kevin Fry.)

157

**Figure 6.12**
A marker sketch including people for scale and detail. (Designer: Kevin Fry.)

**Figure 6.13**
An interiorscape sketch showing a gazebo garden within the Opryland Hotel Atrium, Nashville, Tennessee. (Designer: Kevin Fry.)

159

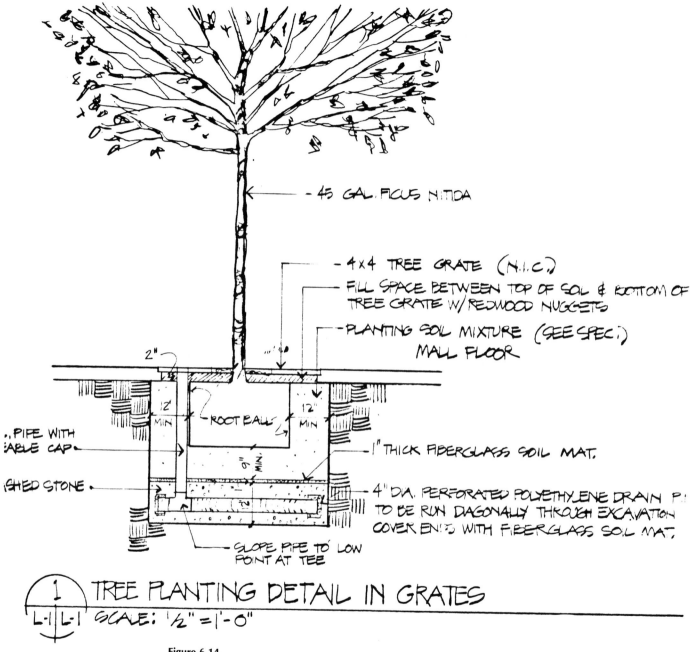

- 45 GAL. FICUS NITIDA

- 4×4 TREE GRATE (N.I.C.)

- FILL SPACE BETWEEN TOP OF SOIL & BOTTOM OF TREE GRATE W/ REDWOOD NUGGETS

- PLANTING SOIL MIXTURE (SEE SPEC.) MALL FLOOR

2"

12' MIN

ROOT BALL

12" MIN

PIPE WITH CABLE CAP

9" MIN

1" THICK FIBERGLASS SOIL MAT.

SHED STONE

4" DIA. PERFORATED POLYETHYLENE DRAIN PIPE TO BE RUN DIAGONALLY THROUGH EXCAVATION COVER ENDS WITH FIBERGLASS SOIL MAT.

SLOPE PIPE TO' LOW POINT AT TEE

**1** TREE PLANTING DETAIL IN GRATES
L-1 L-1 SCALE: 1/2" = 1'-0"

**Figure 6.14**
Planting detail drawings are part of many construction documents. This construction detail shows a floor planter with grate. (Courtesy of Melvin-Simon Associates.)

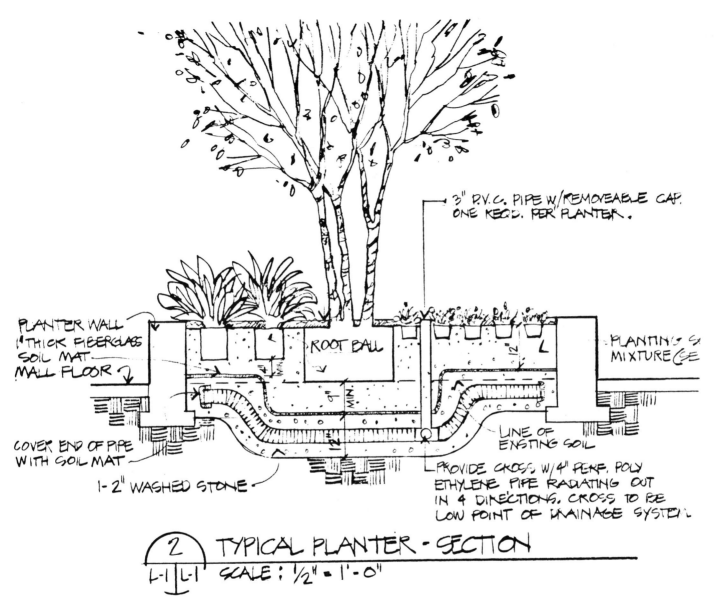

3" P.V.C. PIPE W/REMOVEABLE CAP. ONE REQ'D. PER PLANTER.

PLANTER WALL
1" THICK FIBERGLASS
SOIL MAT
MALL FLOOR

ROOT BALL

PLANTING
MIXTURE

COVER END OF PIPE
WITH SOIL MAT

1-2" WASHED STONE

LINE OF
EXISTING SOIL

PROVIDE CROSS W/4" PERF. POLY
ETHYLENE PIPE RADIATING OUT
IN 4 DIRECTIONS. CROSS TO BE
LOW POINT OF DRAINAGE SYSTEM.

② TYPICAL PLANTER - SECTION
L-1 L-1 SCALE: ½" = 1'-0"

**Figure 6.15**

In comparison with the floor-level planter, detailed in Figure 6.14, this detail illustrates the specifics involved in a raised planter. (Courtesy of Melvin-Simon Associates.)

**6.16**

**Figures 6.16–6.19**

This sequence of illustrations and text show a simple interiorscape proposal for an art museum interior display area. Included is a quick sketch, plan, and elevation. (Designers: Tom Weiler, Judy Watson, and G. M. Pierceall.)

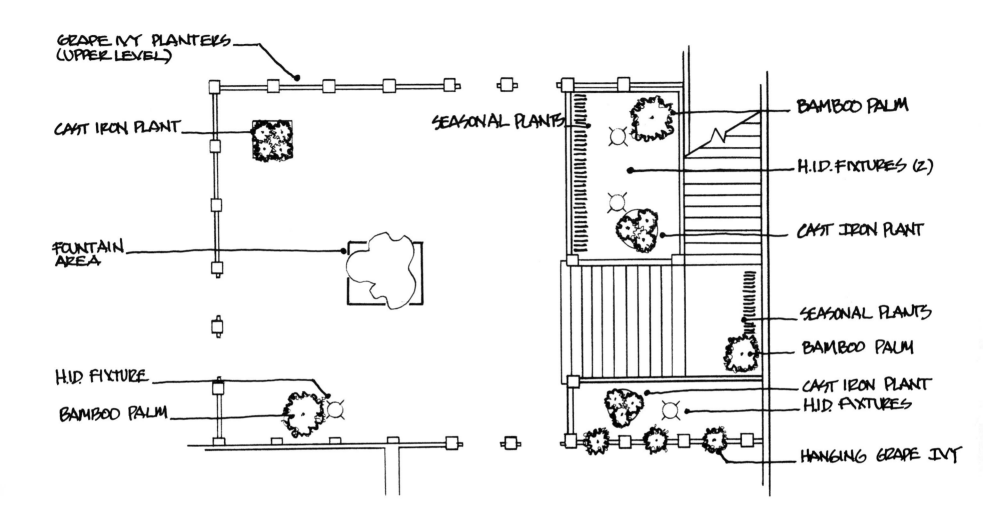

GRAPE IVY PLANTERS
(UPPER LEVEL)

CAST IRON PLANT

FOUNTAIN
AREA

H.I.D. FIXTURE

BAMBOO PALM

SEASONAL PLANTS

BAMBOO PALM

H.I.D. FIXTURES (2)

CAST IRON PLANT

SEASONAL PLANTS

BAMBOO PALM

CAST IRON PLANT
H.I.D. FIXTURES

HANGING GRAPE IVY

FLOOR PLAN CLOWES COURT

SCALE  1/8" = 1'-0"

0    4    8    16

6.17

163

EAST ELEVATION OF CLOWES COURT

SCALE 1/4" = 1'-0"  0  2  4  8

6.18

## ITALIAN GARDENS/COURTYARD

Purpose:          Contemplation, relaxation, entertainment

Layout:           Symmetrical, geometric, simple, formal

Focus:            Water, flat basin or tiered pool, sculpture terra cotta jars with plants

Design Theme:     The courtyard needs a centralized floor level focus. A pool, basin, and/or sculpture could be used. This feature can be flexible as were gardens of the past. Figures included show how this interior Italian garden can look. This feeling can be replicated only partially in an interior environment. The terra cotta jars with plantings and the vining character of wall plants are probably most practical for this area. Considering that the primary focus of this interior courtyard is the art work, plantings should not compete but should complement each other and create a sense of place.

6.19

**Figure 6.20**
While interiorscapes bring a feeling of the outdoors in, some design proposals may include a collaboration between interiorscapers, interior designers, landscape architects, and architects. These sketches done by an interior designer show a comprehensive study of the interior and exterior proposal. (Designer: Renee Zurad.)

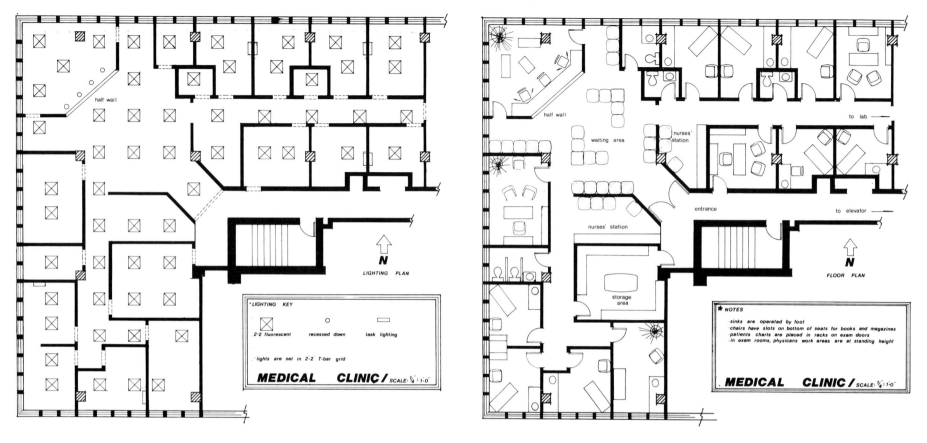

**Figure 6.21**
Skill in reading floor plans and schedules is a requirement of all design professionals. Scaled drawings such as this floor and ceiling plan are the most efficient means to communicate design and to develop as well as evaluate project proposals. (Designer: Renee Zurad.)

## SUMMARY

Designing solely in plan view, even though this is the primary presentation mode of designers, usually limits the client's opportunity to understand a design project space fully. Sketching while designing in plan provides a broader perspective and understanding of existing conditions and proposals developed. Please review these examples and practice your graphic techniques by tracing and composing from these illustrations.

# Chapter 7

# Design Composition and Presentation

Designers use drawings and various other presentation methods to present ideas before they are constructed. Drawings are used to illustrate the intended proposals or design changes in conjunction with written text and/or verbal dialogue explaining what the graphics may not portray. Models may be used as three-dimensional representations of a proposal, presenting scaled scenes of design ideas intended. Drawings and photographs are the primary focus in developments for interior landscape design. Models have limited use due to the time and expense involved in their production. Two-dimensional graphics are the primary presentation mode used by the designer to communicate design proposals before and during implementation.

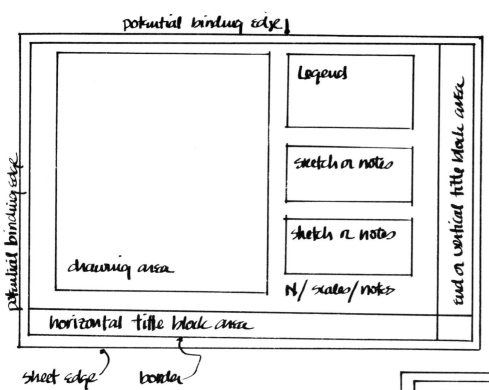

Within the figure (handwritten labels):
potential binding edge
potential binding edge
Legend
sketch or notes
sketch or notes
drawing area
N/ scales/ notes
end or vertical title block area
horizontal title block area
sheet edge
border

**Figure 7.1**

Design drawings usually include basic graphic and drawing components. Usually proposals include borders to give an edge to sheet a drawing area and a title block to identify the client, project, location, and designer. Actual sheet drawing areas can include a plan, section, elevation, or perspective as well as a legend and/or note area for project details or explanation.

**Figure 7.2**

Sheet organization and composition is often as individual as are designers. As is seen in Figure 7.1 and in this figure, the basic graphic and written information should be arranged in a logical and orderly manner.

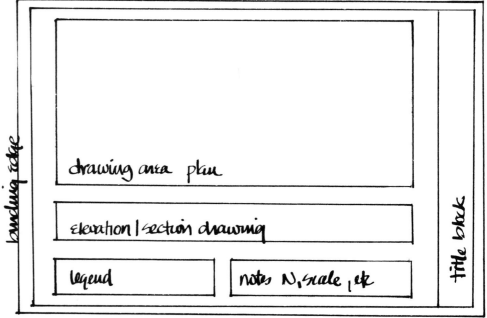

Within the figure (handwritten labels):
drawing area plan
elevation / section drawing
legend
notes N, scale, etc
binding edge
title block

## DRAWING COMPONENTS

The fundamental components found in any design drawing include sheet borders, a title block, the plan or drawing area, and support information such as legends, labels, leaders, scale, compass orientation, and notes (Figure 7.1). The effectiveness of any sheet lies in the organization and composition of its information. The initial step in composing a sheet is to select a drawing surface appropriate for the media to be used. As mentioned earlier, toothed paper for pencil and smooth paper or mylar for ink. The next step is to select a paper size that is in proportion to the drawing to be developed. A variety of sheet sizes appropriate for the project's demands and equivalent to duplication papers are available. Standard ozalid print papers include individual sheets of 8½" by 11", 11" by 17", 12" by 18", 17" by 22", 18" by 24", 21" by 30" 24" by 36", or rolls 30" or 36" wide in almost any length.

The final sheet size should provide adequate space for the drawing area and support information. Thus it is best to have a sheet that is too large and cut it down than to start with a sheet that is too small. The drawing area should be aligned to permit space for adequate labels, leaders, and notes. Areas for a legend and for title block information should be secondary in their location on the sheet. The title block, plan, legend, notes, and sketches, if any, should be composed in a unified manner rather than scattered on the sheet. Figure 7.2 shows a well-developed sheet. If more than one sheet is required for a project, a "base sheet" can be drawn as an original for sepias for the multiple sheets and additions. Use of sepias for information found on more than one sheet saves time and ensures consistency of information. The use of sepias for multiple sheet presentations is illustrated later in this chapter.

### Title Blocks

Title blocks normally include project and sheet information which is supportive to the drawing. Permanent project data that belongs on all sheets includes the project title, project owner and address, project designer, date, and project numbers. Information that may vary with each sheet includes the sheet titles such as the site survey, master plan, and site details. The sheets should also include graphic and written scales and orientation as relatively consistent pieces of information. A title block is most often located on the bottom or right-hand edge of the sheet, as the top and left-hand edges of sheets are normally options as binding edges.

The title block is a continuous block of information proportionate to the sheet and/or drawing sizes. Figure 7.3 shows options for title block location and composition. Title blocks are normally found at the bottom or right-hand sheet edges, which allows easy visibility if multiple sheets are bound at the top or left-hand sides. Related pieces of information should be organized together within the title block.

**Figure 7.3**
Title blocks characteristically are located to the bottom or right-hand edge of design sheets. Title blocks are normally located opposite the binding edge of a proposal package.

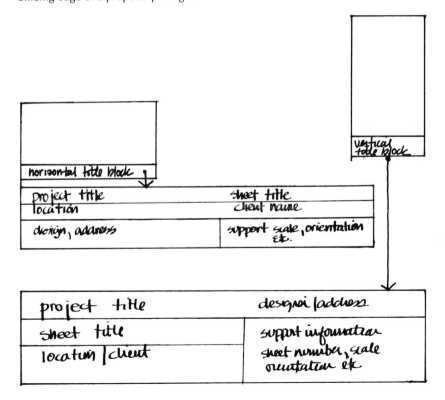

For example, the project title, sheet title, and client–owner information should be grouped together as these pieces of information are related. The project title and sheet title should be predominant since they relate to the project drawing more than the other pieces of information. The project owner, client–owner, and address are secondary to the sheet and project titles, but should be located in the same area within the title block. Composition of other pieces of important data such as the designer's name, project number, and date, as well as the sheet number, scale, and orientation is by priorities of the listings and amount of space available after the project and sheet titles and client information have been organized. Figure 7.4 shows examples of information within title blocks.

**Figure 7.4**

Typical title block information includes data that is not easily drawn or cannot be drawn.

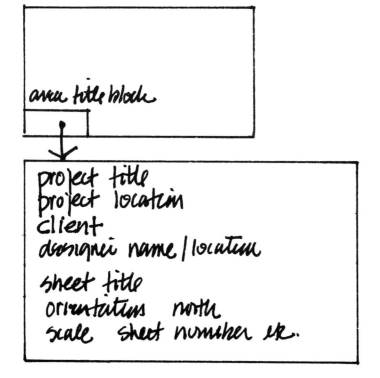

## Borders

Borders are used on a sheet as a frame for information. When developing multiple sheet presentations, the binding edge (top or left sides) will have a wider border than the other edges. Border line sizes depend on the sheet's size and should be proportionate to the other sheet information. After the sheet has its border and title blocks have been defined, the drawing area can be organized.

While the borders and title block are drawn before the actual drawing in a drafting sequence, the size and configuration of the anticipated drawing is considered before borders and title block are finalized.

## Labels and Leaders

Design drawings include support information such as labels, leaders, notes, legends, and titles to explain information that cannot be fully conveyed by graphics. Labels and notes are written descriptions of plan components, materials, or details. A leader is used to connect a label to the specific element that it describes. In laying out labels and leaders, try not to place them too far away from their objects. Long leaders can be confusing and create clutter on a drawing. Notes are normally used to describe the characteristics or function of an area or elements, or to present information that cannot be drawn. Figures 7.5 and 7.6 show examples of sheet support information.

## Lettering

Lettering is a major information and design consideration in the organization and composition of a sheet proposal. Lettering is used principally where graphics or symbols alone cannot explain the information. In a presentation, the lettering and the information conveyed become a compositional element to be organized. Consistent, neat, and organized lettering complements a drawing whereas inconsistent, messy, or haphazard lettering distracts from the overall appearance of the presentation. Lettering, like graphics, requires practice to gain proficiency

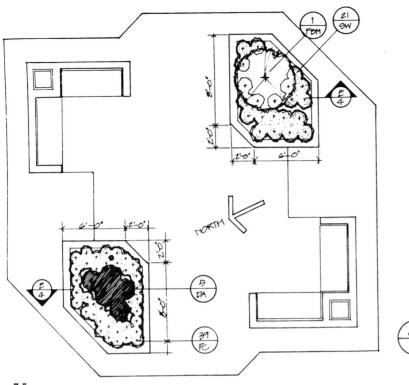

**PLANTER AREA**
SCALE 1/4" = 1'-0"

7.5

**Figures 7.5 and 7.6**
In this project plan, the plant layers and the planting zone details are diagrammed to fully communicate the design and installation intent to the contractor. (Courtesy of Melvin-Simon Associates.)

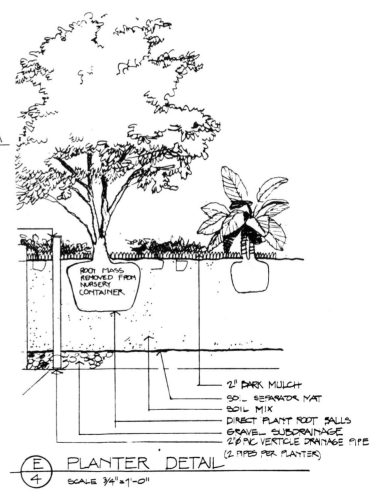

ROOT MASS REMOVED FROM NURSERY CONTAINER

2" BARK MULCH
SOIL SEPARATOR MAT
SOIL MIX
DIRECT PLANT ROOT BALLS
GRAVEL SUBDRAINAGE
2" Ø PVC VERTICLE DRAINAGE PIPE
(2 PIPES PER PLANTER)

**PLANTER DETAIL**
SCALE 3/4" = 1'-0"

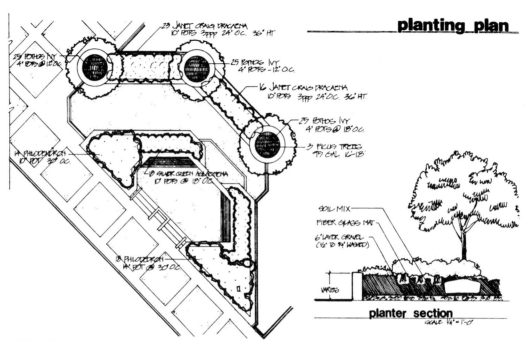

23 JANET CRAIG DRACAENA
10' POTS 3PPP 24' O.C. 36" HT

25 POTHOS IVY
4' POTS @ 18' O.C.

25 POTHOS IVY
4' POTS - 12' O.C.

16 JANET CRAIG DRACAENA
10' POTS 3PPP 24' O.C. 36" HT

25 POTHOS IVY
4' POTS @ 18' O.C.

3 FICUS TREES
45 GAL 16'-18'

14 PHILODENDRON
10' POT 30' O.C.

10 SILVER GREEN AGLAONEMA
10' POTS @ 18' O.C.

18 PHILODENDRON
14' POT @ 30' O.C.

SOIL MIX

FIBER GLASS MAT

6' LAYER GRAVEL
(1/2' TO 3/4' WASHED)

VARIES

**planter section**
SCALE: 1/4" = 1'-0"

## PLANT LIST

| KEY | BOTANICAL NAME | COMMON NAME | CALIPER | HEIGHT | POT SIZE | | OTHER REQUIREMENTS | QUANTITY |
|-----|----------------|-------------|---------|--------|----------|---|---------------------|----------|
| FBM | FICUS BENJAMINA | WEEPING FIG (4'-5' MIN SPREAD) | 4"-6" | 7'-8' | 17" | POT | MULTI-STEM | 7 |
| FBS | FICUS BENJAMINA | WEEPING FIG (7'-8' MIN SPREAD) | ± 4" | 13'-14' | 21"-26"-30" | POT | STANDARD TREE FORM- OVERALL CLEAR TRUNK CLEARANCE OF 7'-6" | 16 |
| CE | CHAMAEDOREA ELEGANS | PARLOR PALM | | 4'-5' | 14" | POT | | 18 |
| DA | DIEFFENBACHIA AMOENA | GIANT DUMB CANE | | 3'-5' | 14" | POT | | 14 |
| FJ | FATSIA JAPONICA | JAPANESE FATSIA | | 2'-3' | 10" | POT | | 30 |
| SW | SPATHIPHYLLUM WALLISII | PEACE LILLY | | | 10" | POT | PLANT 18' O.C. | 72 |
| ACE | AGLAONEMA COMMUTATUM ELEGANS | SILVER EVERGREEN | | 18"-24" | 8" | POT | PLANT 18' O.C. | 68 |
| PC | PHILODENDRON CORDATUM | COMMON PHILODENDRON | | | 4" | POT | PLANT 12' O.C. | 324 |
| HH | HEDERA HELIX | ENGLISH IVY | | | 10" | HB | HANGING BASKET | 84 |

## MATERIALS QUANTITIES ESTIMATE

| | UNIT | |
|---|---|---|
| BARK MULCH | C.Y. | 7.0 |
| GRAVEL MULCH | C.Y. | 2.9 |
| SOIL SEPARATOR MAT | S.Y. | 202 |
| PREPARED SOIL MIX | C.Y. | 149 |
| GRAVEL SUBDRAINAGE | C.Y. | 29 |
| PVC DRAINAGE PIPE | EA. | 52 |
| SELF WATERING PLANTERS | EA. | 42 |

## GENERAL NOTES

1. ALL OVERHEAD SELF-WATERING PLANTERS REQUIRE PLACEMENT OF A PREPARED SOIL MIX.
2. EXACT NUMBER & LOCATION OF HOSE BIBS IN THE MALL REMODEL AREA IS UNKNOWN.

7.6

and skill. Being observant, tracing, and collecting lettering types are means to gaining confidence and experience in lettering and its composition.

The key to good lettering is (1) legibility and (2) consistency. Lettering must be readable and should have consistency of style, height, and weight. Lettering styles selected should be simple and relatively easy to produce. A detailed lettering style may not only be time consuming, but may distract from the drawing's focus. Lettering height or size should be selected relative to its purpose. If for a project title, its size should be relatively large. Most major project titles can be in the range of 1/2" to 1" letters, while labels, notes, and other lettering can be in the 1/8" to 1/4" size range.

Overall lettering heights should be kept consistent through the use of guidelines. Guidelines are usually defined by light pencil lines or the use of graph paper under a drawing to maintain lettering heights, spacing, and widths and their alignment with other sheet elements. After a lettering height has been selected for a particular area in a drawing, cross-bar guidelines where all horizontal portion of letters will cross are also included. Letters such as A, B, E, F, G, H, P, R, and X all have a cross-bar portion that should be consistent within a drawing. The spacing of this cross-bar affects the character of lettering. If the overall height of a letter is divided, the cross-bar can occur in the middle or two-thirds the distance above the base of the letter.

Individual letters should be spaced relative to the words they represent, rather than spaced evenly. When reading we see words, not individual letters; thus, organize and compose lettering accordingly.

Freehand lettering is an important skill to develop because it is quick, once one is proficient, and it gives character to a drawing. A proficiency in freehand lettering helps one learn the skill of composing words from letters. This skill is critical when hand lettering or using preprinted lettering or mechanical lettering sets. See Figure 7.6 for examples of lettering and its composition within proposals.

## Scales

Both written and graphic scales are necessary as part of a drawing's support information. A graphic scale indicates the scale of a drawing and remains consistent even when photographically reduced, so it can be used when an actual scale is unavailable. Examples of graphic and written scales are shown in Figure 7.7. The northern orientation relative to the project site is also associated with sheet scale information.

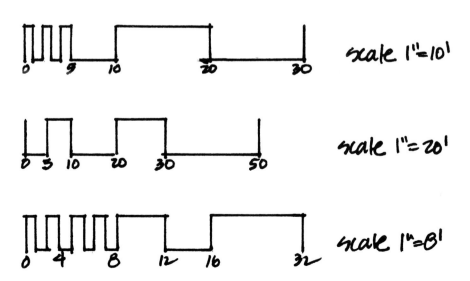

**Figure 7.7**
Written and/or graphic scales are desirable on all drawings. Graphic scales are helpful to illustrate on plans the relative size of components. If drawings are photographically enlarged or reduced a graphic scale is then valid at the changed size.

173

## PRESENTING A DESIGN PROPOSAL

Design proposals often require more than one sheet to completely document and express design ideas and construction details. Interior landscape planning packages may include the following information: a project survey and analysis, design schematics, a master plan, illustrative details and sketches, and construction drawings. The amount of information presented depends on the client's needs, the installation process and budget limitations. If the client–owner has only enough resources for the development of a master plan, then the survey, analysis, and design details may be communicated verbally or may occur on the same sheet as the presentation of design concepts. In any case, make sure you keep project notes to document the design process, client review, and discussions if shortcuts are taken. After the design proposal is presented and approved, construction drawings may or may not be developed depending on the project scale, phasing and/or installation sequences. In addition to the design and/or construction drawings, a title page may be included to reference the project and to list the various sheets that comprise the package. Figures 7.8–7.12 illustrate a multi-sheet design proposal.

## SINGLE SHEET PLANTING PROPOSALS

Design proposals, in contrast to the complete design packages, can be simplified. Figures 7.13 and 7.14 show a project's designs communicated using single pages. To eliminate excessive time spent on design, the graphic production of a title sheet and survey and analysis were dropped, making the master plan the only sheet in the presentation. On this sheet, details were identified through notes or in letter correspondences presented. The graphic style used for symbols and sheet borders were simplified and thus saved time. Overall, the project information is compact yet communicates the plantings and constructed features proposed. This format requires much more explanation as to how the design evolved and more instructions for future design direction. Make sure when you contract to do a project that the design budget is sufficient for development of the design to the extent and detail expected by the client, and that it can be implemented. If the budget and expectations do not match, explain to the client what can be provided within the defined limits. The purpose of a design proposal is to communicate information, not to produce useless drawings.

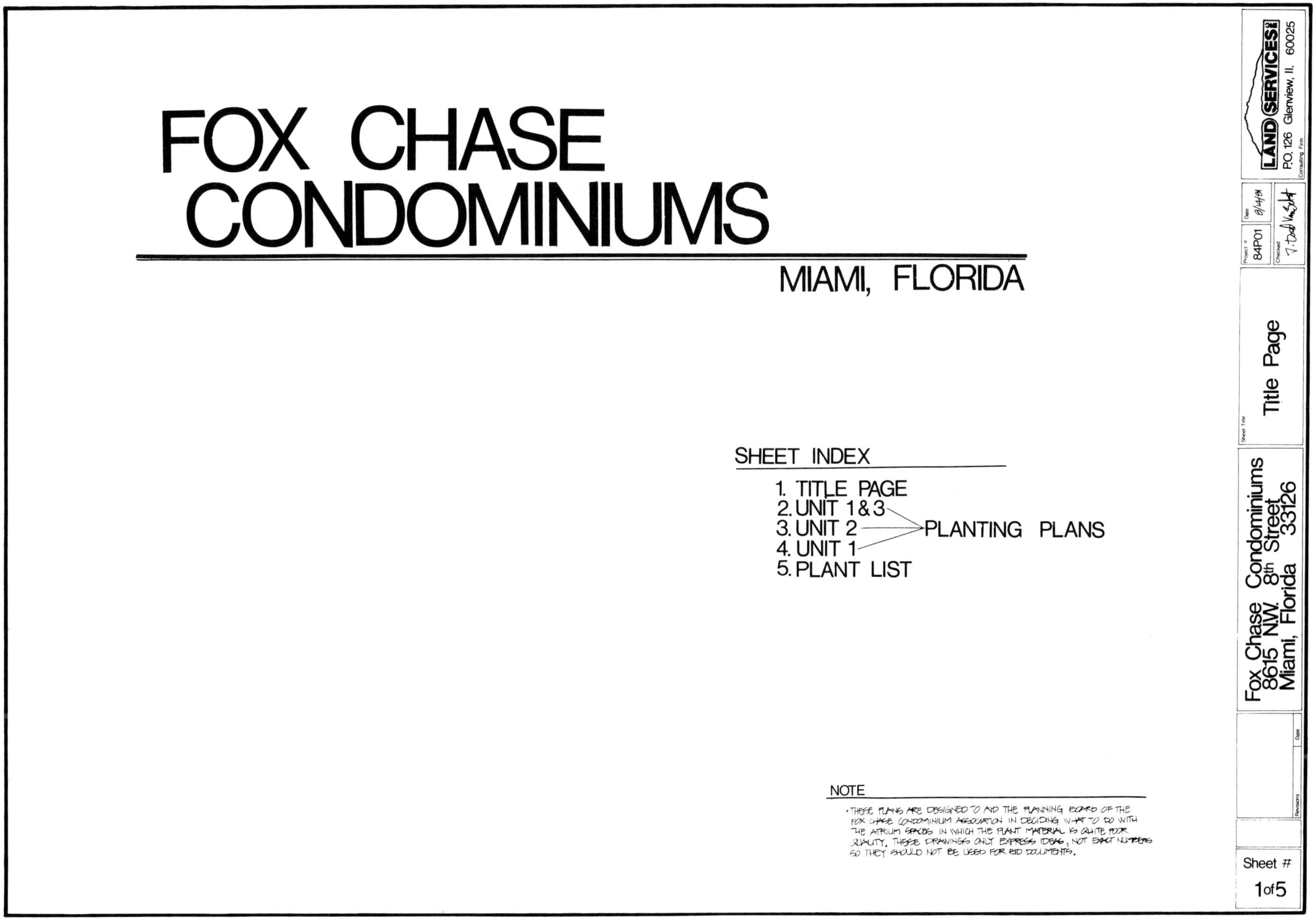

# FOX CHASE CONDOMINIUMS

## MIAMI, FLORIDA

SHEET INDEX

1. TITLE PAGE
2. UNIT 1 & 3
3. UNIT 2 ——————> PLANTING PLANS
4. UNIT 1
5. PLANT LIST

NOTE

- THESE PLANS ARE DESIGNED TO AID THE PLANNING BOARD OF THE FOX CHASE CONDOMINIUM ASSOCIATION IN DECIDING WHAT TO DO WITH THE ATRIUM SPACES IN WHICH THE PLANT MATERIAL IS QUITE POOR QUALITY. THESE DRAWINGS ONLY EXPRESS IDEAS, NOT EXACT NUMBERS SO THEY SHOULD NOT BE USED FOR BID DOCUMENTS.

LAND SERVICES
P.O. 126 Glenview, Il. 60025
Consulting Firm

Project # 84P01
Date 8/14/81
Checked T. Van Zelst

Sheet Title: Title Page

Fox Chase Condominiums
8615 N.W. 8th Street
Miami, Florida 33126

Date
Revisions

Sheet #
1 of 5

**Figure 7.8**

In this condominium planting proposal, three similar atrium areas within a complex are shown. Sheet one is the title page of the proposal defining the project and sheet index. (Designer: D. Van Zelst.)

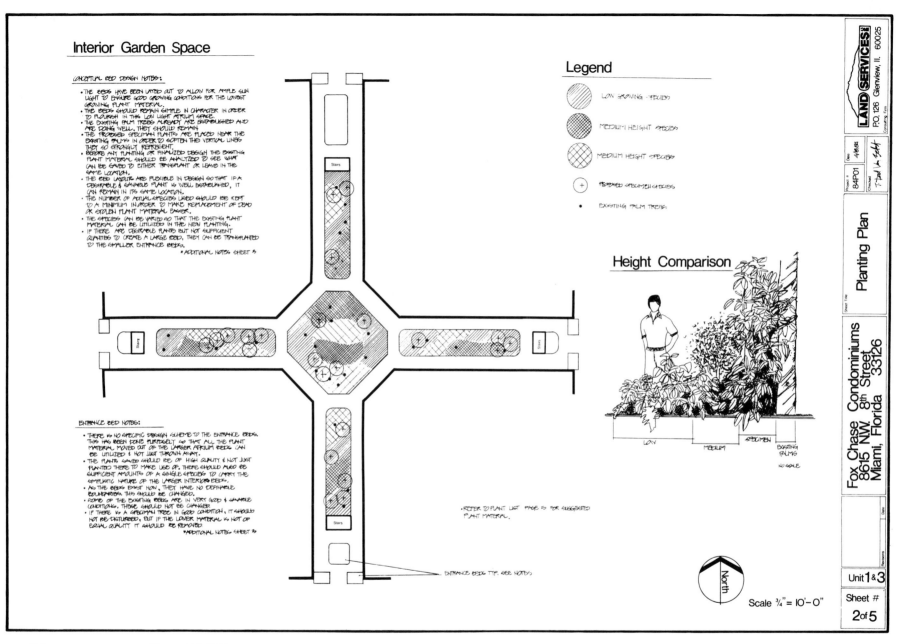

## Interior Garden Space

**CONCEPTUAL BED DESIGN NOTES:**

- THE BEDS HAVE BEEN LAID OUT TO ALLOW FOR AMPLE SUN LIGHT TO ENSURE GOOD GROWING CONDITIONS FOR THE LOWEST GROWING PLANT MATERIAL.
- THE BEDS SHOULD REMAIN SIMPLE IN CHARACTER IN ORDER TO FLOURISH IN THIS LOW LIGHT ATRIUM SPACE.
- THE EXISTING PALM TREES ALREADY ARE ESTABLISHED AND ARE DOING WELL, THEY SHOULD REMAIN.
- THE PROPOSED SPECIMEN PLANTS ARE PLACED NEAR THE EXISTING PALMS IN ORDER TO SOFTEN THE VERTICAL LINES THEY SO STRONGLY REPRESENT.
- BEFORE ANY PLANTING OR FINALIZED DESIGN THE EXISTING PLANT MATERIAL SHOULD BE ANALYZED TO SEE WHAT CAN BE SAVED TO EITHER TRANSPLANT OR LEAVE IN THE SAME LOCATION.
- THE BED LAYOUTS ARE FLEXIBLE IN DESIGN SO THAT IF A DESIRABLE & SAVABLE PLANT IS WELL ESTABLISHED, IT CAN REMAIN IN ITS SAME LOCATION.
- THE NUMBER OF ACTUAL SPECIES USED SHOULD BE KEPT TO A MINIMUM IN ORDER TO MAKE REPLACEMENT OF DEAD OR STOLEN PLANT MATERIAL EASIER.
- THE SPECIES CAN BE VARIED SO THAT THE EXISTING PLANT MATERIAL CAN BE UTILIZED IN THE NEW PLANTING.
- IF THERE ARE DESIRABLE PLANTS BUT NOT SUFFICIENT QUANTITIES TO CREATE A LARGE BED, THEY CAN BE TRANSPLANTED TO THE SMALLER ENTRANCE BEDS.

*ADDITIONAL NOTES SHEET 3

**ENTRANCE BED NOTES:**

- THERE IS NO SPECIFIC DESIGN SCHEME TO THE ENTRANCE BEDS. THIS HAS BEEN DONE PURPOSELY SO THAT ALL THE PLANT MATERIAL MOVED OUT OF THE LARGER ATRIUM BEDS CAN BE UTILIZED & NOT JUST THROWN AWAY.
- THE PLANTS SAVED SHOULD BE OF HIGH QUALITY & NOT JUST PLANTED THERE TO MAKE USE OF. THERE SHOULD ALSO BE SUFFICIENT AMOUNTS OF A SINGLE SPECIES TO CARRY THE SIMPLISTIC NATURE OF THE LARGER INTERIOR BEDS.
- AS THE BEDS EXIST NOW, THEY HAVE NO DEFINABLE BOUNDARIES, THIS SHOULD BE CHANGED.
- SOME OF THE EXISTING BEDS ARE IN VERY GOOD & SAVABLE CONDITIONS, THOSE SHOULD NOT BE CHANGED.
- IF THERE IS A SPECIMEN TREE IN GOOD CONDITION, IT SHOULD NOT BE DISTURBED, BUT IF THE LOWER MATERIAL IS NOT OF EQUAL QUALITY IT SHOULD BE REMOVED.

*ADDITIONAL NOTES SHEET 3

Stairs

Stairs

Stairs

Stairs

- REFER TO PLANT LIST PAGE 5 FOR SUGGESTED PLANT MATERIAL.

ENTRANCE BEDS TYP. SEE NOTES

## Legend

- LOW GROWING - FICUS
- MEDIUM HEIGHT SHRUBS
- MEDIUM HEIGHT SHRUBS
- (+) PROPOSED SPECIMEN SPECIES
- EXISTING PALM TREES

## Height Comparison

LOW | MEDIUM | SPECIMEN | EXISTING PALMS

NO SCALE

LAND SERVICES INC.
P.O. 126 Glenview, Il. 60025
Consulting Firm

Project #: 84P01  Date: 4/16/84
Checked: Ted Van Zelst

Sheet Title: Planting Plan

Fox Chase Condominiums
8615 N.W. 8th Street
Miami, Florida  33126

Revisions | Date

Unit **1 & 3**

Sheet #  **2 of 5**

North

Scale ¾" = 10'-0"

7.9

**Figures 7.9–7.11**

In this planting proposal the same basic drawing was used for all the sheets because the same base floor plan configuration was found in each area. Sepia drawings were used to add the correct orientation and individual garden design to each sheet. Rather than producing detailed planting plans, this proposal illustrates appropriate planting zones. Each area then reflects the light, exposure, and location relative to views, access, and use. A plant scale comparison is included on each sheet to give a feeling of the proposed scale and composition. (Designer: D. Van Zelst.)

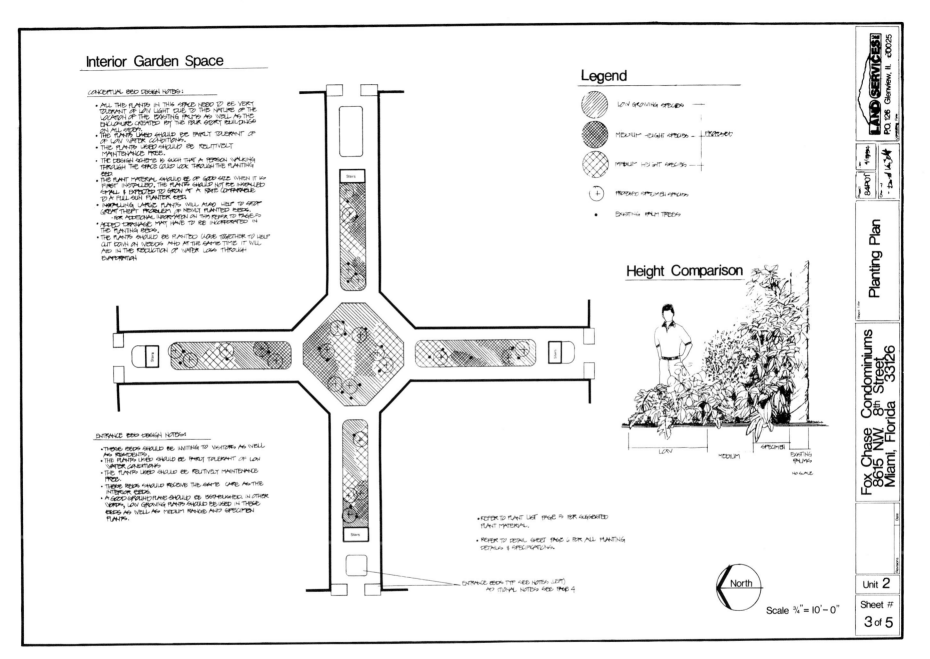

## Interior Garden Space

CONCEPTUAL BED DESIGN NOTES:

- ALL THE PLANTS IN THIS SPACE NEED TO BE VERY TOLERANT OF LOW LIGHT DUE TO THE NATURE OF THE LOCATION OF THE EXISTING PALMS AS WELL AS THE ENCLOSURE CREATED BY THE FOUR STORY BUILDINGS ON ALL SIDES.
- THE PLANTS USED SHOULD BE FAIRLY TOLERANT OF LOW WATER CONDITIONS.
- THE PLANTS USED SHOULD BE RELATIVELY MAINTENANCE FREE.
- THE DESIGN SCHEME IS SUCH THAT A PERSON WALKING THROUGH THE SPACE COULD LOOK THROUGH THE PLANTING BED.
- THE PLANT MATERIAL SHOULD BE OF GOOD SIZE WHEN IT IS FIRST INSTALLED. THE PLANTS SHOULD NOT BE INSTALLED SMALL & EXPECTED TO GROW AT A RATE COMPARABLE TO A FULL SUN PLANTER BED.
- INSTALLING LARGE PLANTS WILL ALSO HELP TO STOP GREAT THEFT PROBLEM OF NEWLY PLANTED BEDS.
  - FOR ADDITIONAL INFORMATION ON THIS REFER TO PAGE 5
- ADDED DRAINAGE MAY HAVE TO BE INCORPORATED IN THE PLANTING BEDS.
- THE PLANTS SHOULD BE PLANTED CLOSE TOGETHER TO HELP CUT DOWN ON WEEDS AND AT THE SAME TIME IT WILL AID IN THE REDUCTION OF WATER LOSS THROUGH EVAPORATION.

ENTRANCE BED DESIGN NOTES:

- THESE BEDS SHOULD BE INVITING TO VISITORS AS WELL AS RESIDENTS.
- THE PLANTS USED SHOULD BE FAIRLY TOLERANT OF LOW WATER CONDITIONS.
- THE PLANTS USED SHOULD BE RELATIVELY MAINTENANCE FREE.
- THESE BEDS SHOULD RECEIVE THE SAME CARE AS THE INTERIOR BEDS.
- A GOOD GROUND PLANE SHOULD BE ESTABLISHED. IN OTHER WORDS, LOW GROWING PLANTS SHOULD BE USED IN THESE BEDS AS WELL AS MEDIUM RANGE AND SPECIMEN PLANTS.

Stairs

Stairs

Stairs

Stairs

ENTRANCE BEDS TYP SEE NOTES (LEFT) ADDITIONAL NOTES SEE PAGE 4

- REFER TO PLANT LIST PAGE 5 FOR SUGGESTED PLANT MATERIAL.
- REFER TO DETAIL SHEET PAGE 6 FOR ALL PLANTING DETAILS & SPECIFICATIONS.

## Legend

LOW GROWING SPECIES

MEDIUM HEIGHT SPECIES — PROPOSED

MEDIUM HEIGHT SPECIES

PROPOSED SPECIMEN SPECIES

EXISTING PALM TREES

## Height Comparison

LOW    MEDIUM    SPECIMEN    EXISTING PALMS

NO SCALE

North

Scale ¾" = 10'-0"

### LAND SERVICES
P.O. 126 Glenview, Il. 3025

Planting Plan

Fox Chase Condominiums
8615 N.W. 8th Street
Miami, Florida    33126

Unit 2

Sheet #
3 of 5

7.10

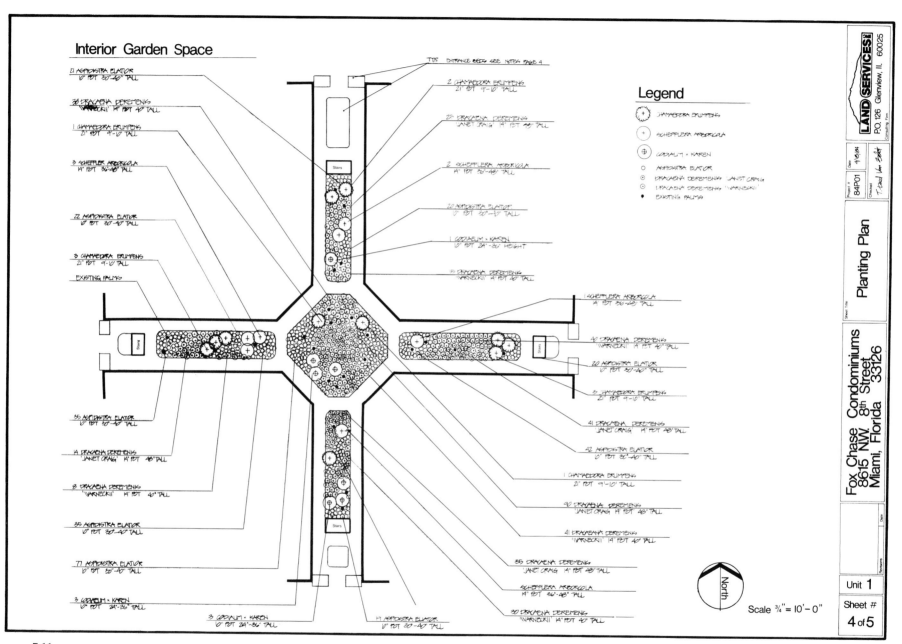

## Interior Garden Space

21 ASPIDISTRA ELATIOR
10" POT 30"-40" TALL

38 DRACAENA DEREMENS
'WARNECKII' 14" POT 40" TALL

1 CHAMAEDORA ERUMPENS
21" POT 9'-10' TALL

3 SCHEFFLERA ARBORICOLA
14" POT 36"-48" TALL

22 ASPIDISTRA ELATIOR
10" POT 30"-40" TALL

3 CHAMAEDORA ERUMPENS
21" POT 9'-10' TALL

EXISTING PALMS

35 ASPIDISTRA ELATIOR
10" POT 30"-40" TALL

14 DRACAENA DEREMENS
'JANET CRAIG' 14" POT 48" TALL

8 DRACAENA DEREMENS
'WARNECKII' 14" POT 40" TALL

35 ASPIDISTRA ELATIOR
10" POT 30"-40" TALL

77 ASPIDISTRA ELATIOR
10" POT 30"-40" TALL

3 CODIAUM × KAREN
10" POT 24"-36" TALL

3 CODIUM × KAREN
10" POT 24"-36" TALL

19 ASPIDISTRA ELATIOR
10" POT 30"-40" TALL

TYP. ENTRANCE BEDS SEE NOTES PAGE 4

2 CHAMAEDORA ERUMPENS
21" POT 9'-10' TALL

25 DRACAENA DEREMENS
'JANET CRAIG' 14" POT 48" TALL

2 SCHEFFLERA ARBORICOLA
14" POT 36"-48" TALL

20 ASPIDISTRA ELATIOR
10" POT 30"-40" TALL

1 CODIAUM × KAREN
10" POT 24"-36" HEIGHT

19 DRACAENA DEREMENS
'WARNECKII' 14" POT 40" TALL

1 SCHEFFLERA ARBORICOLA
14" POT 36"-48" TALL

42 DRACAENA DEREMENS
'WARNECKII' 14" POT 40" TALL

20 ASPIDISTRA ELATIOR
10" POT 30"-40" TALL

3 CHAMAEDORA ERUMPENS
21" POT 9'-10' TALL

41 DRACAENA DEREMENS
'JANET CRAIG' 14" POT 48" TALL

42 ASPIDISTRA ELATIOR
10" POT 30"-40" TALL

1 CHAMAEDORA ERUMPENS
21" POT 9'-10' TALL

90 DRACAENA DEREMENS
'JANET CRAIG' 14" POT 48" TALL

41 DRACAENA DEREMENS
'WARNECKII' 14" POT 40" TALL

35 DRACAENA DEREMENS
'JANET CRAIG' 14" POT 48" TALL

SCHEFFLERA ARBORICOLA
14" POT 36"-48" TALL

30 DRACAENA DEREMENS
'WARNECKII' 14" POT 40" TALL

### Legend

- CHAMAEDORA ERUMPENS
- SCHEFFLERA ARBORICOLA
- CODIAUM × KAREN
- ASPIDISTRA ELATIOR
- DRACAENA DEREMENS 'JANET CRAIG'
- DRACAENA DEREMENS 'WARNECKII'
- EXISTING PALMS

Stairs

North

Scale ¾" = 10'-0"

LAND SERVICES
P.O. 126 Glenview, Il. 60025
Consulting Firm

Project # 84P01
Date 4/6/84
Checked T. Paul Van Schaft

Sheet Title
Planting Plan

Fox Chase Condominiums
8615 NW. 8th Street
Miami, Florida 33126

Unit 1

Sheet #
4 of 5

7.11

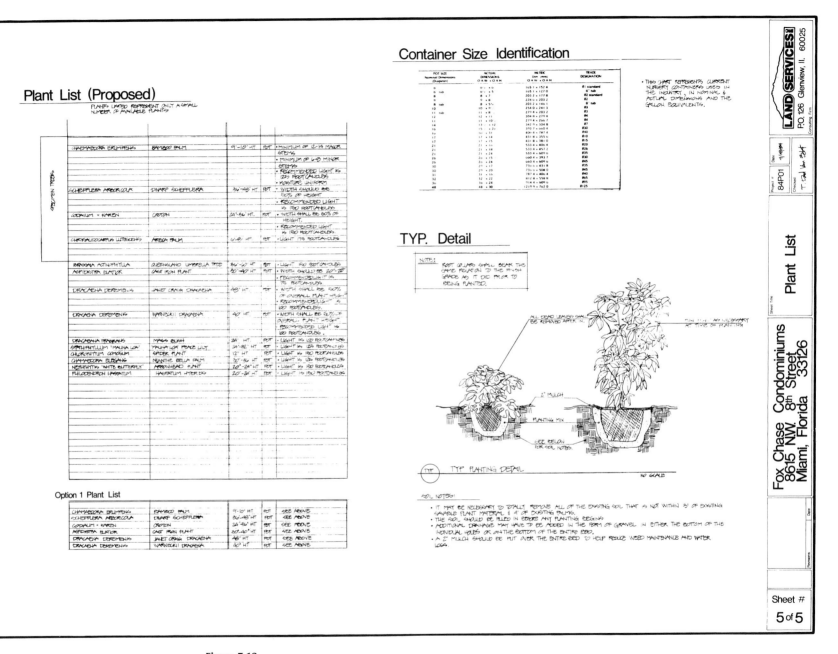

**Figure 7.12**

On this final project sheet a plant schedule, plant alternatives, and planting detail are included. (Designer: D. Van Zelst.)

**SECTION A-A**

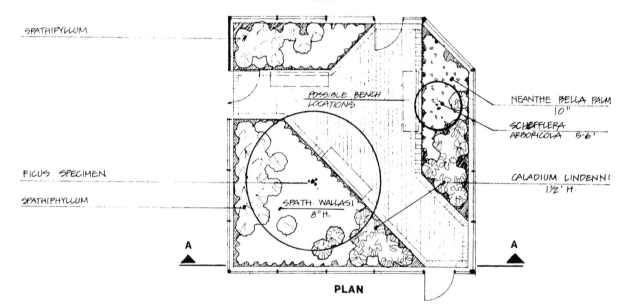

SPATHIPYLLUM

POSSIBLE BENCH LOCATIONS

NEANTHE BELLA PALM 10"

SCHEFFLERA ARBORICOLA 5-6'

FICUS SPECIMEN

SPATHIPHYLLUM

SPATH WALLASI 8" H.

CALADIUM LINDENNI 1½' H.

A                                    A

**PLAN**

INTERIOR LANDSCAPE DESIGN FOR

# THE DUPONT ATRIUM

¼"=1'-0"

BY GARDEN MILIEU INC.

**Figure 7.13**

Some projects are of a scale that only a single sheet is required. This planting plan for the DuPont atrium by Garden Milieu Inc. includes a plan and section to communicate the proposed design scheme. (Courtesy of Garden Milieu Inc.)

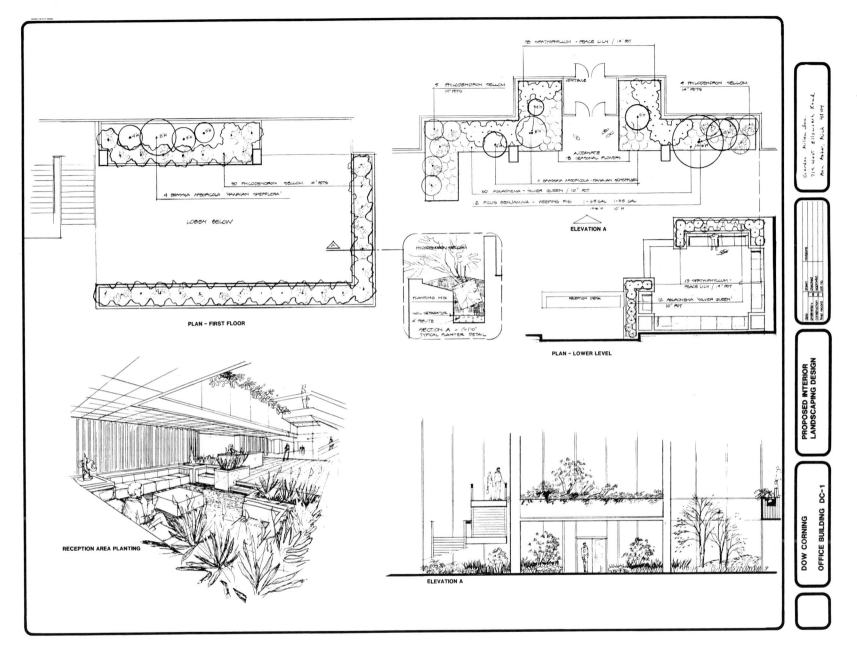

**Figure 7.14**

This interiorscape proposal for the Dow Corning Office Building, also by Garden Milieu Inc., is more detailed. Included is a lower and upper floor plan, elevation, and perspective. (Courtesy of Garden Milieu Inc.)

181

## DESIGN DRAWING OPTIONS

If the scale and intensity of your design services require the production of many proposals a day, an alternative to an original drawing and blueprint copies may be the use of a preprinted design form. This is a preprinted sheet that includes basic title block information, borders, and scale reference to develop quick yet professional looking proposals. An easy sheet size to use is 11" by 17", which equals two 8½" by 11" sheets when folded: this sheet size can be halved and

**Figure 7.15**

These concept drawings illustrate the idea of pre-printed design sheets. These proposed base sheets could include a printed title block and logo with a grid or dot pattern as the basis of scaled drawings. The advantage to these is they can be used on-site for quick concept sketches. Later clients and designers can work out additional or final ideas.

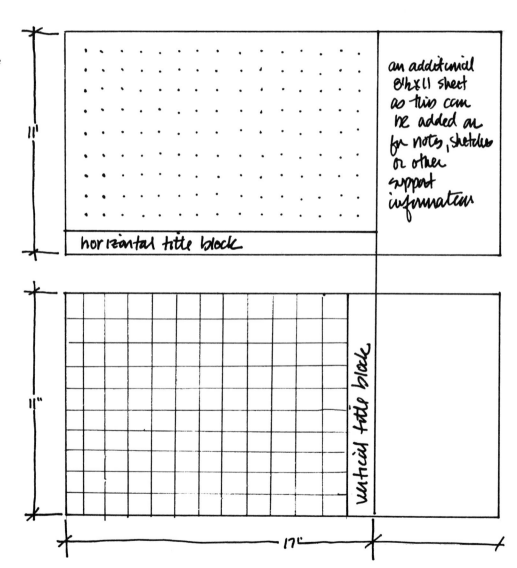

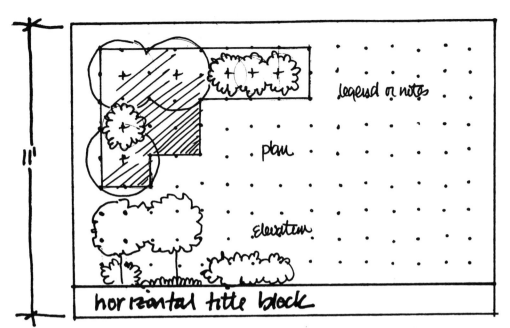

**Figure 7.16**
These examples illustrate how the pre-printed design sheets could be used in sketching out project ideas.

easily stored by clients or designers, and is easy to use in the field with a clipboard. Copies can also be made for the designer's use, with originals for the clients (Figure 7.15).

A preprinted grid or indication of inch subdivisions helps align and scale proposals on the sheet. A colored sheet that includes the company's logo is helpful in communicating your image and services. The colored sheet for presentations also provides a visible background when black and/or colors showing a proposal are added. Markers can be used to easily define plantings in one shade of green, specimen trees in a contrasting color, and accent or other plants in another. Edges can then be added to the colored symbols to define canopy versus ground plane elements and to indicate trunk locations. With practice, designs can even be developed on site or generated in the office, be consistent and professional in format, and yet be cost-effective for the scale and demands of a project (Figure 7.16).

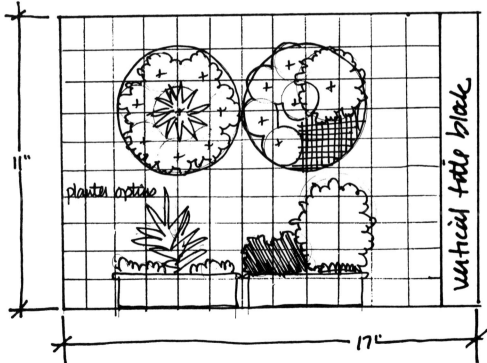

183

In practice, the on-site conceptualization of ideas for small scale design projects is valuable to both the client and the designer. For the client there is an immediate translation of ideas to the specific site situation. To the designer this sequence of inventory, analysis, and development of preliminary ideas is essentially the first step of design process. On-site planning is a method of communication whereby the designer defines and interprets the site conditions in combination with the client's requests. These rough sketches in plan and elevation are then used as a basis for further design and refinement.

## SUMMARY

Graphic presentation of design ideas requires an understanding of the basic components of a drawing and sheet in conjunction with a drafting and design process. Drawing and sheet composition include selection and development of a sheet, border, title block, drawing, labels, and leaders, etc. for a specific project and client.

# Chapter 8

# The Portfolio

The graphics included in this chapter are collected examples of interior design proposals, typical planting plans, sections, and sketches. Please remember that the plans and drawings have been photographically reduced and thus may not be of a scale that you can copy directly. Please review these drawings as incentives for developing your own symbols, styles, and skills in design. In conjunction with these collected ideas start making a design and graphics file of your own as you complete projects and/or see examples that you feel are appropriate to your situation. Graphics can be collected from newspapers, magazines, advertisements, etc. These in combination with design proposals and construction process photographs can develop into a design portfolio. As you develop projects in any area of interiorscaping, showing "visuals" to potential clients is one way of establishing credibility and visibility as a professional. For the designer, supplier, installer, and maintenance personal, reviewing design ideas is the first step in understanding and communicating design.

**Figure 8.1–8.2**

Published projects such as these half-tone pages can be used in portfolios or as public relations brochures. (Courtesy of Land Design/Research, Inc. Columbia, Maryland.)

## Hyatt Regency Chicago

Chicago, Illinois

LDR produced concepts and detailed designs for the major public spaces of the Hyatt Regency Hotel overlooking the Chicago River. As a member of the planning and design team for the 83-acre Illinois Center Air Rights Development, our services included design of the outdoor plazas, the hotel's enclosed walkway and concourses, and the interior lobby spaces.

The main lobby is a dramatic four-level, one-half acre glass atrium. This transparent enclosure furnishes excellent lighting for extensive interior landscaping. The central feature of the atrium is a 4,000 square foot reflecting pool surrounded by three restaurants, a cocktail lounge and the guest registration area. Contemporary-styled staircases, escalators, and a spiral ramp create exciting connections within this large multi-level interior space.

8.1

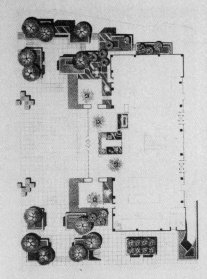

## Illinois Center Development
## Chicago, Illinois

**CLIENT**
Metropolitan Structures, Inc.
Illinois Center Corporation
**PROJECT SIZE**
48 acre site
**SERVICES**
Urban Design Plans,
Contract Drawings
**ARCHITECTS**
A. Epstein & Sons, Inc.
Fujikawa, Conterato,
Lohan, and Associates

8.2

8.3

**Figure 8.3–8.6**
These collected ads from magazines illustrate the
increased awareness and use of plants within interiors.
(8.3 and 8.4: Pace Collection Inc.; 8.5: Lutron
Electronics; 8.6: East Marsh Nurseries)

8.4

8.5

8.6

**8.7**

**Figures 8.7–8.10**

In these line drawings from magazines, line and texture
are the graphic skills used to convey the ideas in the
sketches and diagrammatic illustrations. (Drawings
courtesy of Kennedy, Brown, McQuiston Architects,
E. Schleef, designer: 8.8, ENKA Corporation; 8.9, USA
Corporation; 8.10, Grefco Corporation.)

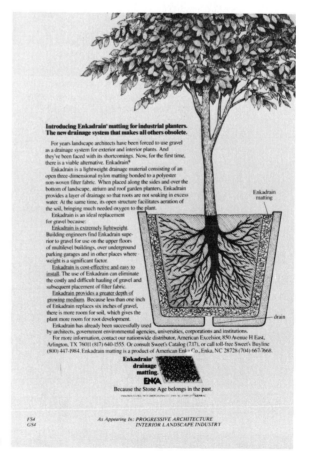

**8.8**

Courts for people in USAA's home office

8.9

8.10

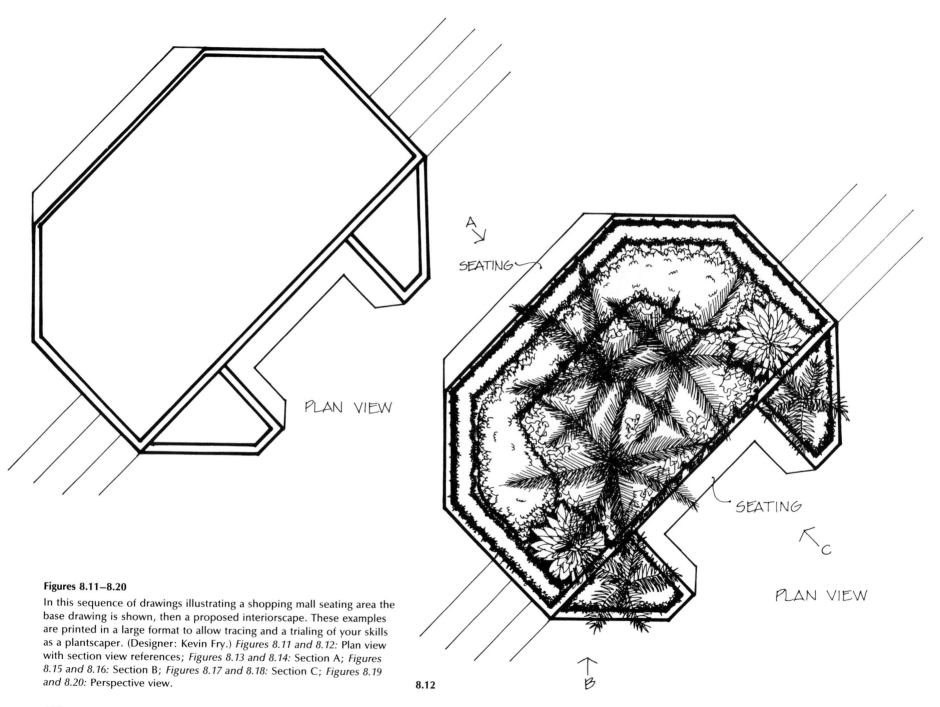

PLAN VIEW

A

SEATING

SEATING

C

PLAN VIEW

B

**Figures 8.11–8.20**

In this sequence of drawings illustrating a shopping mall seating area the base drawing is shown, then a proposed interiorscape. These examples are printed in a large format to allow tracing and a trialing of your skills as a plantscaper. (Designer: Kevin Fry.) *Figures 8.11 and 8.12:* Plan view with section view references; *Figures 8.13 and 8.14:* Section A; *Figures 8.15 and 8.16:* Section B; *Figures 8.17 and 8.18:* Section C; *Figures 8.19 and 8.20:* Perspective view.

8.12

192

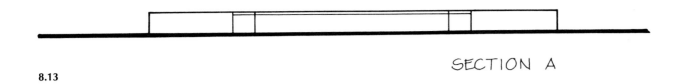

SECTION A

**8.13**

**8.14**                                                            SECTION  A

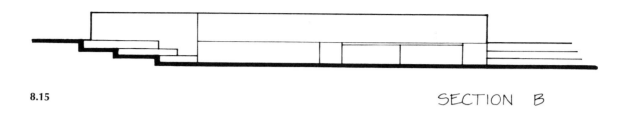

SECTION   B

SECTION B

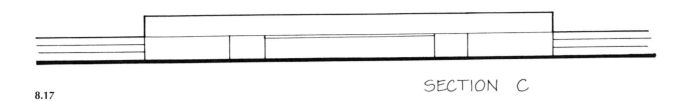

SECTION C

8.17

SECTION C

8.18

195

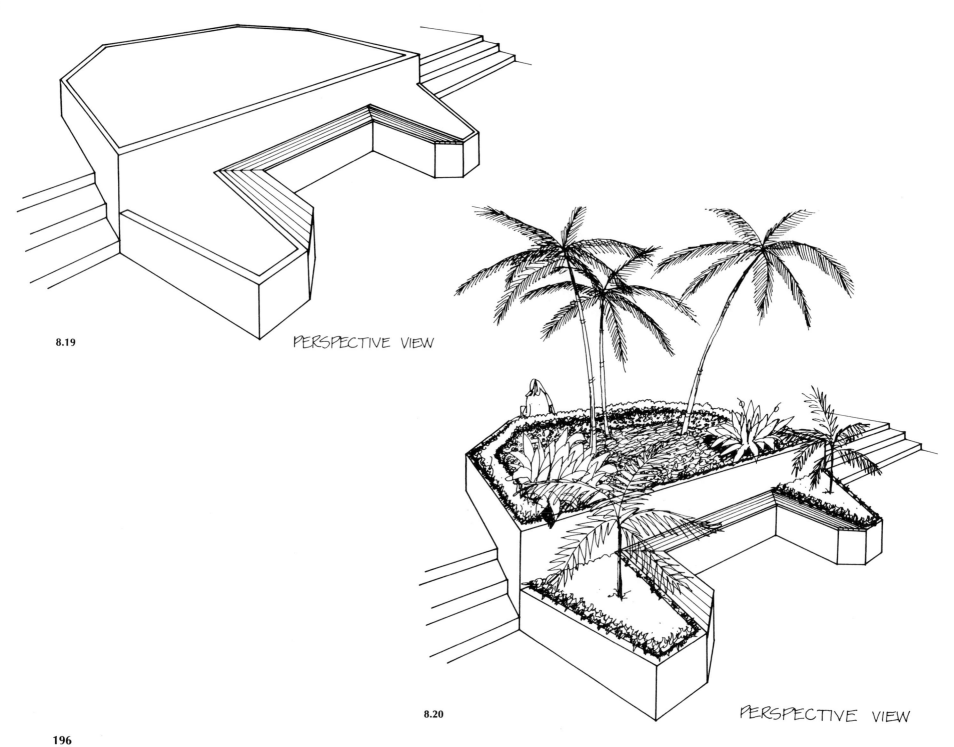

8.19  PERSPECTIVE VIEW

8.20  PERSPECTIVE VIEW

**Figure 8.21**
This interiorscape illustration uses line and texture to define the space and furnishings. (Designer: Roger Winstead.)

**Figure 8.22**
When working with a collaborative design situation, try to have related drawings developed, usually in the same graphic style. This exterior sketch is the entry to the interior seen in Figure 8.21. (Designer: Roger Winstead.)

**Figure 8.23**
This interior sketch uses a variety of line weights, textures, and line shading to create depth in the drawing. (Designer: R. P. Strychalski.)

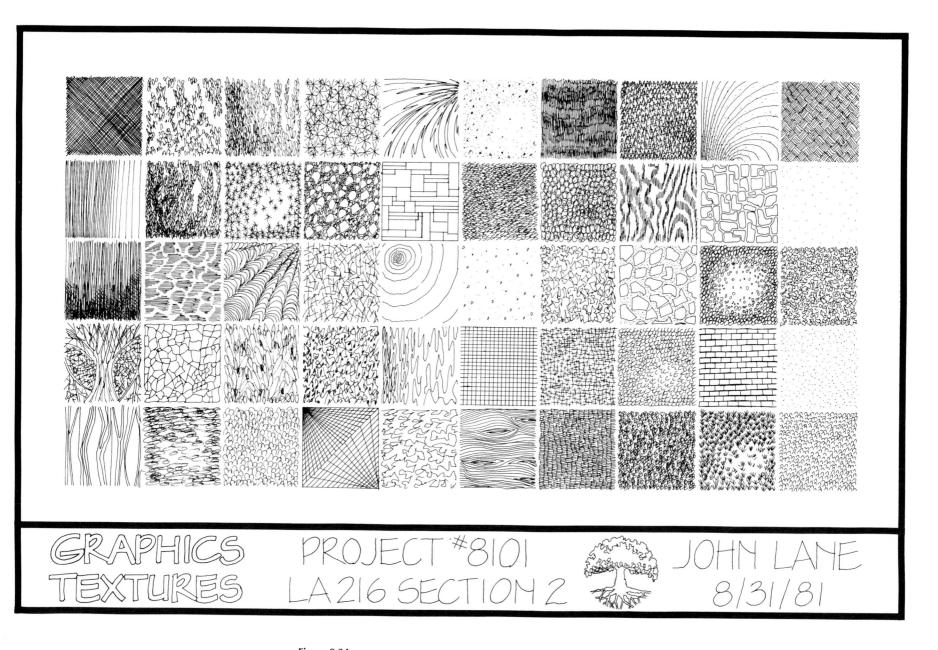

**Figure 8.24**
Practicing textures and developing patterns in a file or catalog format can be a time-saver for current or future project developments. (Designer: John Lane.)

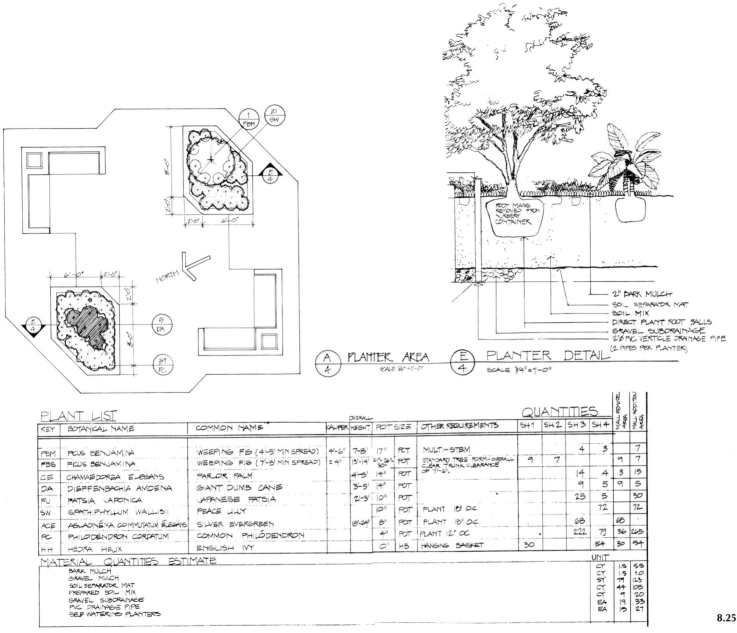

**PLANT LIST** | **QUANTITIES**

| KEY | BOTANICAL NAME | COMMON NAME | CALIPER | OVERALL HEIGHT | POT SIZE | OTHER REQUIREMENTS | SH 1 | SH 2 | SH 3 | SH 4 | MALL REMODEL AREA | MALL ADDITION AREA |
|-----|----------------|-------------|---------|----------------|----------|--------------------|------|------|------|------|------|------|
| FBM | FICUS BENJAMINA | WEEPING FIG (4'-5' MIN SPREAD) | 4'-6" | 7'-8' | 17" | FCT MULTI-STEM | | | 4 | 3 | | 7 |
| FBS | FICUS BENJAMINA | WEEPING FIG (7'-8' MIN SPREAD) | ±4" | 13'-14' | 21"-26"L, 30" POT | STANDARD TREE FORM-OVERALL CLEAR TRUNK CLEARANCE OF 7'-6" | 9 | 7 | | | 9 | 7 |
| CE | CHAMAEDOREA ELEGANS | PARLOR PALM | | 4'-5' | 14" POT | | | | 14 | 4 | 3 | 15 |
| DA | DIEFFENBACHIA AMOENA | GIANT DUMB CANE | | 3'-5' | 14" POT | | | | 9 | 5 | 9 | 5 |
| FU | FATSIA JAPONICA | JAPANESE FATSIA | | 2'-3' | 10" POT | | | | 25 | 5 | | 30 |
| SW | SPATHIPHYLLUM WALLISII | PEACE LILY | | | 10" POT | PLANT 18" O.C. | | | 72 | | | 72 |
| ACE | AGLAONEMA COMMUTATUM ELEGANS | SILVER EVERGREEN | | 18"-24" | 8" POT | PLANT 18" O.C. | | | 68 | | 68 | |
| PC | PHILODENDRON CORDATUM | COMMON PHILODENDRON | | | 4" POT | PLANT 12" OC | | | 222 | 79 | 36 | 265 |
| HH | HEDRA HELIX | ENGLISH IVY | | | 10" HB | HANGING BASKET | 30 | | 54 | | 30 | 54 |

**MATERIAL QUANTITIES ESTIMATE**

| | UNIT | | |
|---|------|------|------|
| BARK MULCH | CY | 1.5 | 5.5 |
| GRAVEL MULCH | CY | 1.5 | 1.0 |
| SOIL SEPARATOR MAT | SY | 79 | 123 |
| PREPARED SOIL MIX | CY | 44 | 108 |
| GRAVEL SUBDRAINAGE | CY | 9 | 20 |
| PVC DRAINAGE PIPE | EA | 19 | 33 |
| SELF WATERING PLANTERS | EA | 15 | 27 |

A/4 PLANTER AREA SCALE 1/4" = 1'-0"

E/4 PLANTER DETAIL SCALE 3/4" = 1'-0"

2" BARK MULCH
SOIL SEPARATOR MAT
SOIL MIX
DIRECT PLANT ROOT BALLS
GRAVEL SUBDRAINAGE
2" Ø PVC VERTICLE DRAINAGE PIPE (2 PIPES PER PLANTER)

ROOT MASS REMOVED FROM NURSERY CONTAINER

## GENERAL NOTES

1. LAYOUT AND DETAIL INFORMATION OF EXISTING MALL PLANTER AREAS WAS TAKEN FROM PRINTS ENTITLED COLLEGE MALL SHOPPING CENTER REMODEL BY KEN CARR & ASSOCIATES, INDIANAPOLIS, DATED FEBRUARY 21, 1980

2. LAYOUT AND DETAIL INFORMATION OF MALL ADDITION PLANTER AREAS WAS TAKEN FROM PRINTS ENTITLED COLLEGE MALL SHOPPING CENTER BUILDING EXPANSION BY GEUPEL DEMARS, INDIANAPOLIS, DATED 11-12-79.

8.25

**Figures 8.25 and 8.26**

Design proposals usually require more than plan drawings. In these projects the design intent is conveyed by the plan, section, and written plant schedules. Included are plant lists, materials estimates, and project notes. (Courtesy of Melvin-Simon Associates.)

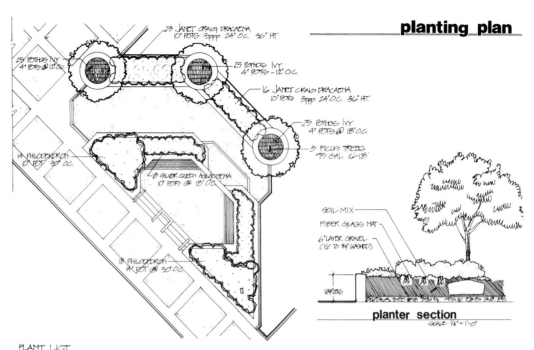

# planting plan

**23 JANET CRAIG DRACAENA** 10' POTS 3PPP 24' O.C. 36" HT

**25 POTHOS IVY** 4' POTS @ 12' O.C.

**25 POTHOS IVY** 4' POTS -12' O.C.

**16 JANET CRAIG DRACAENA** 10' POTS 3PPP 24' O.C. 36" HT

**25 POTHOS IVY** 4' POTS @ 18' O.C.

**3 FICUS TREES** 45 GAL. 16-18'

**14 PHILODENDRON** 10' POT 30' O.C.

**18 SILVER GREEN AGLAONEMA** 10' POTS @ 18' O.C.

**18 PHILODENDRON** 4" POT @ 30' O.C.

SOIL MIX
FIBER GLASS MAT
6' LAYER GRAVEL (1/2 TO 3/4 WASHED)
VARIES

## planter section
SCALE: 1/4" = 1'-0"

## PLANT LIST

| KEY | BOTANICAL NAME | COMMON NAME | CALIPER | HEIGHT | POT SIZE | | OTHER REQUIREMENTS | QUANTITY |
|-----|----------------|-------------|---------|--------|----------|--|--------------------|----------|
| FBM | FICUS BENJAMINA | WEEPING FIG (4'-5' MIN SPREAD) | 4'-6" | 7-8' | 17" | POT | MULTI-STEM | 7 |
| FBS | FICUS BENJAMINA | WEEPING FIG (7'-8' MIN SPREAD) | ± 4" | 13-14' | 21"-26"-30" | POT | STANDARD TREE FORM - OVERALL. CLEAR TRUNK CLEARANCE OF 7'-6" | 16 |
| CE | CHAMAEDOREA ELEGANS | PARLOR PALM | | 4-5' | 14" | POT | | 18 |
| DA | DIEFENBACHIA AMOENA | GIANT DUMB CANE | | 3-5' | 14" | POT | | 14 |
| FJ | FATSIA JAPONICA | JAPANESE FATSIA | | 2-3' | 10" | POT | | 30 |
| SW | SPATHIPHYLLUM WALLISII | PEACE LILLY | | | 10" | POT | PLANT 18" O.C. | 72 |
| ACE | AGLAONEMA COMMUTATUM ELEGANS | SILVER EVERGREEN | | 18"-24" | 8" | POT | PLANT 18" O.C. | 68 |
| PC | PHILODENDRON CORDATUM | COMMON PHILODENDRON | | | 4" | POT | PLANT 12" O.C. | 304 |
| HH | HEDRA HELIX | ENGLISH IVY | | | 10" | HB | HANGING BASKET | 84 |

## MATERIALS QUANTITIES ESTIMATE

| | | UNIT | |
|--|--|------|--|
| BARK MULCH | | C.Y. | 7.0 |
| GRAVEL MULCH | | C.Y. | 2.5 |
| SOIL SEPARATOR MAT | | S.Y. | 202 |
| PREPARED SOIL MIX | | C.Y. | 149 |
| GRAVEL SUBDRAINAGE | | C.Y. | 29 |
| PVC DRAINAGE PIPE | | EA. | 52 |
| SELF WATERING PLANTERS | | EA. | 42 |

## GENERAL NOTES

1. ALL OVERHEAD SELF-WATERING PLANTERS REQUIRE PLACEMENT OF A PREPARED SOIL MIX.
2. EXACT NUMBER & LOCATION OF HOSE BIBS IN THE MALL REMODEL AREA IS UNKNOWN.

**8.26**

**Figure 8.27**
Freehand sketches can be used to communicate the basic essence of a proposal. Here soft-tipped markers are used to create the leaf and plant forms. (Designer: Kevin Fry.)

**Figure 8.28**

In this line drawing only a portion of the project is shown. The porch railing is used as framing for the conservatory. (Designer: Kevin Fry.)

**Figure 8.29**
This silhouette sketch recreates the essence of this interior gazebo setting area. (Designer: Kevin Fry.)

**Figure 8.30**
This sketch emphasizes the fountain, sculpture, and water feature. The planting is only outlined as background for the sketch. (Designer: Kevin Fry.)

**Figure 8.31**
This outline drawing is given scale with the use of figures on the benches. (Designer: Kevin Fry.)

**Figure 8.32**
This scene illustrates the water feature, the brick wall, and the massed
background plantings. (Designer: Kevin Fry.)

**Figure 8.33**
This atrium planting sketch in pencil conveys plants in a softer mode.
(Designer: Kevin Fry.)

**Figure 8.34**
This pencil sketch in a more simplistic style conveys the essence of a court seating area with canopy tree. (Designer: Kevin Fry.)

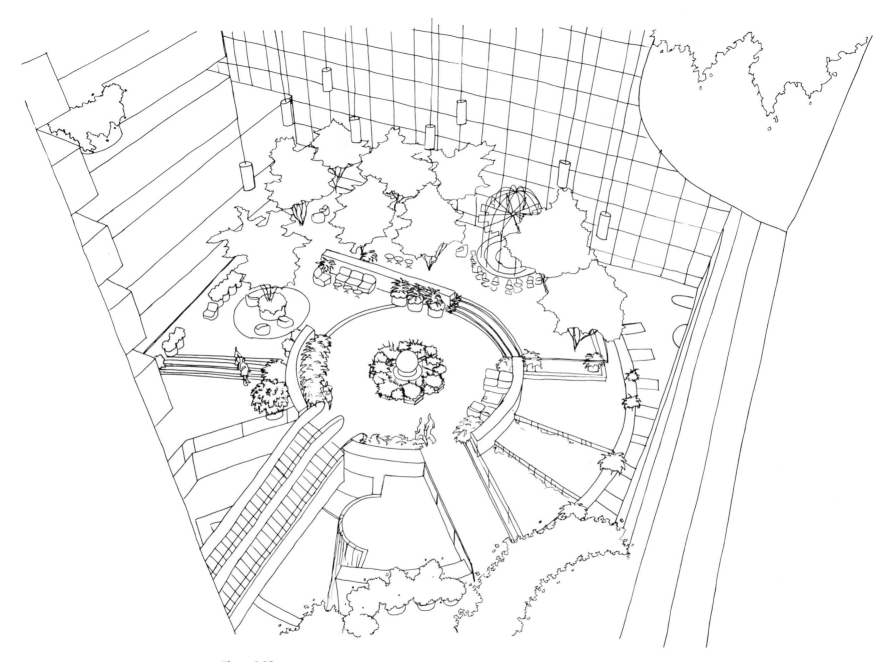

**Figure 8.35**
This aerial perspective is based on a slide that was projected and traced.
The sketch shows the basic outline of atrium areas and plantings.
(Designer: Kevin Fry.)

**Figure 8.36**
This lounge area is an enlargement of an area from the previous illustration. At this size more detail can be included. (Designer: Kevin Fry.)

**Figure 8.37**
To fully communicate the atrium space, this upper view of the space is
drawn in pencil. (Designer: Kevin Fry.)

**Figures 8.38 and 8.39**

These line drawings illustrate the renovated and designed atrium at the Butler Building in Minneapolis, Minnesota. The atrium, which was carved through a warehouse building, provides an ideal space for balcony planters. (Designer: Kevin Fry.)

8.38

8.39

**Figure 8.40**

This halftone image is an interior proposal for a restaurant. The mediums used were sharpie and colored markers to create a basic design concept. (Designer: Renee Zurad.)

**Figure 8.41**
This smaller-scale interior uses a simple marker style. Note that the treatments of the furnishings, plants, floor, and window are representational, not exact. (Designer: Renee Zurad.)

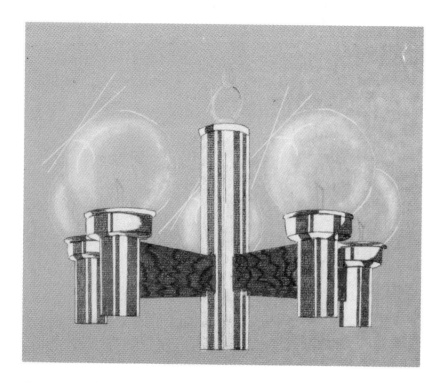

**Figures 8.42 and 8.43**

Material representation is a graphic skill which is often
necessary to illustrate design ideas. In these drawings,
markers are used to convey marble, brick, glass, and
chrome. In Figure 8.43 the delineation of shadows helps
define the light source, the space, and other textures.
(Designer: R. Mumaw.)

8.42

218

8.43

# Chapter 9

# Catalogue of Design Ideas

A collection of interior planting design projects is included to illustrate the actual application of interiorscape concepts. The projects include offices, shopping areas, hotels, and other public applications of interiorscaping. When reviewing these examples, start to evaluate the planning, graphics, and design considerations used in the proposal. Hopefully the variety of proposals can serve as a resource book of ideas for you and potential clients.

## OFFICES

**Reception area: (Figure 9.1).** This reception area at Tropical Plant Rentals includes a focal point photo of the Deere Company Atrium as developed by T. P. R. This photo exhibits the quality of design and installation they provide.

**Figure 9.1**
This reception area includes floor plants, a live flower arrangement, and a photo graphic to communicate a positive image and feeling as you arrive. (Tropical Plant Rentals, Chicago, Illinois.)

The desk is accented by a live flower arangement; an upright ming aralia provides framing and background in the corner. The scheme is simple and can easily be changed when needed.

**Reception area: (Figure 9.2).** This multi-level entry to the Lumberman Insurance Office in Indianapolis, Indiana is seen from an upper balcony level view. The unified plantings not only help tie the floors together visually but provide that needed "green" accent. The movable floor plants at the reception level and on the balconies allow plant cycling within the space if necessary.

**Figure 9.2**
An inviting foyer and balcony planting (Courtesy of Engledow Inc.)

**Reception area: (Figures 9.3 and 9.4).** This small office is developed using the open office system with three-quarter walls and plants as space definers. Figure 9.3 illustrates the architectural and aesthetic uses of plants within the otherwise stark interior. Figure 9.4 show the use of plantings to separate the reception and work areas.

**Banking facility offices: (Figure 9.5).** This interior is an open office area in a bank. The interior scheme includes wooden furniture and movable wooden planters as space dividers. The permanent plantings include dracaenas for the low light situation with mums for seasonal additions of color. A brass container with palm in the foreground accents this account manager's space, while the simpler plantings and planters are used to provide separation. The planting height still allows enclosure and supervision within the office area.

**Atrium areas: (Figure 9.6).** This office atrium includes movable planters throughout its space to allow for maximum use flexibility and potential plant cycling: moving plants from low light to higher light situations. The plants at the ground floor and banners from above provide both scale and visual interest. The plantings on the upper level provide accents for clients on that floor, as well as visual links between the floors as clients look across the atrium.

9.3

**Figure 9.3 and 9.4**

This reception area is accented with floor planters and a wall divider planter. Due to the low lighting, these plants most likely will be used on a rental basis to maintain plant quality and design integrity. (Courtesy of Engledow Inc.)

9.4

**Figure 9.5**
Business offices such as this bank space often use plants for their attractiveness. Here, the plants also serve as a space divider. (Courtesy of Engledow Inc.)

**Figure 9.6**
This triangular-shaped atrium and plantings include groups of plants situated on brick surfaces in the corridor. The surfacing reduces water damage and allows for varied plant arrangements. (Courtesy of Engledow Inc.)

**Atrium area: (Figure 9.7).** This commercial area is a renovated building with an atrium addition. As you look at the photo, the image you see is actually mirrored glass reflecting the balcony areas adjoining the space, as well as the space behind the camera vantage. The office areas seen in the lower portion of the photo are visible because the interior lights are illuminated. This atrium concept, developed by Melvin Simon of Indianapolis, Indiana is diagrammed in Figure 9.8.

9.7

**Figure 9.7 and 9.8**

This atrium, which is part of the renovation of an existing building, includes a mirrored rear wall to reflect light into office areas. Figure 9.8 illustrates this concept and the total atrium within the building.

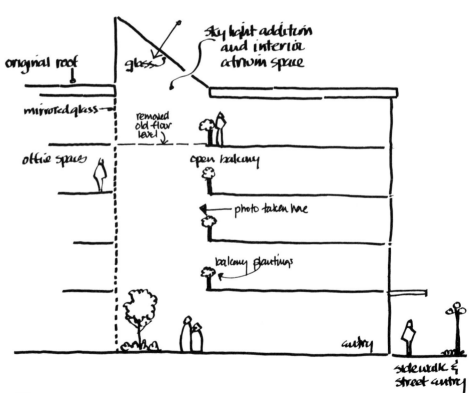

9.8

9.9

**Figure 9.9 and 9.10**
In these general office areas both designed planters and individual plants are included to accent the interior.

**Office corridors: (Figure 9.9).** This photo illustrates the use of pothos in built-in planters along the corridor. The plants provide visual relief along the linear walkways and, through the upper glass areas, for the office personnel on the adjoining side. When the plantings become too leggy they are pruned or replaced.

**Office spaces: (Figure 9.10).** In this office area potted plants are included in combination with files as dividers. Plants are located so that no file drawer conflicts with vining plants.

9.10

9.11

**Office cafeteria areas: (Figure 9.11).** Client and employee areas are the usual locations for intensive office plantings. Here the cafeteria is complemented with flexible plantings that can be cycled for light, to allow adaptable use of the space.

**Office cafeteria areas: (Figures 9.12 and 9.13).** In these cafeteria areas skylights provide an accent and illumination for plant growth. In Figure 9.12 the light is natural and thus of sufficient intensity to grow trees from species and understory plants. In Figure 9.13 the skylight is artificial; the low light necessitates low light plantings with no large canopy plantings to shade plants.

**Figures 9.11–9.13**
These cafeteria planting situations illustrate three light sources. Included are window walls, which give natural side light, a skylight, which provides natural overhead illumination, and artificially-illuminated skylights.

9.12

9.13

**9.14**

**Figures 9.14–9.21**
This sequence of photos communicates the milti-level atrium, created as
a focus to interior office spaces. The space, while providing a view for
interior offices, is a central building focus as well. (Location: John Deere
Corporation, Moline, Illinois.)

**Office atrium.** One of the ultimate office atriums developed in the 1970's by the Deere Corporation in Moline,
Illinois is illustrated in Chapter 1, Figures 1.6 and 1.7, and in
this resource section. The main building exterior was developed using simple lines by architect Eril Saranan. The atrium
shown in Figures 9.14–9.21 is central to an office addition
adjoining this primary building. The atrium was developed
to provide a view of plantings for people in interior office
spaces, and provide corridor and cafeteria focus. Figure 9.14
illustrates the view as you enter the brick area. As you move
to the right in the space you cross a mirrored walkway
through the plantings. Figure 9.15 conveys your vantage
from the bridge and provides a dramatic view of the atrium
space and garden (Figures 9.16–9.18). As you move to the
lower garden areas the stepping stones lead you to a terrace

**9.15**

9.16

9.17

9.18

9.19

9.20

space adjoining the cafeteria (Figure 9.19). In the planting design details even the spaces between stepping stones have a ground planting (Figure 9.20). The overall effect is of a dynamic space with form, textural, and color interest that is in scale with the space and people who use it (Figure 9.21).

9.21

9.22

**Figures 9.22 and 9.23**
High traffic sales areas often include plants as a focal point and as accents to attract customers to these areas. (Photos by D. G. Smith.)

9.23

## SHOPPING/COMMERCIAL AREAS

**Store interiors: (Figures 9.22–9.25).** Plantings have become a part of the customer and sales areas within the retail industry. Figure 9.22 illustrates the use of potted plants in the high traffic cosmetic sales area in a department store.

Figure 9.23 shows large floor plants used as transitions between furniture sample rooms. The plants add scale and a human element that nothing else can provide. Store illumination can influence the effectiveness of plants as is seen in Figures 9.24 and 9.25. These plants are in adjoining niches yet the illumination influences their appearance greatly.

**9.24**

**9.25**

**Figures 9.24 and 9.25**
Lighting affects how plants look in an interior. In this comparison of plantings, the photo with accent lighting creates a much better impression. (Photos by D. G. Smith.)

**Store accessways: (Figure 9.26).** The architecture of this escalator area is accented by designed permanent planters. The stepped plants provide interest, enclosure, and scale to the area as people move through it. In Figure 9.26 showing the entrance to a mall anchor store, the transition between levels is achieved with light standards, terraced stairs, and some plantings. Note that the planters at the columns near the store entry are underscaled for the vertical dimension of the space.

**Store court area: (Figure 9.27).** This urban shopping court is the accessway and focus of stores and corridor balconies. The permanent plantings include simple sculptural palms, with seasonal accents of potted floor plants provided for scale and transition. The floor accent pots of seasonal color include varying sizes and shapes of containers for material and textural accents within the space.

**Figures 9.26 and 9.27**

Mall store entries should be planted to focus patrons to the doors. Planting alignments and heights should not hide the doors or the company's name, but should frame the view.

9.27

9.26

**Figures 9.28 and 9.29**
Individual design details and compositions often vary from project location to location. In these photos the design concept of the architecture and plantings are quite different. The variations are often due to budget differences that reflect the economics of the locale. (Photos by Richard Wade, Melvin-Simon Associates.)

**Mall/store entry.** Figures 9.28 and 9.29 illustrate two mall locations with variations in the treatment of anchor store entry–corridor spaces. Figure 9.28 shows an anchor store with very large plantings at the structural building columns. This scene is contrasted to a similar entry with a diagonal skylight, plantings, seating areas, and a floor pattern which creates interest in the store front space (Figure 9.29).

9.28

9.29

**9.30**

**Mall corridor areas.** Figures 9.30 and 9.31 illustrate the before and after renovation of a mall corridor. Included were changes in the floor surfacings, ceilings, and lighting, with the addition of skylights, new site furnishings, and plantings. Figure 9.30 shows the original permanent seating areas, planters, and artificial lighting. The lighting and dark color scheme made the space dull and unflexible. The renovation as illustrated in Figure 9.31 in another corridor area includes lighter colored floors and a ceiling with natural skylights which helps the overall appearance. The flexible planters and seating areas allow for more adaptive uses such as temporary display shows, while providing more open circulation and views to stores.

**Figures 9.30 and 9.31**

Corridor areas, just as in the store entrance examples, show variations between locales. Project location, budget, and management often influence design and development. (Photos by Richard Wade, Melvin-Simon Associates.)

**9.31**

**9.32**

**Figures 9.32 and 9.33**
Planter selection and placement within architectural spaces should relate
to the floor plan, traffic floor surfacing, and ceiling details. The examples
show two approaches to similar mall situations (Photos by Richard Wade,
Melvin-Simon Associates.)

**9.33**

**Mall court areas.** Figures 9.32 and 9.33 illustrate how
architectural and planting changes can occur in the design
and development of malls. The entry area in Figure 9.32
shows the original artificial light and a rectangular ceiling–
floor design. Figure 9.33 shows a comparable space developed with a diagonal ceiling–floor pattern to contrast with
the rectangular corridor and store fronts.

9.34

**Mall furnishings: (Figures 9.34 and 9.35).** The plants, plantings, seating, trash receptacles, and so on can be a unifying element within the complex. These photos show how the repetition of planters and furnishings adds contemporary accent, unifying the renovated mall court and adjoining corridor spaces.

**Shopping court theme: (Figures 9.36–9.40).** In the Country Club Plaza shopping area of Kansas City, Missouri, an architectural theme of brick, tile, and wrought iron has given this area unity and notoriety since its development in the early 1920s (Figure 9.36). The attention to detail as a tradition is continued in new additions and in the renovation of spaces. In the redevelopment of a store area the Seville Square Complex was developed (Figure 9.37). The kiosk and pavement pattern establishes a theme that starts at the sidewalk and is carried into the newly created spaces and atrium. (Figure 9.38). The space was opened to the roof

**Figures 9.34 and 9.35**
Interior mall fixtures, planters, benches, trash receptacles, and so on should be selected and located to complement the space. Functionally they should work with traffic and should consider the sight lines of shoppers. (Photos by Richard Wade, Melvin-Simon Associates.)

9.35

9.36

**Figures 9.36–9.40**

In this photo sequence, the distinctive brick and tile detailing of the building exterior is extended into the store spaces of Country Club Plaza in Kansas City, Missouri. In this renovated structure, the construction material selection, planters, and plants reinforce the detailed theme established for the locale.

9.37

9.38

to allow a shaft of light to fall to the floors below, creating a pleasing focus for the four story building (Figure 9.39). The selection of plantings and containers helps reinforce the theme and add life to the space while matching the established architectural theme. In other situations the architecture and interior may make such a strong architectural or design statement that little or no plantings may be the best choice, as seen at the American Restaurant at the Crown Center in Kansas City, Missouri (Figures 9.41 and 9.42).

9.39

9.40

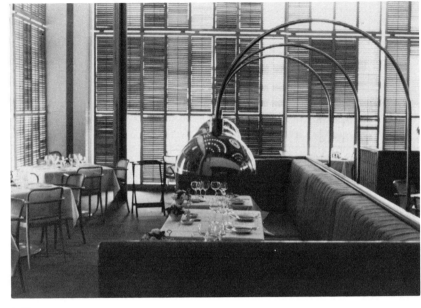

**9.42**

**Figures 9.41 and 9.42**
The American Restaurant at the Crown Center in Kansas City, Missouri, is a designed interior that uses only table flowers as plant accents. The project location and design focus is on the food, interior design, and city view beyond the restaurant walls.

**9.41**

These photos illustrate the exterior and the detailed interior design. The only plants used are at the reception area off the elevator, adjoining the lounge. Selected flower accents at the tables are the only dining room additions. The theme of the interior views is the city skyline, thus few interior plantings are included.

9.43

## HOTELS

**Lobby and reception areas: (Figures 9.43–9.45).** The simple architectural lines of this hotel lobby area can be seen in the design and construction materials as well as the massed plantings (Figure 9.43). As a contrast in size and design, the lobby–atrium area seen in Figures 9.44 and 9.45 has simple lines yet includes a distinctive theme of massed plantings as a central focus. Screening, seasonal accents, and sculptural plants complement the space. As a seasonal accent the hotel has used a pyramid poinsettia display.

**Figures 9.43–9.45**
A lobby and reception area, where groups of people gather, provides a great opportunity for showy interiorscape displays.

9.44

9.45

**Lobby atrium/restaurant area.** In this hotel, the atrium is also the primary restaurant as seen in Figures 9.46–9.49. The space provides daily client services as well as being the focus of a Sunday brunch for the community, as is staged in Figure 9.46. The upper space areas provide a lounge area at night. The main floor area is divided into subspaces using built-in planters, screens, and potted plantings. This multiple use concept is also seen in the conservatory at the Opryland Hotel. The 2-acre planted conservatory with two level walkways, plantings, and fountains provides a central focus to the entry. The entire facility, with adjoining rooms, is an attractive background for an excellent ground-level restaurant (Figures 9.50–9.52).

9.47

**Figures 9.46–9.49**

In this hotel/commercial office atrium, plantings are used both aesthetically and functionally. Plants on tables serve as accents, and floor and area planters are designed as space definers and for scale in the four-story atrium.

9.46

9.48

9.49

**Figures 9.50–9.52**

The Opryland Hotel atrium includes a two-level walk through the garden area and restaurant. These zones are defined and complemented by the selection and composition of the plantings within the overall atrium.

9.50

9.51

9.52

9.53

## CONSERVATORIES, ATRIUMS

**Atriums/conservatories.** Growing plantings indoors is not a new concept: the Linnaean House built in the early 1900's at the Missouri Botanic Garden illustrates the development of plants and gardens within buildings (Figures 9.53 and 9.54). These same concepts have been applied in the newly constructed entry and education center at the Garden in the Ridgeway Center (Figures 9.55–9.57). The vaulted ceiling skylight provides a distinctive architectural and plant environment statement. Open and skylighted spaces are becoming part of architecture as seen at the University of Houston at Clear Lake City atriums (Figures 9.58 and 9.59).

**Figures 9.53 and 9.54**
Historically, early conservatories were structurally heavy due to their construction of brick, narrow side windows, and partial steel and glass roofs. This type of construction is seen at the Linnaean House at the Missouri Botanic Garden, St. Louis, Missouri.

9.54

244

**Figures 9.55–9.57**
To contrast these early conservatories, the newly-constructed Ridgeway Center at the Missouri Botanic Garden provides a dramatic conservatory and entry to the gardens.

9.55

9.56

9.57

9.58

9.59

**Figures 9.58 and 9.59**
At the University of Houston, Clear Lake City, two atriums provide an interior focus for faculty and students alike. The designed atrium skylight area provides the necessary ingredient for plant success.

The benefits of natural light for people and plants and the potential passive solar gain are concepts being incorporated into a residential design as seen in Figures 9.60 and 9.61, and Figures 1.31 and 1.32 in Chapter 1.

**Skylights.** The use of natural light for illumination, effect, and plant growth in architecture can be seen in the Loews-Antiole Hotel in Dallas. As you view the building from the expressway (Figure 9.62) the skylight roof is a de-

9.60

**Figures 9.60 and 9.61**
Passive solar considerations and numerous plants are a part of the home environment in this single-family residence.

9.61

9.62

structive element of the building. The resulting interior space is an atrium of ten stories as seen in Figure 9.63. Because of the distance from the light source to the ground, the plant selection and design needs to be organized with the high light plants to the north edge so they receive maximum light. If skylights are glazed or mirrored surfaces, an accurate evaluation of actual interior light is necessary. Often the glazing can reduce available light by 70%. Skylights in architecture can also be used as accents to define open spaces, as seen in the Herbarium Building at the Missouri Botanic Garden (Figures 9.64–9.66). The skylight relates to a central axis of the building and provides illumination, yet there are minimal plants. In this case the function of the building—preservation of herbarium specimens—limits plant use due to insect and disease related implications.

**Figures 9.62 and 9.63**
In commercial and institutional buildings, skylights and the resulting interior atriums are becoming common. Here in The Loews-Antitole Hotel in Dallas, Texas, the interior atrium provides a relaxing lounge area and dramatic view for guests from surrounding balconies.

9.63

## SUMMARY

Hopefully these examples have been helpful in conveying the design applications of plantings indoors. As you develop projects take before, during, and after photos to create your own design resource book. You may also use these examples to convey design concepts of similar project spaces to prospective design clients. Remember that examples help convey concepts better than verbal or written explanations.

9.64

9.65

9.66

**Figure 9.64–9.66**
At the Herbarium Building on the grounds of the Missouri Botanic Garden, glass side walls reflect the garden surroundings. An interior skylight brings natural light into the interior for employees and patrons alike.

# Chapter 10

# Shopping Malls

Shopping and commercial areas are one of the major interiorscape focus areas within the interior planting industry. Included in this chapter are two case study examples of shopping mall interiorplantscaping. The first is an example of how maintenance and management practices can dilute and destroy the initial planting design concepts. The second is a planting project for a mall with plans, details, and before, during, and after photos of its development.

Shopping malls, as any design situation, change over time influenced by the changes in use, management, and maintenance practices. The regional shopping mall included in this discussion illustrates changes in the visual character of the primary court areas and corridor spaces. The basic floor plan of the two-story mall is illustrated in Figure 10.1. As you review this scheme the planting court areas at the ends of the mall and the central diagonal area will be illustrated in photos. The time span represented in the photos is

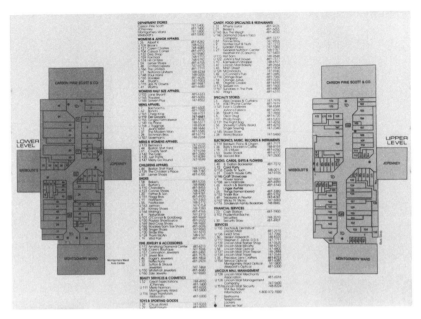

**Figure 10.1**

Mall floor plans such as this locator directory illustrate the mall's overall layout, its levels, store locations, and corridor spaces, all of which involve human traffic and potential plantings.

one year after opening vs. six years after opening. Figures 10.2–10.4 illustrate the image and design changes that have occurred in the court area outside an anchor store. Once the focus of the court space, the fountain is now cluttered with too many different plant species. The once lively space is now made static by an overly-complex planting. A simple massing of a few species would be better.

The architectural design of the mall has exceptional skylights and light for plant growth as seen in Figure 10.5. Basic maintenance and grooming practices have had their toll on the plantings as seen in Figures 10.6 and 10.7. The primary practices have encouraged leggy-looking tree forms rather than using a thinning practice which permits light to reach lower plant areas, thus creating a denser specimen. This area shown is the upper level of the fountain court area seen

**Figure 10.2**

This stair and anchor store entry court included planting and a water feature as part of the initial design.

**10.3**

**Figures 10.3 and 10.4**
Many years after the mall's opening, design and development decisions caused dramatic planting changes in this court area from what was seen in Figure 10.2. The added plantings were made simpler and massed so that the area would be visually more attractive within the space.

**10.4**

**Figure 10.5**
The skylights that were part of the mall's original architecture provide the natural light necessary for plant growth and development. If plant selection and placement is not appropriate, the results can be visually distracting.

10.7

10.6

**Figures 10.6 and 10.7**
These seating area photos illustrate an initial planting, and the same area many years later. The canopy fig trees have clumped leaf patches, most likely due to pruning practices. Poor maintenance causes the plants to shade lower leaf areas out. Pruning practices should strive to open the crown areas up to allow adequate light through the crown, thus keeping lower branches vital and attractive.

in Figures 10.2–10.4. Another fountain area in an anchor store entry court was also filled in with plantings (Figures 10.8 and 10.9). The resulting one-sided planting is due to lack of light for plants in the back side of the planter.

In the central diagonal court areas of the mall, escalators connect shoppers with the two levels. Figures 10.10 and 10.11 show a comparison of the upper level landing before and after. The before (Figure 10.10) shows a scaled space subdivided by movable plants and seating areas. Today this area is stark and open (Figure 10.11).

**10.8**

**Figures 10.8 and 10.9**

This court area once included a fountain that has since been planted. The area was not initially planned as a planter and thus has inadequate light. On the store side of the planter the plants create a poor visual image. Plant survival on this shaded side of the planter (as viewed when exiting the store) will be limited.

**10.9**

**10.10**

**Figures 10.10 and 10.11**
Once, when shoppers reached the upper level from the escalator, floor planters and fixtures greeted patrons. The planters also defined a seating area. Today, this area is open and barren.

**10.11**

To create a transition between the two levels the original design included sculptural elements projecting up and down from the various levels. Figures 10.12 and 10.13 illustrate an effective use of a floor sculpture and mobile type sculpture elements in combination with floor plantings. One last planting area that has changed is seen in Figures 10.14 and 10.15. Here, due to whatever reason, the plantings have been changed from a simple bold mass planting to a mixed assortment which doesn't have the same mass or visual effect.

10.13

10.12

**Figures 10.12 and 10.13**
Original mall sculptures help to visually and physically connect two-level shopping zones. A wooden mobile is seen in Figure 10.12 and a brass and stainless steel sculpture is shown in Figure 10.13.

10.14

**Figures 10.14 and 10.15**
Over the lifetime of a planting, individual planters may have to be renovated. Here is a comparison of an initial and a renovated planting. The initial planting used a bold specimen plant with finer-textured and shade-tolerant ground covers. The replacement planting texture is too fine and doesn't create a focal point.

In each of the situations illustrated the changes are not an error of the facility management but of the plant maintenance and installation which developed interior plant decorations rather than design. This is an example of how design knowledge is important from a maintenance standpoint to maintain the design continuity and integrity that was initially established. In contrast to this example a newly completed mall planting package is included for your review.

## REGIONAL SHOPPING MALLS

Melvin Simon and Associates, an Indianapolis, Indiana based development company, prides themselves on "building tomorrow, today" in the design and planning of their commercial centers and regional shopping malls. One such example of their design expertise is the East Towne Mall in Knoxville, Tennessee. The site improvement consultants for this project were David Krause and Associates, Birmingham, Michigan.

10.15

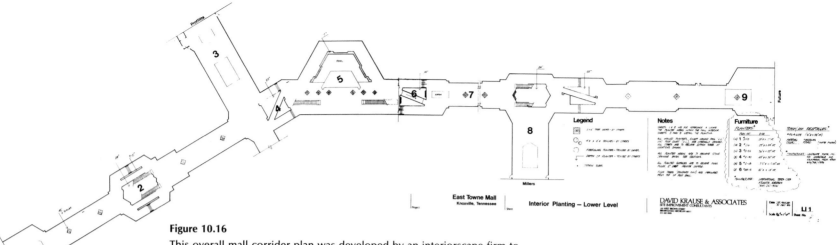

**Figure 10.16**

This overall mall corrider plan was developed by an interiorscape firm to communicate the plantings to be developed. The plan shows lower-level planters, escalator courts, stairs, and other floor or ceiling openings that relate to the lower and upper mall levels. (Designer: David Krause & Associates, Birmingham, Michigan, and Melvin-Simon Associates, Indianapolis, Indiana. East Towne Mall, Knoxville, Tennessee.)

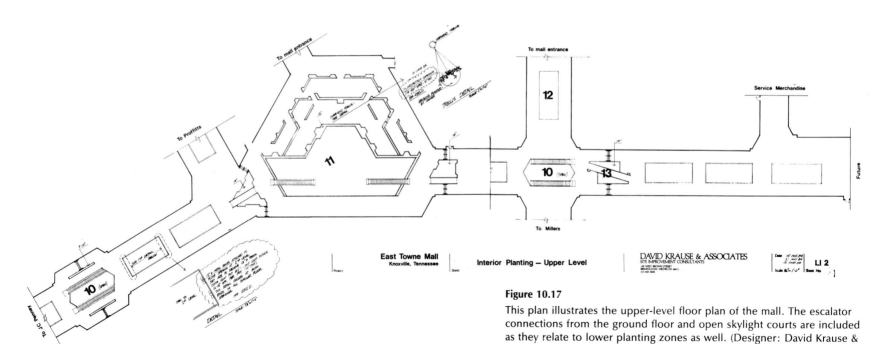

**Figure 10.17**

This plan illustrates the upper-level floor plan of the mall. The escalator connections from the ground floor and open skylight courts are included as they relate to lower planting zones as well. (Designer: David Krause & Associates, Birmingham, Michigan, and Melvin-Simon Associates, Indianapolis, Indiana.)

**Figure 10.18**
This is the originally drafted sheet for the lower-mall floor. The overall corridor floor plan was cut using match lines rather than in one long segment, for sheet efficiency. This page is the first of five project sheets. (Designer: David Krause & Associates, Birmingham, Michigan, and Melvin-Simon Associates, Indianapolis, Indiana.)

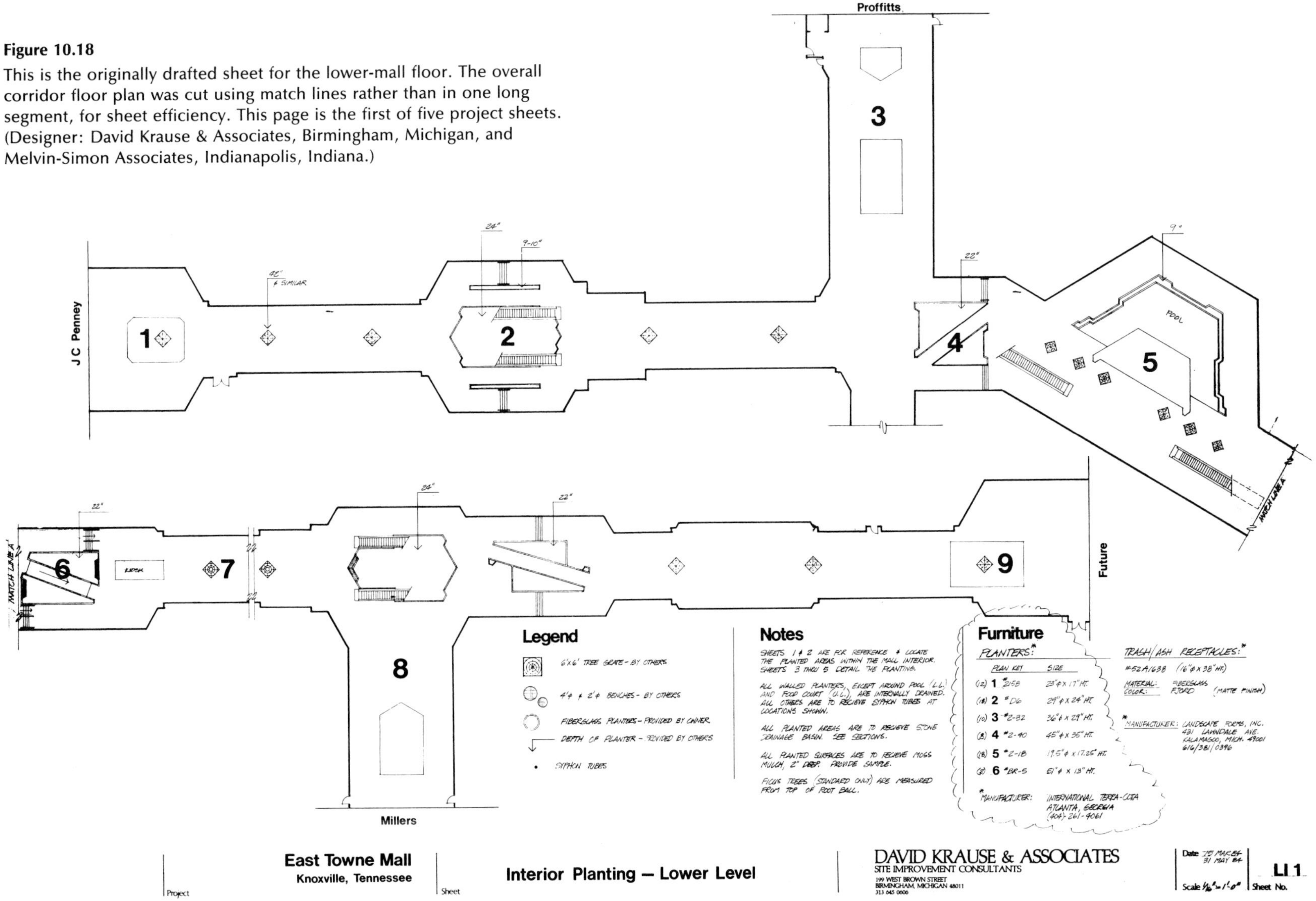

East Towne Mall
Knoxville, Tennessee

Interior Planting — Lower Level

DAVID KRAUSE & ASSOCIATES
SITE IMPROVEMENT CONSULTANTS

LI 1

The interior planting design for East Towne Mall is shown in Figures 10.16 through 10.22. Figure 10.16 includes the lower-level planting proposal with the upper level seen on sheet LI2, Figure 10.17. These two illustrations are not in the same sheet configuration or organization as initially drafted by DKA. The original drawings, which were 24 by 36 in size, were laid out with the mall corridor cut into two segments using match lines to align the parts. This organization was used for sheet efficiency while illustrating the proposal at the largest scale representation. These actual sheet layouts are seen in Figures 10.18 and 10.19. The upper and lower level planting details are shown on Sheets LI3, LI4, and LI5 (Figures 10.20–10.22). Enlargements of specific planting plan areas are seen in Figures 10.23–10.27).

259

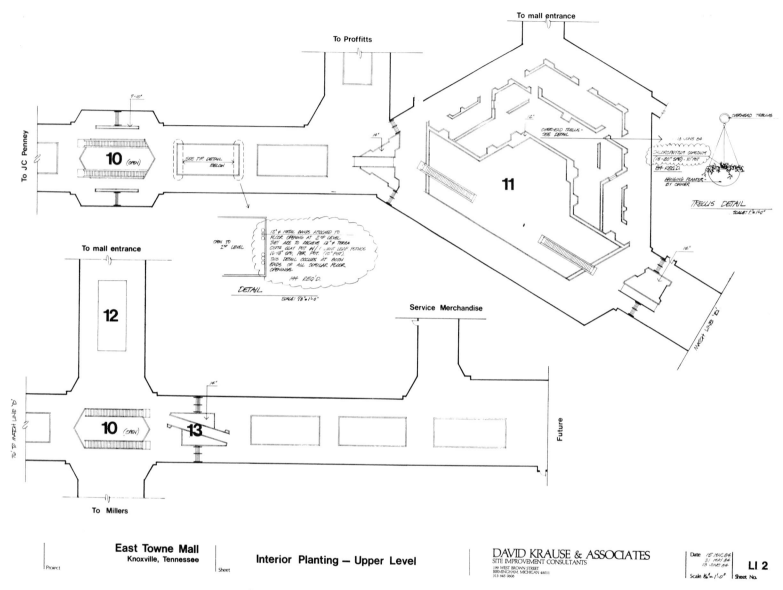

East Towne Mall
Knoxville, Tennessee

Interior Planting — Upper Level

DAVID KRAUSE & ASSOCIATES
SITE IMPROVEMENT CONSULTANTS
199 WEST BROWN STREET
BIRMINGHAM, MICHIGAN 48011
313 645 0606

LI 2

**Figure 10.19**

This drawing, sheet 2, shows the upper-mall level, also using cut and match lines. In both Figures 10.18 and 10.19 the drawings show more detail than can be seen in Figures 10.16 and 10.17. The reference numbers of these plans then relate to court enlargements. (Designer: David Krause & Associates, Birmingham, Michigan, and Melvin-Simon Associates, Indianapolis, Indiana.)

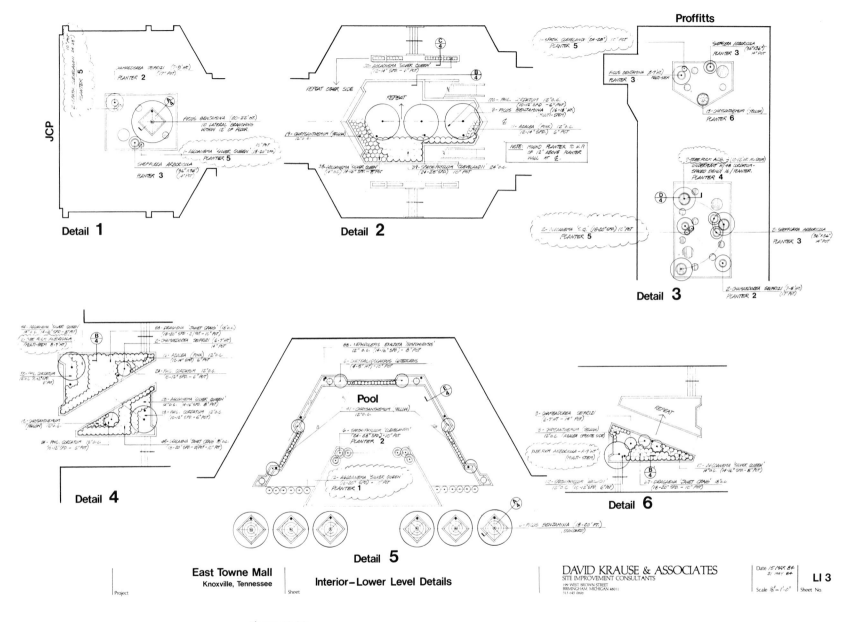

**Figure 10.20**
Sheet 3 of the design proposal includes details of individual court areas.
The detail numbers are referenced to sheet 1, the lower-level plan in
Figure 10.18. (Designer: David Krause & Associates, Birmingham,
Michigan, and Melvin-Simon Associates, Indianapolis, Indiana.)

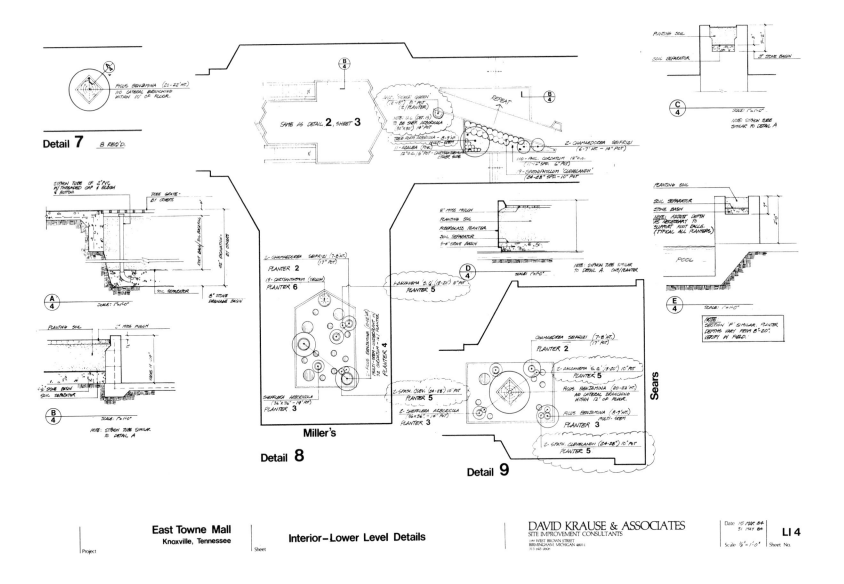

**Figure 10.21**

Sheet 4 includes additional lower-level details of courts and planter areas, and one referenced to Figure 10.19. (Designer: David Krause & Associates, Birmingham, Michigan, and Melvin-Simon Associates, Indianapolis, Indiana.)

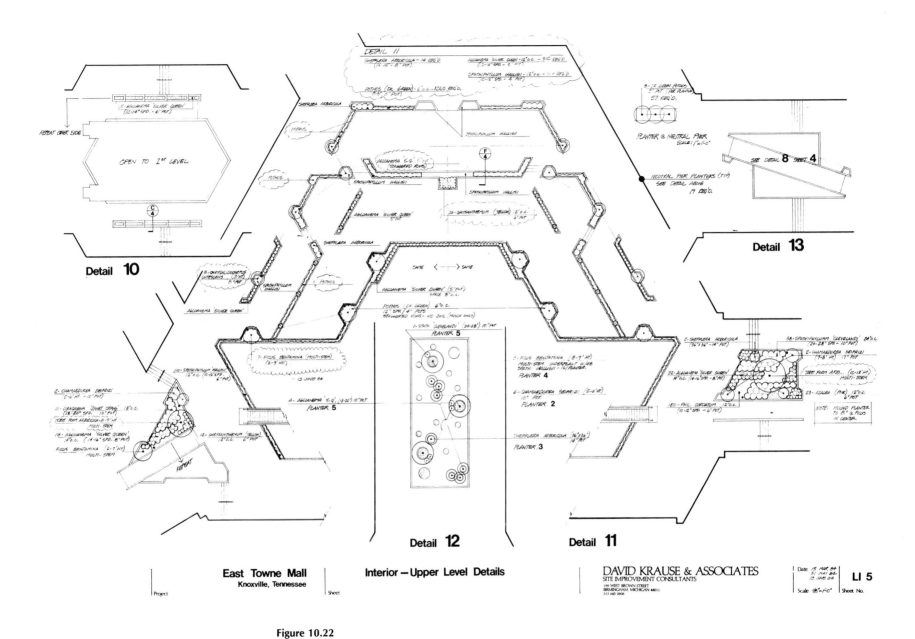

Detail **10**

Detail **12**

Detail **11**

Detail **13**

East Towne Mall
Knoxville, Tennessee

Interior — Upper Level Details

DAVID KRAUSE & ASSOCIATES
SITE IMPROVEMENT CONSULTANTS
199 WEST BROWN STREET
BIRMINGHAM, MICHIGAN 48011
313 645 0606

LI 5

**Figure 10.22**
Sheet 5 illustrates the upper-level food court planters and corridor areas.
The details are tightly organized on the sheet for efficiency. (Designer:
David Krause & Associates, Birmingham, Michigan, and Melvin-Simon
Associates, Indianapolis, Indiana.)

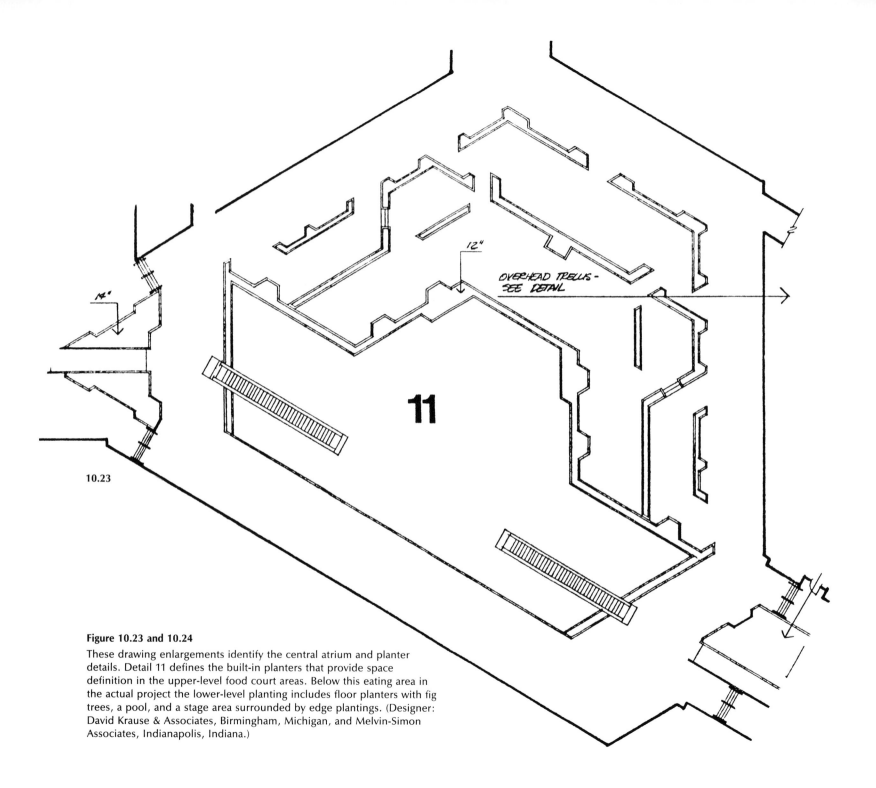

12"

OVERHEAD TRELLIS-
SEE DETAIL

14"

11

10.23

**Figure 10.23 and 10.24**
These drawing enlargements identify the central atrium and planter details. Detail 11 defines the built-in planters that provide space definition in the upper-level food court areas. Below this eating area in the actual project the lower-level planting includes floor planters with fig trees, a pool, and a stage area surrounded by edge plantings. (Designer: David Krause & Associates, Birmingham, Michigan, and Melvin-Simon Associates, Indianapolis, Indiana.)

264

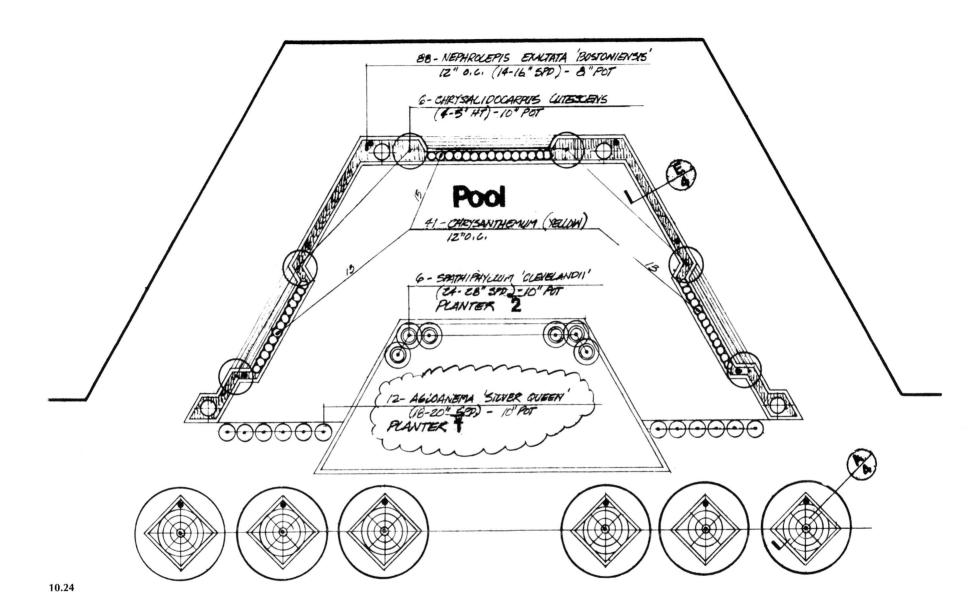

88 - NEPHROLEPIS EXALTATA 'BOSTONIENSIS'
12" O.C. (14-16" SPD) - 8" POT

6 - CHRYSALIDOCARPUS LUTESCENS
(4-5' HT) - 10" POT

**Pool**

41 - CHRYSANTHEMUM (YELLOW)
12" O.C.

6 - SPATHIPHYLLUM 'CLEVELANDII'
(24-28" SPD) - 10" POT
PLANTER 2

12 - AGLOANEMA 'SILVER QUEEN'
(18-20" SPD) - 10" POT
PLANTER 1

10.24

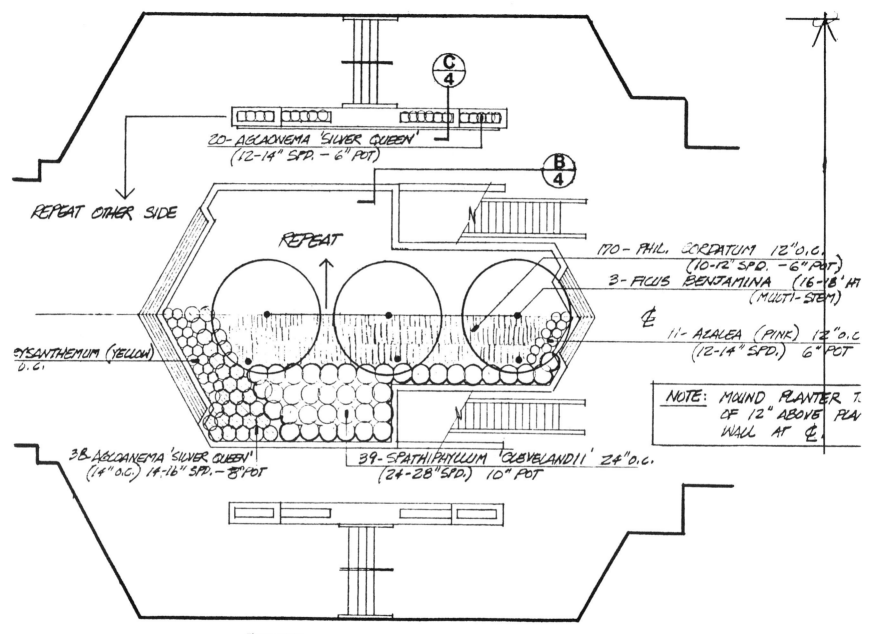

C/4

20 - AGLAONEMA 'SILVER QUEEN'
(12-14" SPD. — 6" POT)

REPEAT OTHER SIDE

REPEAT

B/4

170 - PHIL. CORDATUM 12" O.C.
(10-12" SPD. — 6" POT)

3 - FICUS BENJAMINA (16-18' HT)
(MULTI-STEM)

¢

11 - AZALEA (PINK) 12" O.C.
(12-14" SPD.) 6" POT

NOTE: MOUND PLANTER T.
OF 12" ABOVE PLAN
WALL AT ¢.

CHRYSANTHEMUM (YELLOW)
O.C.

3B AGLAONEMA 'SILVER QUEEN'
(14" O.C.) 14-16" SPD. — 8" POT

39 - SPATHIPHYLLUM 'CLEVELANDII' 24" O.C.
(24-28" SPD.) 10" POT

**Figure 10.25**

Many of the mall's plantings are concentrated where people gather: the escalator, stairs, ramps, and seating areas. Detail 2 illustrates the symmetrical ground plantings used on the lower level. This area is viewed from the escalators and open court area above. (Designer: David Krause & Associates, Birmingham, Michigan, and Melvin-Simon Associates, Indianapolis, Indiana.)

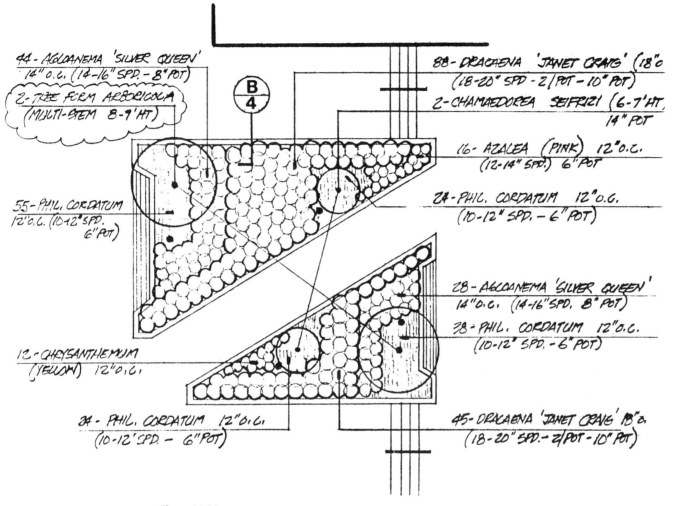

44 - AGLOANEMA 'SILVER QUEEN'
14" O.C. (14-16" SPD. - 8" POT)

2 - TREE FORM ARBORICOLA
(MULTI-STEM 8-9' HT)

55 - PHIL. CORDATUM
12" O.C. (10-12" SPD.
6" POT)

12 - CHRYSANTHEMUM
(YELLOW) 12" O.C.

24 - PHIL. CORDATUM 12" O.C.
(10-12' SPD. - 6" POT)

B
4

88 - DRACAENA 'JANET CRAIG' (18"0
(18-20" SPD - 2/POT - 10" POT)

2 - CHAMAEDOREA SEIFRIZI (6-7' HT,
14" POT

16 - AZALEA (PINK) 12" O.C.
(12-14" SPD.) 6" POT

24 - PHIL. CORDATUM 12" O.C.
(10-12" SPD. - 6" POT)

28 - AGLOANEMA 'SILVER QUEEN'
14" O.C. (14-16" SPD. 8" POT)

38 - PHIL. CORDATUM 12" O.C.
(10-12" SPD. - 6" POT)

45 - DRACAENA 'JANET CRAIG' 18"0.
(18-20" SPD. - 2/POT - 10" POT)

**Figure 10.26**
This planter detail conveys the repetition of plantings between planters
to visually link separated corridor areas. This repetition also provides
some unity. The planters are used in a design sense as a transition and a
separation between stairs, ramps, and seating. (Designer: David Krause &
Associates, Birmingham, Michigan, and Melvin-Simon Associates,
Indianapolis, Indiana.)

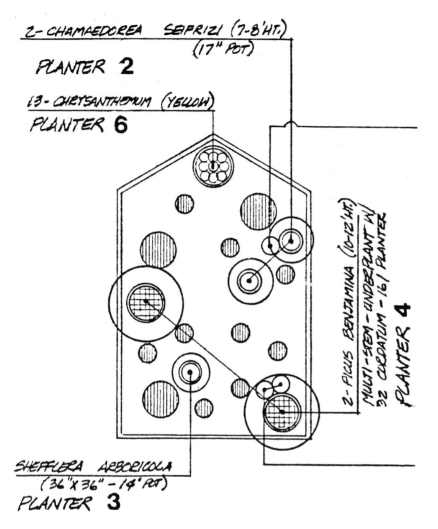

2 - CHAMAEDOREA SEIFRIZI (7-8'HT.)
(17" POT)

PLANTER **2**

13 - CHRYSANTHEMUM (YELLOW)

PLANTER **6**

2 - FICUS BENJAMINA (10-12'HT.)
MULTI-STEM - UNDERPLANT W/
32 CORDATUM - 16.1 PLANTER

PLANTER **4**

SHEFFLERA ARBORICOLA
(36" X 36" - 14" POT)

PLANTER **3**

**Figure 10.27**

On the lower level, the entries to anchor stores use plantings that are simple and uncluttered. Additional detailing in floor surfacings and seating are included as accents. (Designer: David Krause & Associates, Birmingham, Michigan, and Melvin-Simon Associates, Indianapolis, Indiana.)

**Figures 10.28 and 10.29**

In the design and construction process, the exterior detailing for plantings planned in the parking lots establishes a theme for the planting repeated indoors. (Photos by Richard Wade/Chris Thoe.)

10.28

10.29

**10.30**

**Figures 10.30 and 10.31**
These photos illustrate the dramatic changes in the central atrium area from the early construction of a mall. (Photos by Richard Wade/Chris Thoe.)

The photos which convey the actual project illustrate the basic construction sequence from the building shell through interior furnishing. Making up the central court and building, Figures 10.28–10.31 show before and after results of the basic exterior and the stark interior skeleton of the framework structure. As the construction process progresses the court area results in the shell: a two level interior mall with court space and balconies as seen in Figures 10.32 and 10.33.

**10.31**

10.32                                       10.33

**Figures 10.32 and 10.33**
Designed projects such as shopping malls take planning, design,
detailing, and foresight to create the results seen in these photos.
(Photos by Richard Wade/Chris Thoe.)

At the interior finishings stage of the construction the central court and planting pits are established and are starting to take shape as seen in Figures 10.34–10.37. The construction detail for the planting pit can be seen in Figure 10.21 Sheet C14, detail 7, and section illustration A/4. As the construction and interior finishes continued the court areas, balconies, and corridors started to take form with dry wall, railings, floor surfacings, planters, and wall surfacings as seen in Figures 10.38–10.40. As the interiorspaces develop an observer can see how planning and design has transformed the central court from the area already seen to the finished spaces and areas seen in Figures 10.41–10.43.

10.34

10.35

10.36

**Figures 10.34–10.36**

The central focus of the mall's lower and upper levels is the central atrium. These photos illustrate the construction sequence mid-way in the development process. (Photos by Richard Wade.)

**Figure 10.37**

If plants are to be used in floor planters, the details have to be included early at the planning and design stages of the architecture, before construction begins. (Photo by Richard Wade.)

10.38

10.39

**Figures 10.38–10.40**
Finish details of walls, ceilings, and lighting start to give form to the interior space and planters areas. (Photos by Richard Wade.)

10.40

**10.41**

**10.43**

**10.42**

**Figures 10.41–10.43**
The finished central atrium creates a people and plant place. The food court seating and lower-level stage and pool areas are accented by the plantings and water. (Photos by Chris Thoe.)

**10.44**

**10.46**

**10.45**

**Figures 10.44–10.49**
These photos illustrate the simple yet detailed development of the central court area. Floor and ceiling materials provide a background for permanent and movable plantings. The ceiling mobile and the water add color and sound to the space. (Photos by Chris Thoe.)

The central focus within East Towne Mall is seen in the central court with its tent-like interior ceiling, waterfalls, lower pool area, and upper seating/eating areas. The details are seen in Figures 10.18–10.22. The balcony and seating area below includes a waterfall source as seen in Figures 10.44–10.49, with the pool and stage area shown in Figure 10.49. One nice aspect of the stage area is that it can be transformed into seasonal display, as seen in the photo.

**10.47**

**10.48**

**10.49**

**Figures 10.50 and 10.51**
The fabric ceiling mobile provides scale, color, and movement to the open ceiling space. (Photos by Chris Thoe.)

10.50

10.51

Overall, the attention to pavement, ceiling, planting, and accessories in the mall makes it a striking contemporary setting. The central court has a light, open feeling due to the use of illumination and the soft fabric ceiling. This space is further accented by a mobile sculpture floating in the space (Figures 10.50 and 10.51). The shiny ceiling materials in other corridor areas provide some reflected light, making the skylighting and artificial illumination seem more striking (Figures 10.52 and 10.53).

Other mall and planting details include the escalator planting seen in plan, Figure 10.18 and 10.20 details and in Figures 10.54 and 10.55. The planting scheme in the escalator area uses a canopy of ficus to scale the space and a simple ground plane planting of permanent and seasonal plantings. Note how a mirrored surfacing under the escalators was specified to reflect any light and to visually enlarge the space by reflecting the ground bed plantings. Some planting areas in the mall's corridors do not have direct nat-

**10.52**

**10.54**

**10.53**

**10.55**

**Figures 10.54 and 10.55**
Escalator court areas include plantings that are seen from both the lower and upper mall levels. Note that under the escalators the additional lighting and mirrored surfaces give this otherwise dark area an added dimension. (Photos by Chris Thoe.)

277

**10.56**

ural illumination except at the bed edges. In these cases the larger plant materials are kept to the lightest edges, with more low light species towards the center of the beds. The planting detail 4 is seen in Figure 10.20 in conjunction with Figures 10.56 and 10.57.

Anchor stores in the mall have a simple and uncluttered entry planting as seen in Figures 10.58 and 10.59, The Miller's department store. The plan detail of this area is seen in the enlargement shown (Figure 10.27). With this design scheme of varied size plants and containers to provide scale, visual interest and good sight lines to the store entry and display windows are developed similarly (Figures 10.60–10.62). The most extensive plantings are in the central court areas which have maximum exposure to people, movement, and the skylights. More simplicity prevails in the level transition areas of the escalators and corridor accessways.

Through the plans and photos of the East Towne Mall you can see the need and utility for planning and design and

**Figures 10.56 and 10.57**
Within some corridor areas a change of planters is one small floor-level change that creates a separation between the stair and ramp arrangements. The planter edges also include benches with lighting accents beneath them. (Photos by Chris Thoe.)

**10.57**

278

**10.58**

**Figures 10.58 and 10.59**

At this anchor store, the lower and upper views of the store are open. Taller plants are used to frame, not cover, the entry. The plan detail of this area can be seen in Figure 10.27.

**10.59**

10.60                     10.61                          10.62

**Figure 10.60–10.62**

At store entries the floor, ceiling, fixtures, and plants need to accent and complement the entry. In these photos the components collectively help accent and emphasize the store entry. (Photos by Chris Thoe.)

the detail information used in the coordination of a project of this scale. If you as an interiorscape designer get involved with a project of this scale photography can be an exceptional communication skill in conveying design ideas. Figures 10.63 and 10.64 illustrate a photo embellishment technique you can use to express the design and development ideas you have for a space. The parallel "after" shot can then be used as a tool in discussing design ideas in similar projects.

10.63

**Figures 10.63 and 10.64**
In these photos of a food court area the before and after comparison is a
vivid example of how plants can improve a people space. (Photos by
Richard Wade.)

10.64

## SUMMARY

Interiorscaping is a profession involved in the design and development of interior spaces that attempt to bring the outdoors indoors through the use of tropical plantings. The professionals may include architects, landscape architects, interior designers, plant specialists, and maintenance personnel. Key words in understanding the planning, design, development, and care of interiorscapes are diversification and specialization. Interiorscapes should be attractive, functional, and manageable in terms of the people and plants. The ultimate test of any interiorscape is time, both short-term and long-term: Does the proposal initially work as expected, is it attractive, and can it be maintained?

As the profession of interiorscaping evolves, the introduction of new technologies and perspectives concerning design will add to the current considerations and techniques. As a practicing professional be open to new information and considerations that affect the industry and the interior planting profession. As a designer always have a goal, project the ultimate, then revise for reality—accomplishing your goal through creative problem-solving, design process. In staged or phased proposals, if you only design for the available funds, the client doesn't know what to do beyond your initial recommendations. Be an anticipator, be the "devil's advocate," both positive and negative. The industry is diversified in its wide range of professionalism and the variety of project situations and potential plantings and schemes to consider. Specialization is related to the expertise required in the planning, design, and developments of interiorscapes as well as the specialties represented in the plant production and maintenance of interior plantings. Role-play: put yourself in the position of the client, the users, an installer, and maintenance personnel or building managers. As a designer you're the client's representative in defining, interpreting, selecting, and developing the space. Lastly, learn from others and your own experiences. Past design and installation evaluations can be teaching tools in bettering your design perspective and problem-solving skills for the development of future design proposals. Evaluate other design situations, basing your review on basic design elements, principles, and the design context and situation. You can always learn something that applies to a design situation somewhere. Remember to be interdisciplinary: if you don't know the answer seek another professional's advice; it doesn't make you a lesser person. Lastly, remember that design is for people's use and enjoyment.

# Chapter 11

# Industry Images and References

## COMPANY LOGOS

Figures 11.1–11.4 illustrate coordinated company logos. In each case, the company conveys their specialty in their name and in associated graphics used on vehicles and public relations materials. A concerted effort in communicating professionalism is an important part of the development within the interiorscape industry. Another important consideration in presenting yourself as a professional is keeping current on trends and topics within the industry. Professional associations like the Associated Landscape Contractors of America–Interior Landscape Division (ALCA–ILD) provide materials such as *A Guide to Specifications for Interior Landscaping* (Figure 11.5), as well as other institutional leaflets. Industry publications can also be sources of new information to pass on to your clients. Such publications may include *Interior Landscaping Industry, Interiorscaping, Florida Foliage, Florida Nurseryman, American Nurseryman,* and *Nursery Manager* (Figures 11.6–11.9).

11.1

**Figures 11.1 and 11.2**
Interiorscape company names and logos are important design
considerations because they communicate the nature of the business.
(Tropical Plant Rentals, Chicago, Illinois.)

11.2

**Figure 11.3**

The Tropical Plant Rentals logo seen in the previous figures is repeated on brochures, stationery, and other office materials. (Tropical Plant Rentals, Chicago, Illinois.)

**Figure 11.4**
In the design of this interiorscape brochure, the emphasis is on their
plant leasing program. (Engledow Associates, Indianapolis, Indiana.)

**Figure 11.5**

Professional associations such as the ALCA–ILD (Associated Landscape Contractors Association–Interior Landscape Division) provide educational materials and references. You can use these materials as company and employee resources. Shown is the ALCA-ILD, *A Guide to Specifications for Interior Landscaping*.

**Figure 11.6**

*Florida Foliage,* published by the Florida Foliage Association, 114 E. Fifth Street, Apopka, Florida, 32703

**Figure 11.7**

*Florida Nurseryman,* 5401 Kirkman Road, Suite 650, Orlando, Florida 32819

288

**Interior landscaping issue**

Interior landscaping at the Hyatt Regency Chicago

**Figure 11.8**

*American Nurseryman,* published by American Nurseryman Publishing Company, 111 North Canal Street, Chicago, Illinois 60606

**Figure 11.9**

*Nursery Manager,* published by Branch-Smith Publishing Company, P.O. Box 1868, Ft. Worth, Texas 76107

Bedding/Pot Plants - 10
Foliage Plants - 20
Supplies - 42
Trees/Shrubs - 28
Tricks of the Trade - 50
Upcoming Events - 36

# NURSERY MANAGER
## FORMERLY SF&N MAGAZINE

May 1985                                                                      $3.00

A new middleman may be in your future, trends show

How good is the quality of your water supply?

## Greenhouses
**A survey of manufacturers shows who's buying and why**

11.10

Published references and texts may also be part of your professional departure when proposing interiorscapes. Included in the following figures are graphics and design books, as well as books on specific interiorscaping topics. Figures 11.10 and 11.11 illustrate a few of the basic landscape design graphic references available.

**Figures 11.10 and 11.11**

These graphic references are two of the many example books available to help designers with ideas for presentations. The other graphic and design references noted are only a sampling of the many books available. (*Plan Graphics* by PDA Publishers, drawing by Jeff Gebrian, CR 3 Design. *Perspective Sketches* by PDA Publishers, drawing by Janet Shen, Perkins & Will.)

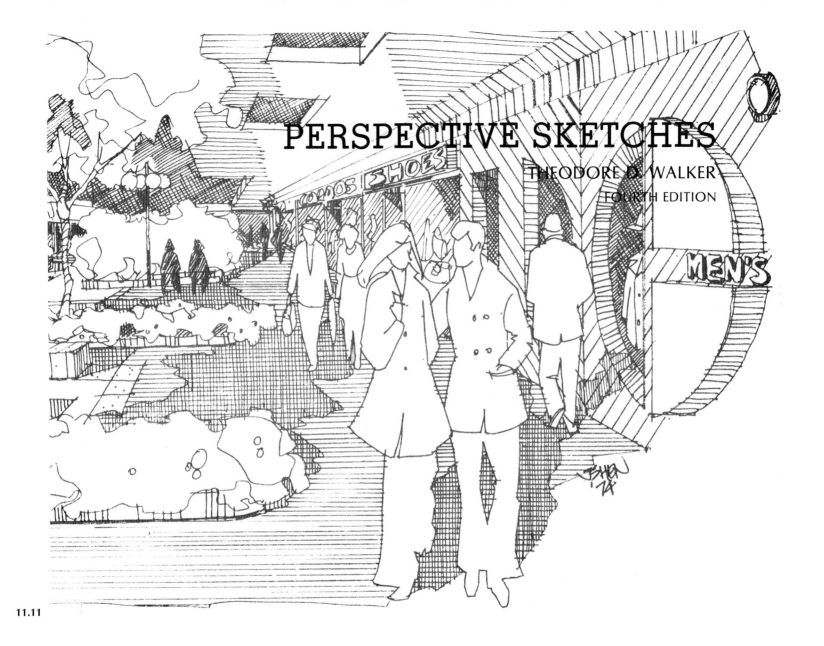

# PERSPECTIVE SKETCHES

THEODORE D. WALKER

FOURTH EDITION

11.11

# Graphic and Design References

*Interior Planting Line Art,* by Upper Level Graphics, published by Environmental Design Press, 1980.

*Perspective Sketches,* by Theodore D. Walker, published by PDA Publishers, 1975.

*Plan Graphics,* 3rd ed. by Theodore D. Walker, published by PDA Publishers, 1985.

*From Line to Design,* by Scott Van Dyke, published by PDA Publishers, 1982.

*Plan and Section Drawing,* by Thomas C. Wang, published by Van Nostrand Reinhold Co, 1980.

*Pencil Sketching,* by Thomas C. Wang, published by Van Nostrand Reinhold Co, 1977.

*Sketching with Markers,* by Thomas C. Wang, published by Van Nostrand Reinhold Co, 1981.

*A Graphic Vocabulary for Architectural Presentation,* by Edward T. White, published by Architectural Media, 1972.

*Drawing Interior Architecture,* by Norman Diekman and John Pile, published by Whitney Library of Design, 1983.

*Design Presentation,* by Ernest Burden, published by Mc-Graw-Hill Book Company, 1984.

*Projection Drawing,* by Thomas C. Wang, published by Van Nostrand Reinhold Co, 1984.

*Rendering Standards in Architecture and Design,* by Stephen W. Rich, published by Van Nostrand Reinhold Co, 1984.

*Design Drawing,* by William Kirby Lockard, published by Van Nostrand Reinhold Co, 1974.

*Interior Plantscapes,* by George H. Manaker, published by Prentice-Hall, Inc., 1981.

*Designing the Interior Landscape,* by Richard L. Austin, published by Van Nostrand Reinhold Co, 1985.

*Interior Landscaping,* by Tok Furuta, published by Reston Publishing Company, Inc., 1983.

*Interior Plantscaping,* by Richard L. Gaines, published by Architectural Record Books, 1977.

*Residential Landscapes: Graphics, Planning, and Design,* by G. M. Pierceall, published by Reston Publishing Company, 1984.

*Atrium Buildings,* by Richard Saxon, published by Van Nostrand Reinhold Co., 1983.

*The Glass House,* by John Hix, published by the Massachusetts Institute of Technology, 1974.

*The New Atrium,* by Michael J. Bednar, published by Mc-Graw-Hill Book Company, 1986.

# Appendix

# Large Tree Installation

**Figure A.1**
Large tree installations may require the use of cranes to assist with
planting and to reduce plant damage.

**Figure A.2**
Interior staging is critical in preventing damage to floors, walls, and ceiling; here, the floor is planked.

**Figure A.3**
After the tree is in place, soil and crown work is required.

**Figure A.4**
After the tree is placed it is selectively pruned for light penetration. Soil
addition and cleanup of the areas are also completed.

**Figure A.5**
After installation of these smaller trees within the entry the
installation of the larger specimen is contemplated.

**Figure A.6**
On the street the tree has arrived stored in the truck transport with awaiting boom crane in place.

**Figure A.7**
Planning and staging of equipment and people is necessary for a project installation of this size.

**Figure A.8**
As the specimen is removed, note the wrapping of the tree crown and trunk for protection.

**Figure A.9**
Accessibility is a pre-condition of an installation of this size.

**Figure A.10**
The tree is transfered from the large crane outdoors to the small equipment inside.

**Figure A.11**
Planking provides access to the planter and reduces damage to finished floor areas.

**Figure A.12**
Before uprighting, the crown is unwrapped and damaged branches are
removed.

A.13

**Figures A.13 and A.14**
Straps are adjusted to upright the specimen.

A.14

A.15

**Figure A.15**
Before installation the fiberglass container is cut away to allow the roots to be inspected and possibly pruned before being planted in the new container.

**Figure A.16**
Final contemplations and evaluations of soil depths are completed before the tree is installed.

**Figure A.17**
The tree is uprighted.

**Figure A.18**
The tree is installed in the planter.

**Figure A.19**
The crane is used as a support while the tree is balanced within the container.

**Figure A.20**
With the specimen uprighted, the final ties are cut.

**Figure A.21**
Once the crown is unfolded it is selectively pruned for better form and
for light penetration to lower crown areas.

**Figure A.22**
The planning, scheduling, and installation is completed.

A.23

**Figures A.23 and A.24**
Smaller job sites may require varied equipment to match the materials and spaces.

A.24

**A.25**

**Figure A.25 and A.26**

These are additional examples of a one- and two-point perspective.
Other examples are in Chapter 5, Figures 5.18 and 5.19.

EG 321 | 1009

A.26

319

**Figure A.27**

---

## SITE AND PLANTER ANALYSIS CHECKLIST

### Site Analysis—Architectural and Environmental Systems

I. Environment

  A.  Light: intensity, color, duration
    1) natural: (roof, windows) plants within 45° angle area of vertical window top
    2) artificial: type, ease of lamp replacement
    3) dust level: dust acts as a light filter or shade

  B.  Temperature: heating or air cooling
    1) day: night
    2) holiday
    3) hot or cold drafts: heaters, or near doors to outside

  C.  Potential evapotranspiration
    1) percent of interior volume to be filled by plants; plant drying by environment
    2) greater in heating season
    3) drafts

  D.  Water: manual preferred for control and tidiness
    1) quality: toxins, salts, pH
    2) pipe size and pressure, especially for automated systems
    3) proximity of outlets, no more than 100 ft. away
    4) provisions for drainage from plantings, e.g., floor drains
    5) perhaps tempered to about 70°F

  E.  Air exchange
    1) oxygen and carbon dioxide levels
    2) water vapor reduction–reduction of condensation
    3) avoid musty odor of soil
    4) avoid chlorine gas build-up around swimming pools (about $\frac{1}{10}$ air exchange/minute)
    5) avoid concentrations of cleaning compound vapors ($NH_3$, carbon tetrachloride)

  F.  Pest management
    1) filtering of air system to prevent spread of biotic pests
    2) isolation from the building air movement system if volatile pesticide or pesticide sprays, dusts, fogs, aerosols, etc. are used

II.  Ability of structure to hold plant or planter weight (wet soil $\simeq$ 80 lb/cu ft, plants about 90% water or about 64.5 lb/cu ft of solid plant)

III.  Resistance of materials on walls and floors near plants to mold or algae growth, warping, water marking; e.g., slate, brick, tile, terrazzo, concrete, vinyl, teak, cypress, redwood; no creosote on wood

IV. Loading Shelter (for winter movement of plants into building)

V. Ease of mobility of plants through building

VI. Traffic patterns; mechanical damage

VII. Potential for theft; e.g., small plants near door

VIII. Access to plant for general maintenance and foliar cleaning

IX. Storage area for maintenance equipment, supplies, and chemicals, including fertilizers and pesticides

## Planter Analysis—may need to buy planter or have it built

I. Plant Growth Characteristics
   A. Volume: root volume should be $\frac{1}{3}$—$\frac{1}{2}$ foliar volume
   B. Depth (anchorage): 3–4 ft for large plants
   C. Drainage (water removal and salt leaching): fiberglass soil separator mat between growing medium and drainage site

II. Construction Material
   A. Non-decomposable: stainless steel, copper, fiberglass, urethane, ceramic, concrete
   B. Non-toxic: no creosoted wood
   C. Porosity: porous types will stain floor
   D. Non-flammable
   E. No sharp edges

III. Growing Medium
   A. Hydro-culture
      1) nutrient solution without salt residue
      2) sufficient plant anchorage system: container depth, buoyancy of medium
   B. Medium
      1) high porosity and water-holding characteristics
      2) easy wetting and rewetting
      3) high ion exchange capacity or periodic addition of slow-release fertilizer
      4) slow rate of organic matter decomposition (oxidation); e.g., fibrous peatmoss
      5) optimum nutrient levels before planting (see production handout): soil test or use packaged mix of known characteristics
      6) pH 5.5–6 before planting
      7) non-flammable

IV. Mobility

# INTERIOR PLANTINGS: THE INTERIOR ENVIRONMENT

Thomas C. Weiler, Horticulture
Gregory M. Pierceall, Landscape Architecture
Judith A. Watson, Interior Design
*Purdue University*

Interiorscaping brings "gardens" inside, and landscaping companies increasingly are asked to design, install, and maintain these interior plantings. We will discuss both the horticultural and design aspects of this topic and will start with a description of the interior environment.

Urban residents are estimated to spend 90% of their time indoors and are said to be unhappy when isolated from nature. Interiorscaping is one way of fulfilling the need to associate with natural components. Since interiors are often designed for human comfort, not plant growth, plants must be selected and maintained with the purpose of the space as well as cultural conditions in mind. Plants thrive at high humidities, but the relative humidities of most interiors are 30–40%. This is the range preferred for human comfort and the preservation of furnishings. While tropical plants are intolerant of temperatures much below 60°F, room and building temperatures are often lowered at night or during office holidays. Light levels acceptable for reading and other human activities are insufficient to keep many plants alive. Awareness of these incompatibilities is essential to successful interiorscaping.

Interiors, like greenhouses or growth chambers, are controlled environments. Above-ground factors such as relative humidity, air temperature, oxygen and carbon dioxide, and air pollutants are carefully regulated by HVAC (humidity-ventilation-air conditioning) systems. The below-ground environment, which consists of soil, water, and nutrients, is controlled by soil mix, type of container, and watering and fertilizing schedules. Interiors also are biotic environments involving people, plants, and sometimes pests. Pests such as mealy bugs, scales, and spider mites thrive without natural predators. Pesticides are used for control. Researchers have also introduced beneficial predatory organisms as a means of lowering pest populations. In short, the interior is an ecosystem that we can manage.

The quantity of light that plants receive deserves special emphasis. Plants manufacture food from the energy of sunlight, carbon dioxide, and water. They respond to the total amount of light received each day—the more sunlight, the better most plants grow. Total light per day is the product of the intensity of light times its duration. In horticultural language:

total light/day = footcandles of light × hours of light/day

Thus, the total light for a day with 50 footcandles of light for 12 hours equals 600 footcandle hours/day. Although this is more than enough to light hallways or for reading, it is hardly enough light for plants.

Light meters aid in judging light levels. Artificially-lit spaces are easy to analyze by multiplying the light reading by the number of hours of illumination. Spaces lit all or in part by natural light are much more difficult to analyze. Here, experience is extremely valuable, but the following are also helpful as guidelines.

1. Light strikes the plant vertically or laterally. Bottom leaves drop when light enters from above the plant (vertically) and filters through the canopy leaving little light to sustain bottom leaves. Conversely, if light strikes the profile of the plant (laterally), plants will bend in the direction of the light. Parts of the plant missed by the light will suffer. So the way in which light strikes plants is important. If light comes from the side, a quarter-turn of plants weekly usually maintains form.

2. Skylights are rarely as effective as they seem. Greenhouse roofs admit a great deal of light because they cover the whole space, and roof pitch is engineered to optimize light penetration. Skylights often cover only a small percentage of the roof area and light only the area immediately below them. Most skylights are so far above the plantings that the light is lost either by scattering or by tall plants shading lower plants. Therefore, skylight configuration and placement must be carefully studied before plants are chosen, and the amount of light may need to be augmented.

3. Southern exposures provide maximum light. Since interior plants typically suffer from too little light, southern exposures make possible the most diverse selection of plants. East and west exposures are adequate for many plants, while northern exposures considerably limit plant selection.

4. Window treatments and trees beyond windows reduce light. Trees, especially evergreens, building overhangs, tinted glass, and curtains filter out valuable light for plantings. These factors must be taken into account when evaluating interior light.

5. Light levels vary with the seasons and are lowest during winter. Winter light is less than half that of summer because we are further from the sun, the sun is lower in the sky, cloudiness is greater, and hours of light/day are fewer. Either plants must be selected for the winter light conditions or plants must be relocated to brighter areas for that season.

We have emphasized that the interior is an ecosystem in which light is the most important consideration. The following plant specification lists recommend minimum light levels to keep plants alive 3–5 years.

## LIGHT SPECIFICATIONS FOR INTERIOR PLANTS

TOLERANT OF LOW LIGHT (require at least 300–2400 footcandle hours/day)

*Large plants (5–25 feet tall)*
   *Chamaedorea erumpens* - Bamboo Palm
   *Chamaedorea seifrizii*
   *Dracaena fragrans* 'Massangeana' - Corn Plant

*Intermediate-sized plants (3–5 feet tall)*
   *Brassaia arboricola* - Asian Umbrella Tree
   *Dracaena reflexa* - Malasian Dracaena
   *Howea forsterana* - Forster Sentry Palm

*Small plants (1/2–3 feet tall)*
   *Aglaonema commutatum* - 'Treubii' - Variegated Chinese Evergreen
   *Aglaonema modestum* - Chinese Evergreen
   *Aspidistra elatior* - Cast Iron Plant
   *Chamaedorea elegans* - Parlor Palm
   *Dracaena thalioides* - Lance Dracaena
   *Epipremnum aureum* - Golden Pothos
   *Philodendron scandens* (subsp. *oxycardium*) - Heart-Leaf Philodendron
   *Sansevieria trifasciata* - Snake Plant

TOLERANT OF MEDIUM LIGHT (require at least 2400–6000 footcandle hours/day

*Large plants (5–25 feet tall)*
   *Araucaria heterophylla* - Norfolk Island Palm
   *Brassaia actinophylla* - Australian Umbrella Tree

*Caryota mitis* - Clustered Fishtail Palm
*Chrysalidocarpus lutescens* - Butterfly Palm, Areca Palm
*Ficus benjamina* - Weeping Fig
*Ficus elastica* - India Rubber Tree
*Ficus lyrata* - Fiddle-Leaf Fig
*Ficus retusa* - Indian Laurel
*Monstera deliciosa* - Split-Leaf Monsters
*Rhapis excelsa* - Slender Lady Palm

*Intermediate-sized plants (3–5 feet tall)*
   *Chamaerops humilis* - European Fan Palm
   *Cycas revoluta* - Sago Palm
   *Cyperus alternifolius* - Umbrella Plant
   *Dieffenbachia maculata* - Spotted Dumb Cane
   *Dizygotheca elegantissima* - False Aralia
   *Dracaena deremensis* 'Janet Craig' - Janet Craig Dracaena
   *Encephalartos ferox* - Encephalartos
   *Livistona chinensis* - Chinese Fan Palm
   *Pandanus veitchii* - Veitch Screw Pine
   *Philodendron domesticum* - Spade-Leaf Philodendron
   *Philodendron selloum* - Saddle-Leaf Philodendron
   *Phoenix roebelenii* - Miniature Date Palm
   *Pittosporum tobira* - Japanese Pittosporum
   *Polyscias balfouriana* - Balfour Aralia
   *Polyscias filicifolia* - Fern-Leaf Aralia
   *Polyscias fruticosa* - Ming Aralia

*Small plants (1/2 - 3 feet tall)*
   *Aechmea* spp. - Vase Plant
   *Asparagus densiflorus* 'Sprengeri' - Sprengeri Fern
   *Chlorophytum comosum* - Spider Plant
   *Cissus antarctica* - Kangaroo Vine
   *Cissus rhombifolia* - Grape Ivy
   *Cordyline terminalis* - Tree-of-Kings
   *Cryptanthus* spp. - Earth Star
   *Dracaena surculosa* - Gold-Dust Dracaena
   *Episcia* spp. - Flame Violet
   *Fatsia japonica* - Japanese Aralia
   *Ficus pumila* - Creeping Fig
   *Maranta leuconeura* (var. *kerchoviana*) - Rabbit's Tracks
   *Pedilanthus tithymaloides* - Devil's Backbone
   *Peperomia obtusifolia* - Pepper-Face
   *Philodendron wendlandii* - Wendland's Philodendron
   *Pilea cadierei* 'Minima' - Aluminum Plant
   *Pilea depressa* - English Baby's Tears
   *Pilea serpyllacea* - Artillery Plant
   *Plectranthus australis* - Swedish Ivy
   *Rhoeo spathacea* - Oyster Plant

*Senecio mikanioides* - German Ivy
*Spathiphyllum clevelandii* - White Peace Lily
*Syngonium angustatum* - Arrowhead Vine
*Tolmiea menziesii* - Piggyback Plant
*Tradescantia albiflora* - Giant White Inch Plant
*Zebrina pendula* - Inch Plant

REQUIRE HIGH LIGHT (require at least 6000 footcandle hours/day)

*Large Plants* (5–25 feet tall)
*Beaucarnea recurvata* (var. *intermedia*) - Elephant Foot Tree
*Cereus peruvianus* - Hedge Cactus
*Citrus limon* 'Ponderosa' - Ponderosa Lemon
*Coffea arabica* - Coffee Tree
*Epiphyllum oxypetalum* - Night Blooming Cereus
*Grevillea robusta* - Silk Oak
*Podocarpus macrophyllus* (var. *maki*) - Buddhist Pine
*Tabernaemontana divaricata* - Crape Jasmine

*Intermediate-sized plants* (3–5 feet tall)
*Codiaeum variegatum* (var. *pictum*) - Garden Croton
*Euphorbia lactea* - Dragon Bones

*Euphorbia trigona* - African Milk Tree
X*Fatshedera lizei* - Pagoda Ivy

*Small plants* (1/2 - 3 feet tall)
*Agave americana* - Century Plant
*Aporocactus flagelliformis* - Rattail Cactus
X*Citrofortunella mitis* - Calamondin Orange
*Crassula argentea* - Jade Plant
*Crassula lycopodioides* (var. *pseudolycopodioides*) - Princess
  Pine
*Echinocactus grusonii* - Barrel Cactus
*Echinopsis multiplex* - Pink Easter-Lily Cactus
*Ferocactus acanthodes* - Barrel Cactus
*Hedera helix* - English Ivy
*Justicia brandegeana* - Shrimp Plant
*Opuntia microdasys* - Bunny Ears
*Pellionia daveauana* - Trailing Watermelon
*Phalaenopsis* spp. - Moth Orchid
*Sedum morganianum* - Burro's Tail
*Streptocarpus* × *hybridus* - Cape Primrose

# DESIGN CONSIDERATIONS FOR INTERIOR PLANTSCAPING

Judith A. Watson, Interior Design
Gregory M. Pierceall, Landscape Architecture
Thomas C. Weiler, Horticulture
*Purdue University*

Technological advances in the architectural, engineering, and ornamental horticulture industries have opened the way for more extensive and diversified interior planting projects. The demand for interior plantscaping has caused designers to explore the aesthetic and functional contributions which plants can make to interior environments. Initially plants were used to provide a naturalistic setting in commercial interior spaces. Because many commercial spaces are often windowless or lack a direct view of the outdoors, the mere presence of plants may relieve the stress of a complex working environment by creating a view. Plants may be employed as transitional elements between outdoors and indoors as well as between various interior levels. These common elements add to the continuity between the land, building, and interior spaces. Plants may also serve functional needs such as screening or subdividing areas (defining space), directing traffic movement, or calling attention to stairs or glass for safety reasons. Finally, plants contribute to the aesthetic quality of a space by adding color, texture, shape, or by serving as a focal point. There are good reasons for incorporating plants into interior design schemes. To do a good job, however, one must first have a good understanding of design principles as they pertain to interior spaces.

Making the transition from exterior to interior landscaping is not as simple as one might think. Interior environments, like landscaped outdoor areas, are planned environments where every detail is reviewed to create a total setting. Unlike exterior areas, where plants play a major role in defining, texturing, and coloring space, in interior environments they are only one of many design components. One of the major reasons for this fact is the reduced scale within the confines of the architectural structure. Interior space is predefined according to the needs of the people who will use the space. Many human and design needs, such as function and style, have higher priority than plants. The interplay between the architectural space, its surface materials, furnishings, and accessories is carefully balanced to achieve the overall effect desired by the client and designer.

The primary goal in selecting plant materials for interior environments is to relate plants to the space and furnishings. Most commercial interiors have been ordered in a particular fashion by a design team to reflect the client's needs. Plants must blend with the intended design scheme. Assuming cultural and functional factors have already been assessed, the process of selecting appropriate plant materials begins.

Regardless of whether the plant is freestanding or in a predesigned planter, a preliminary space analysis is crucial to proper selection. This analysis is done by on-site inspection or examination of the designer's drawings. To achieve unity, both the interior space and plants should be analyzed to determine their compatibility.

The starting point is to examine the interior space and record crucial data such as size, shapes, textures, and colors. First, note the overall dimensions and try to pinpoint the scale and proportions of the space. Scale refers to the relative size, and proportion refers to the relationship between parts. If you classify the space as large or small, in comparison to human scale, then you are considering relative size or scale. A hotel lobby with a sixteen-story ceiling is a large-scale space, whereas one of the individual suites would be considered small-scale by comparison. When describing a space as long and narrow or squarish, you are considering proportion—the relationship between different elements such as height, width, and depth. These dimensions are important because plant size is relative to the size of the space. For example, an eight-foot Schefflera would seem large in an ordinary room with average ceiling heights, but small in a lobby space with an eighteen-foot ceiling.

Also consider the furnishings. Is the furniture massive or dainty in relation to the space (scale)? Are furniture pieces long and low or short and boxy (proportion)? Compare the relative amount of furniture and decorative elements to the amount of space (proportion). Are there too many items in the room or too few? Consider that people also will occupy space. In other words, try to put into words the spatial relationships of the interior and its components.

Then, try to continue this order when adding plants. For example, a massive, bold plant next to a dainty, delicate chair will be out of scale. A tall, narrow Cane plant next to a long, low sofa will be out of proportion. Likewise, too many or too few plants can be out of proportion to the size of the space. Consider also the relationship between plant and container; be sure the container is an appropriate size and shape. Then relate the plant and container unit to the other interior components as well as the space. This will contribute to overall unity.

Repetition is another unifying element. One often encounters a repetition of shapes and lines in interiors. Sometimes there is a major vertical emphasis dictated by windows or paneling. Likewise, curved shapes may be reiterated in both the architecture and the furnishings. Plants can reflect these characteristics. First, you must recognize a repetitive factor and then decide whether other elements should blend with it or contrast with it. For example, a strong horizontal balcony line can be broken up by vines with a linear, vertical nature (contrast). Also, a strong vertical window pattern can be softened with horizontal planters all across the bottom sills (contrast).

In relation to plants, form is the overall, three-dimensional effect conveyed by their height, shape, and density. Plants can be placed in four basic categories: upright (taller than wide), spreading (same height and width), prostrate (linear horizontal emphasis), and vining (linear vertical emphasis). Certain forms are more appropriate than others in different situations. An upright plant would work better in a narrow hallway because it would not interfere with traffic patterns as much as a spreading plant. A spreading plant would look better on a bank of office files than an upright plant because it would hug the surface and blend with the file structure. A dense plant works well for screening, whereas an open plant should be selected where visibility beyond the plant is desirable. Therefore, it is important to consider plant form in terms of function as well as how the form relates to architectural features and other interior components.

Another important design consideration is contrast. Contrast is all-important to highlight plants. Textural and color differences are helpful in creating contrast. Again, analyze the room's visual textures (patterns)—the sensation it evokes by appearance, not touch. For example, a stone fireplace appears coarse and rough textured. A plant such as Monstera can be considered coarse in comparison to a fine-textured fern. If a room is texturally plain, a highly-textured plant serves as a nice contrast. However, in a room with a busy, complex appearance with many textures and patterns, the same plant would be lost.

As far as color is concerned, the main consideration is value difference. Value is the lightness or darkness of a color. In plant groupings, select plants of differing green values to set them apart from each other. Be careful, when placing plants against various backgrounds, to select a lighter or darker value plant than the value of the surface behind it. In addition, colored plants can be used for accent, such as a red plant in a predominantly grey or beige interior. Try to use variegated plants in simpler, plainer settings, and avoid grouping differently-variegated specimens.

These are some of the major facets to explore in considering plants as design elements. It is difficult to separate the various aspects and principles of design; however, much of design has to do with observation and common sense. Start by observing planting schemes until you can distinguish the good ones from the bad. You can then begin to analyze why the good ones are effective to broaden your own expertise.

Plant form is an important consideration in a narrow space such as this hallway. The low, spreading saddle leaf philodendron (*Philodendron Selloum*) on the left would be damaged by traffic; while the ming aralia (*Polyscias Fruticosa*) on the right is less disruptive and more related to the form of the space.

# INTERIOR PLANTSCAPING: THE DESIGN PROCESS

G. M. Pierceall, Landscape Architecture
Judith A. Watson, Interior Design
Thomas C. Weiler, Horticulture
*Purdue University*

The process of selecting plant materials and placing them appropriately in interior locations is based on several factors. Many variables influence plant selection and location: the client's needs and preferences, physical features of the space, and related environmental conditions inside and outdoors. Space and client information must be collected, analyzed, synthesized, and evaluated to make the best plant placement decisions. This design process may be organized in several ways. The following suggested approach to this process is followed by a sample case of a professional office space.

## PROBLEM IDENTIFICATION

The first stage of any design project is defining the problem. An evaluation is made of exactly what services the client is requesting. In relation to interior plantscaping, there are several design possibilities: 1) *new plantings*—selecting plant materials for free-standing units or built-in planters in an existing interior; 2) *renovation*—replacing or reorganizing existing plant materials; or 3) *planting design*—creating a specific planting effect during the developmental stages of an interior project. Design opportunities may also consist of a combination of these options.

## RESEARCH

In most cases, the client's request is straightforward, "add plants to improve the overall quality of a space." This takes us to the second stage of the design process, researching problem parameters and analyzing possibilities. Designers investigate and use two primary areas as sources of information: the physical features of the interior and the client's needs and preferences. They begin by gathering the pertinent data about the interior environment. This includes: 1) *architectural information* such as wall, floor, and ceiling surface materials, dimensions, and window locations (from sketches of floor plans and elevations); 2) *environmental data* such as the type of heating and cooling system, location of vents, artificial light, orientation, and climatic conditions; and *characteristics of interior components* such as style, furniture, color scheme, and window treatments.

The needs and preferences of the client are best determined through a personal interview. Budget is the concern mentioned by the client most often, so the various plant purchase or lease arrangements and maintenance options should be discussed. Determine the client's plant preferences as well as ideas about seasonal and permanent plantings. Information relating to the type of business, clientele, and company image is helpful in deciding on plant choices and a design scheme. A general review of operational procedures aids the understanding of interior traffic patterns and activity areas.

## ANALYSIS

After information has been gathered, it is time to analyze the data and determine its implications—stage three of the design process. List the information according to resources and constraints imposed by the client's needs or space limitations. At the same time add notes on how these will affect the selection of plant material.

## SYNTHESIS

As the fourth stage of a design process, synthesis consists of generating and evaluating alternatives by combining the constraints and resources with design objectives. This is probably the most challenging stage, where design principles are applied to the collected data to determine how the plants can best be used in the interior. Be sure the design proposal relates to the design objectives. Both aesthetic and functional contributions of plants should be considered.

Implementation of these goals is best explored through sketches. Listing alternatives and indicating the advantages and disadvantages of each possibility is also useful.

## SOLUTION: PLANTSCAPING PROPOSAL

In the final stage of the design process, the best alternatives are presented in the plantscaping proposal. See the proposal and illustrations in the case history which follows.

## Case Study—Office Interior Plantscape

**Problem**

The owner, who also occupies this professional office, has requested plantscaping services. Figure 1, a drawing of the interior, illustrates a great opportunity for the addition of plants to serve both aesthetic and functional objectives. The main areas of the office have adequate natural light, thus plant selections should include moderate to low light species.

**Research**

For stage two, collection of physical and client data, the basic considerations are listed here:

*Physical Environment*

1. Architectural information (see drawings for details)
2. Environmental data: baseboard heating; cooling vents overhead; closed system; artificial and natural light; winter relative humidity about 30%
3. Furnishings: few textures (patterns), neutral color scheme

*Client Needs*

1. Lease arrangement
2. Image to convey: efficient and organized
3. Plant preferences: to be specified by plantscaper, and to include some seasonal flowering specimens
4. Clientele: primarily adults
5. Moderate budget

## Analysis

*Constraints*

1. Lighting: limited; client approves of supplemental lighting as needed
2. Water source: necessary to install tap in storage room
3. Floor surface; carpet; nonporous saucer or containers needed
4. Low winter relative humidity; select plants accordingly
5. Air vents overhead; place plants to avoid cool drafts

*Resources*

1. Moderate budget, adequate for size of space
2. Leasing plan with professional maintenance
3. Ample room for plants
4. Storage space available for supplies
5. Window orientation: south and west
6. No window treatment
7. Few textures, neutral color; permit greater emphasis on plants

**Synthesis**

The following design objectives have been chosen for this case study:

- Direct traffic from the entry, past lounge to receptionist (functional)
- Screen secretarial work station from lounge (functional)
- Block passage under stairwell because of low clearance (functional)
- Provide transitional elements between levels (aesthetic)
- Soften appearance of spaces by adding textural interest (aesthetic)
- Establish focal points throughout the office where needed (aesthetic)

The design objectives should be integrated when alternatives for each area are considered. As an example, two options for the balcony ledge are compared here.

**Option 1, Hanging Baskets.** Hanging baskets in the opening above the ledge could interfere with views, disrupt architecture line, and create a closed environment which conflicts with the intended openness of the architecture. This option was discarded in favor of Option 2.

**Option 2, Recessed Ledge Planter.** A ledge planter would permit hanging plants to hug the ledge and grow downward, complementing the architectural line. The plants would not interfere with the view between levels and would break the monotony of the balcony wall by adding textural interest.

**Solution and Plantscaping Proposal**

Floor plans, room sections, elevations and perspective drawings potentially can be included in a professional design solution. Typically the comparison of a floor plan with and without plants is helpful to clients. Elevations and perspective drawings that include plantings and people for scale also complement floor plans. The floor plans, sections, elevations and perspectives collectively help illustrate room size, scale, area heights, shapes and the setting in which plants and people interact. The project drawings for this proposal can be seen in Chapter 3, Figures 3.50–3.52.

**Figure A.31**

These two sketches of an interior illustrate the uses of line, and line with texture, to convey design ideas. (Designer: Jay Hood.)

**Figure A.32**
This line drawing is a concept proposal for an interior design firm.
(Designer: Todd Wilson.)

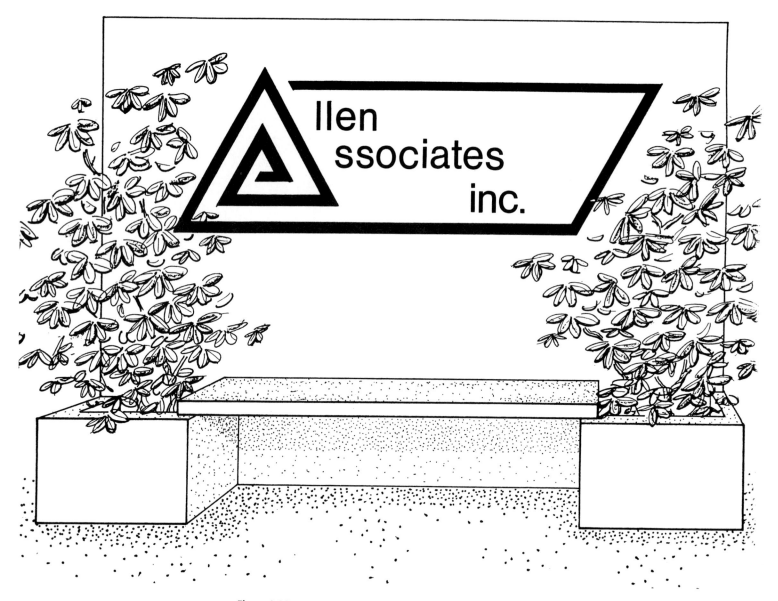

**Figure A.33**
This line drawing is a logo idea for an interiorscape firm. (Designer: Kraig Allen.)

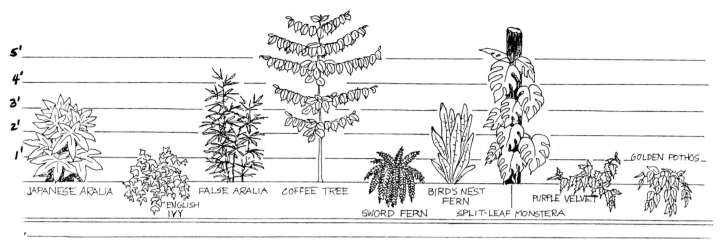

A.34

**Figures A.34–A.36**

These plant form drawings illustrate the relative size of individual plant species, as measured by the background grid. When designing with plants, their relative size is an important consideration. (Designer: Terry Mulvaney.)

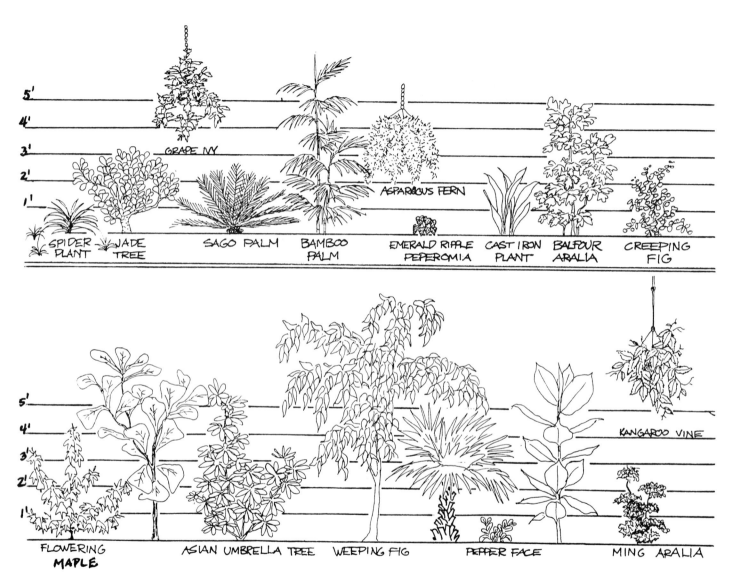

5'
4'
3'
2'
1'

GRAPE IVY

ASPARAGUS FERN

SPIDER    JADE      SAGO PALM    BAMBOO    EMERALD RIPPLE   CAST IRON   BALFOUR    CREEPING
PLANT    TREE                    PALM      PEPEROMIA        PLANT       ARALIA     FIG

5'
4'
3'
2'
1'

KANGAROO VINE

FLOWERING        ASIAN UMBRELLA TREE   WEEPING FIG    PEPPER FACE      MING ARALIA
MAPLE

A.35

334

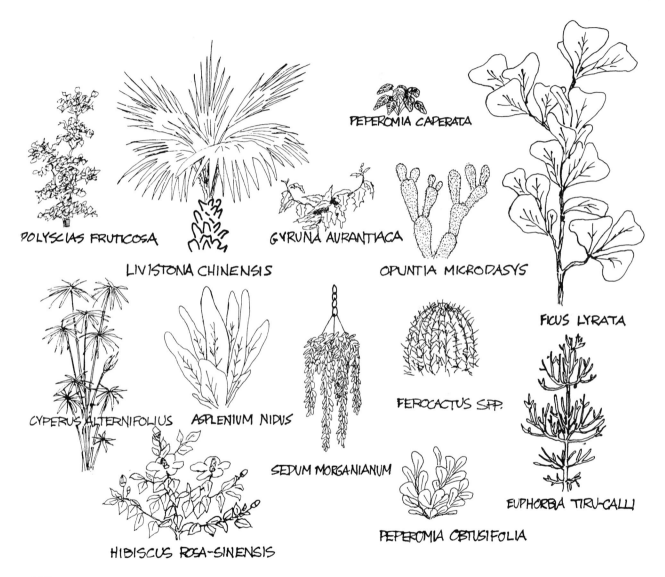

POLYSCIAS FRUTICOSA

LIVISTONA CHINENSIS

GYRUNA AURANTIACA

PEPEROMIA CAPERATA

OPUNTIA MICRODASYS

FICUS LYRATA

CYPERUS ALTERNIFOLIUS

ASPLENIUM NIDUS

SEDUM MORGANIANUM

FEROCACTUS SPP.

EUPHORBIA TIRU-CALLI

PEPEROMIA OBTUSIFOLIA

HIBISCUS ROSA-SINENSIS

A.36

# Index